LORD MAHAVIRA

LORD MAHAVIRA

Edited by
Dr. Shiv Gajrani
Dr. S. Ram

Commonwealth

Lord Mahavira

First Published : **2012**

ISBN 81-311-0010-3

Published by :

Ajay Verma
For COMMONWEALTH PUBLISHERS
4831/24, Prahlad Street,
Ansari Road, Darya Ganj,
New Delhi - 110002
Ph. : 23272541, 23257835
Fax : 91- 011- 23257835
e-mail : campusbooks@hotmail.com

Typesetting by :

Arjun Computers
Delhi - 110051

Printed at :
Roshan Offset Printers
Delhi

Preface

Lord Mahavira is considered as the prominent founder of Jainism. With his pious life and disciplined behaviour he soon attracted millions of people in the Indian sub-continent. By his tours in several regions of India, he happened to give a call for leading the high degree of character. Indeed people were much impressed by him and he created numerous devoted followers who spread the message of their Guru.

Divided into two sects, one sect, *viz.*, the true disciples, do not wear any clothes. They are confined mostly to their *maths*, and sometime they are invited in the homes of Jains who show much love and respect for them.

They do not accept any kind of gift from anybody. They eat once in a day. They do not prolong their stay in the domestic environment. Above all they preach chastity, truth and discipline in one's life. All these qualities have been depicted in this volume.

We have collected the material from several academic institutions and research centres. These are the Nehru Memorial Museum and Library, Sapru House Library, Central Secretariat Library, Jawaharlal Nehru University Library, Indian Council of Historical Research Library and Delhi University Library and feel much beholden to the members of the staff of these institutions for their help during my researches. We are grateful to the several eminent authors whose writings have been used in this volume.

Dr. Shiv Gajrani
Dr. S. Ram

CONTENTS

1 EARLY CAREER

I

Lord Mahavira, the last pontiff of Jains, was born in Bihar six hundred years before Christ. He was elder contemporary of Buddha and came from the clan of Lichhavi Kshatriyas, well known for its spirit of independence and democratic state. His father, Siddhartha was a member of the great republic of Vaishali constituted by nine Malli and nine Lichhavi kingdoms. Vaishali is now a small village known as Vasala. It is situated 30 miles north of Muzaffarpur in Bihar. Mahavira was born in Kshtriyakunda, which was a suburb of Vaishali.

Deeply imbibed with the great spirit of democracy, Mahavira could not tolerate inequality, not only between man and man, but between man and animal also. His heart pained at the pathetic sight of animals beings sacrificed for the sake of human enjoyments. His mind revolted against the social injustice perpetrated to the female and Sudras. He did not like the slavery of man to god and goddesses, and though that man himself is the moulder of his destiny. He wanted to introduce drastic reform in the human outlook and in the standards of valuation. But, he thought, only a strong soul could implement reforms, and the strength of soul lies in its purity. A soul guided by prides and prejudices, carried by favours and frowns, induced by desires for sensual enjoyments and perverted by such other weaknesses cannot purify the society. Consequently, he decided to renounce the worldly pleasures, and practice penances for self-chastisement.

Upto the age of thirty years he lived as a householder. But he thought possession as a bond of soul. A prince is imprisoned in the walls of his vain glory. He cannot breathe in free air. Dispossession is necessary condition for free thinking and free living; and no correct attitude can be had without perfect freedom in thought and life. A prince has many fears; at the same time he is fear to many. He cannot give the message of fearlessness to the afraid. He cannot be a devotee of Universal friendship. Mahavira became an ascetic, a mendicant possessing nothing, not even a begging bowl, a perfect *nirgrantha.*

After getting freedom from external boundaries he started his struggle against the inner enemies.

Non-violence was the first and formosts object of his practices. He thought that no man could be non-violent as long as he bears slightest malice towards his severest enemy. Non-violence, he admitted, is not confined to non-killing of or non-injury to others, which is only its only external form. Its real and positive form is the purity of heart, that one does not wish ill even of his enemy. During the period of his meditations he was tortured, insulted and beaten by different types of people. A cowherd thirst a spike into his ears, swarms of bees stung him. Chanda Kausika, the venomous snake, bit him; the people of Radha set dogs and inflicted other injuries on his body; but his tranquility was undisturbed. He did not feel the slightest malice against anybody. On the other hand, he wished emancipation of those misguided souls, who were committing such acts out of ignorance. A sinner, he thought, is a diseased person, deserving our sympathy and love. One should wish for his recovery from the disease and not be angry upon him. " I cherish friendship with all the beings and enmity to none."—This was the keyword of Mahavira during his practices.

Most of his time during the long period of twelve years of spiritual practices, passed in penance and meditation. He kept long fasts ranging upto six months and took food only a few times. These severe practices gave him strength, so much, so that physical discomforts had no meaning for him. He distinctly realized that soul is separate from the body, and any injury to the body has no relation with soul. Attachment is the weakness of man and he had risen above all attachments.

At the age of forty-two, on the bank of Sadanira, he got enlightenment and became *Arhan,* a perfect soul, worthy of worship. He realized that every soul possesses, by nature, four infinites, *i.e.* Infinite Knowledge, Infinite Intuition, Infinite Bliss and Infinite Energy. This nature of soul is obscured by the *Karmic* matter. As soon as the soul is purified of this dirt, it regains the four infinites. It should be therefore, the aim of every soul to make an effort to get rid of *karmic* influence. Having realized the truth, he started for propagation of his mission.

The mission of Mahavira can be summed up in one word and that is *Samata* (equality). It is the essence of democracy. The entire system of Jainism, its philosophy, its logic and its ethics, is dominated with this spirit. The "*Samayika*" prescribed as a daily *rite* for Jains is nothing but a practice for implementing the spirit of equality into life. *Mitti me savvabhutesu* (I have friendship with all beings) is the strain of Jain prayers.

Non-violence is the first offshoot of the principle of equality. One should feel for others in the same way as he feels for himself. You do not like to injury to your own body, mind and soul, Similarly, others also don't like it. It is, therefore, an imperative duty of a democrat that he should not injure anybody, in body as well as feelings. According to Jainism injury is a very wide term. It covers not only physical injury but that of mind and soul also. When you attach the feelings of a person you injure his mind. The principle of non-injury even to the mind has laid the foundation of Jain logic in the form of non-absolutism (*anekantavada*). It means that all our judgments are relative and nothing is absolute. The same thing, which is good for you, can be bad for your colleague, and the latter also has got a perfect right to form his judgment according to his choice. In spite of apparent contradiction both judgments are correct in their own relations Nevertheless, people try to impose their views on other, fight for it and attack their opponents vehemently. The principle of non-absolutism teaches that in place of rebuking our opponent we should try to understand him, study the circumstances, environment and the mental make-up under which he is speaking. We must honour the mind of our opponent as we do our own. If there is something really wrong in it, we can try to correct it without losing respect for intellect of the individual. The way of denouncing one's views is the way of injury to his mind. Thus a philosophical interpretation of the non-injury to mind is a remarkable contribution of Mahavira.

There are two causes of conflicts in the world. A man or a nation fights against other man or nation either induced by his self-interest or by the desire of domination or to impose his own views on the other. Mahavira has covered both of these causes in his definition of non-violence. A person cherishing friendship towards all beings can injure the interest of none. Everybody's interest becomes his own interest. He resolves to abstain from hurting anybody's interest whether it is an individual, community, or nation. There are other people holding that truth is confined to their own convictions. They denounce the views of others and wish to impose their own. They are not induced by some external interest; yet, their egoism compels them to be so vehement. If logic is not sufficient to bring others to their views they resort to sword. Thus, a religion, the saviour of mankind becomes the cause of bloodshed. Mahavira prescribed non-absolutism as a remedy for these conflicts of thought.

Social equality comes next in the mission of Mahavira. He preached that there is no distinction of caste, creed or sex in the domain of spiritual realization. Purity of soul is the only criterion in this field. Everybody, whether a male or female, a Brahmana or the so-called untouchable possess the same right to study religious scriptures, practice prescribed therein and attain salvation thereby. Mahavira is not particular even about his creed. He admits that any person with the desired purification of soul can attain salvation. It does not matter whether he is in the uniform of a Jain monk or householder or belongs to the order of some other sect.

Next, we find in Mahavira a strong devotion of self-reliance. It is said that when he started his life of penances and was open to hardships, Indra, the king of gods, came to him and offered his assistance in wording off the intruders. Mahavira did not accept the offer and said, "A traveller on the path of inner realization does not seek external assistance."

In a society where pleasure of gods was essential for prosperity and other gains, he announced for the first time, "O man, you and none else, are the maker of your destiny." The self of man is his friend and the same is his enemy. It is a friend when directed towards right path and enemy when directed to the wrong path. Mahavira recalled the inner-strength of man and released him from the slavery of gods and goddesses. He did not believe even in God as the Creator. The man himself moulds his future as he desires. None can grant him boons or shower curses if his own actions do not deserve them. This is how the Jain theory of *Karman* developed; according to which the future of a man is decided by his present and past actions. The Jain theory of *Karman* is altogether different from fatalism where future of a being is sealed, leaving no scope for efforts. According to Jainism the fruit of *Karman* is not altogether unchangeable. It can transferred from a stronger intensity to the milder one, from longer duration to a shorter one and can be rendered quite fruitless through penances and other practices. Thus, Jainism leaves enough scope for personal efforts, not overlooking the influence of former actions. Thus, the Jain theory of *karman*, places entire responsibility of pleasure of pain on the individual.

The mission of Mahavira can be summed up in the following four respects, and I believe, they are the *summun bonum* of democracy :

1. Respect for life.
2. Respect for mind.
3. Respect for soul.
4. Respect for personal potencies.

This is short account of the mission of Mahavira. It is wrong to confine him to a particular sect or creed. He was a leader of mankind and showed the path of true democracy. He lived and preached the path of non-violence which has been the foundation of India in the past. It is time that our nation realizes the importance of his mission and tries to implement it in life.

II

A DEMOCRATIC FESTIVAL

Equality (*Samata*) is the nucleus of Jainism. Its religion and the philosophy, *i.e.* way of life and the view of life both are evolved from this very central point. Jaina logic, metaphysics, religion, ethics, mystic practices and all other aspects move around this pivot. Every monk and lay follower of Jainism pronounces the pledge of universal friendship every morning and evening in his daily *rites* for self purification. No body can claim to be a Jain who does not purify his heart of all hatred and enmity and joins the tie of friendship with all beings at least once a year. Every Jain in this day goes with folded hands to his straitened neighbour, asks his forgiveness and starts a new chapter of friendship.

The daily worship of Jains is known as Samayika. They worship Samata *i.e.* the feeling of equality and it is the essence of friendship. The feeling of equality involves the following four respects :

1.Respect for Life

This is the essence of Ahimsa, which is the sum total of Jain ethics.

2.Respect for Mind

This is the basis of Jain theory of non-absolutism (*Anakantavada*) the sum total of Jain a logic.

3.Respect for Personal Effort

The Jain theory of *Karma* is based on the idea that a being himself is responsible for his happiness and miseries. He himself is the maker of his hell or heaven.

4.Respect for Spiritual Potency
Every soul, according to Jainism, possesses unlimited potencies. Fundamentally all souls are equal. The difference shows only the stages of development. Jainism does not accept any difference of caste or creed on the basis of birth.

The above four respects constitute the fundamentals of democracy which the modern man has yet to learn.

Similarly, Jainism emphasises on personal or inner friendship *i.e.* accordance in mind, speech, and action, the code generally neglected by the modern leader of humanity.

The festival of Paryushana symbolizes all the ideals stated above. It falls on the 5th bright day of every Bhadrapada in the last days of rainy season.

It is observed by keeping fast for the whole day and night up to the next sunrise and holding *Pratikramana* in the evening. Almost all the family members go without meals and a majority of them even without water. The youngsters also follow the tradition according to their ability. If they do not feel strong enough to pass the entire day without meals they confine themselves to one meal. Those with advanced practice observe the fast even for a longer period. *Athai i.e.,* a fast for eight days is very common. The entire day is devoted to listening to religious sermons and introspection. The observance begins eight day earlier and an atmosphere of penance, piety, charity, philanthropy and brotherhood prevails.

Pratikramana is an important ceremony meant for self-purification. Literally, it means retracing or going back. It is a retrace of the soul to its natural purity, which has been spoiled or diverted by passions and longings for external objects. While observing *Pratikramana* a devotee repents for his past sinful activities and decides not to commit them again. He enumerates all the probable possible slips in his vows, regrets and makes a decision not to repeat them. It is a procedure to take an account of the past spiritual advancement and make a new start. The monks and the devotees with vows of a householder observe this *rite* daily. Other observe it fortnightly, after a period of four months or annually on the day of *Paryushana.* In the annual *Pratikramana* the progress of whole year is taken into account.

The last but the most important item of this ceremony is the announcement of forgiveness and friendship. The devotee announce :

"I forgive all beings. May all the beings forgive me. I hold friendship with every being and enmity with none." The heart of Jainism lies in this announcement. Nobody can claim to be a Jain who does not make this announcement on the day of *Paryushana.*

The above announcement is not confined to verbal expression. It is followed by real practice. As soon as the *Pratikramana* is over, every devotee approaches the individuals sitting by and asks for their forgiveness with folded hands. He begins a new chapter of friendship with them. The distant ones are approached next day personally or through a letter. This time-honoured custom is prevalent even in these days of religious disbelief.

Four Categories

According to Jainism there are four stages of ethical development based on the gradual removal or subsidence of passions.

They are :

(a) A devotee without vows.

(b) A devotee with vows of a household.

(c) A devotee with vows of an ascetic.

(d) The perfect soul.

Corresponding to the above there are four degrees of passions.

(a) Anantanubandhi,

(b) Apratyakhyanavarana,

(c) Pratyakhyanavarana, and

(d) Sanjwalana.

Anantanubandhi is the strongest form of passion. A person

with this degree is away from the path of self-development. He cannot be a true aspirant and thus excluded from the spiritual brotherhood of Jains. The strongness of passions is measured in their intensity to cloud the spiritual qualities as well as their duration. The attitude of a person with the first degree is always perverted. He is engrossed in anger, conceit, crookedness and greed. Under the effect of passions he forgets his own nature and roams in a state of restlessness like a person under intoxication. Even when the emotions are pacified, he never realizes the mistake and tries to justify his acts committed in that state. He is never reluctant to repeat those very acts again. The Jain technical term for such an attitude is *Mithyadrsti i.e.,* a perverted attitude.

As for duration, it is roughly said that a passion enduring for a period of more than one year is to be regarded as of the first degree. Here lies the importance of *Paryushana.* A Jain should not perpetuates enmity towards anybody for a period of more than one year. On the day of *Paryushana* he must ask forgiveness of all others and himself forgive them. The chapters of enmity, hatred, greed and such other passions must be closed and a new chapter of friendship should begin. As a matter of fact it is a festival of forgive-and-forget. We must forget the injuries inflicted on us by others and forgive them. Similarly, we should express our sincere regret for the harm done to others ask for their forgiveness and thus, begin new year with a pure and loving heart.

Background Story

There is a significant historical incident attached to this festival.

There was a beautiful maid-servant in the court of king Udayana, the ruler of Sindha. Chandapradyotana, the ruler of Ujjain, heard about her charm and wanted to bring her to his harem. Once, when Udayana was away, he enticed the girl and brought her to Ujjain.

Udayana felt it as his disgrace and ordered his troops for a march. His mighty force invaded the capital of Chanda forced him to surrender. He was taken as a prisoner and the troop marched back. While they were on the way, the holy day of *Paryushana* came. Udayana was a staunch devotee of Lord Mahavira and faithfully observed the vows of a householder. He could not think of passing this important festival unobserved. A halt was ordered and tents were pitched. Udayana kept fast throughout the day and observed *Partikramana* in the evening. He recited the hymn of universal brotherhood and announced that 'he forgave all the beings, that all the beings might forgive him, that he had friendship for all and enmity for none.' While he was reciting the above verse Chandaprodyota came to his mind and the incident pinched him in the heart. He thought his declaration fictitious as long as Chanda was his captive. He went to the camp of Chanda, set him free and asked forgiveness with folded hands. Chanda kept mum. He was feeling deeply the injury incurred in the loss of kingdom. Udayana was wise enough to know his heart from the face. He restored Chanda to his throne honourably, gave him the hand of that beautiful maiden and repeated the request for forgiveness. Ultimately, Chanda was satisfied and then only the ceremony was thought to be complete. The festival of *Paryushana* brought their enmity to an end and a new chapter of friendship began.

Mysterious Origin

The origin of this very important festival is shrouded in mystery. Even the Jaina records do not supply much reliable material. They mention it only as the last day of the rainy halt prescribed for *Munis*, which was later extended to four months.

One notable factor of this festival is that the same is observed as *Rishi Panchami* in the Vedic tradition. It indicates a common background. Rishabhadeva, the first of the twenty-four Jain *tirthankaras* (pontiffs), is respected equally in Vedic tradition. He is not only mentioned in the *Rigveda* but, is described as God incarnate in the *Bhagavata* also which devotes *seven chapters* (*Ch. II to IX of Fifth Skandha*) to his life. Another point of his life is that he preached not only the path of asceticism or renunciation but guided his subjects in the development of a society as well. He taught them the method of cultivation, kindling fire from sticks, weaving, making earthen wares and such other industries. He instituted the system of marriage and arranged the society into castes (*varna*) on the basis of occupation. He himself followed the order of *Ashramas* (four stages of life and took to asceticism (*sannyasa*) in his last days only. Thus he represented both the Shramanic culture of asceticism and renunciation as well as Brahmanic culture of prosperity. Consequently, he got a respectable place in both the traditions. On this basis, Pandit Sukhlal, the renowned scholar of Indian Philosophy and a man of great vision, suggests *Rishabha Panchami* as the origin of *Rishi Panchami*.

Whatever may be its origin, it is a common heritage of Both the great traditions of India. It carries a message of spiritual purification and universal love. It possesses the elements of being observed as an international festival of peace and love. It can convey the Indian ideal of truth and non-violence to other countries. It is time our leaders pay attention towards festival of this type which have made India a spiritual teacher of the entire world.

III

Siddhartha, the father of Mahavira, also known as Sreyamsa and Jasamsa in the Shvetambara Granthas, was a Kshatriya ruler of a place called Kundalpura situated in that part of Northern India which was called Pavan in very ancient times and Videha or Magadha in later times. He belonged to the clan of Gnatrikas who are also known as Natikas in the Buddhist works, and who were a powerful clan in ancient times. Many of the ruling dynasties of later times are said to have sprung from this clan, and even the ruling chiefs of those times, who were also related to him through his wife, belonged to this clan. It is why Mahavira has been very often called Gnatriputra or Nataputta in the Buddhist works. The Digambaras also call him a Haribansi and even a Nathbansi. As to his gotra it is asserted on both hands that he was Kashyapa. In Buddhist works his gotra is confounded with that of his pupil Sudharmacharya and is, therefore, said to be Agnivaishayana. The description of the magnificence of his palace, the ceremonious rejoicings with which the birth of Mahavira was celebrated and the grandeur and pomp of his court, make us believe that Siddhartha was a powerful monarch of his time and his metropolis, Kundalpura, a big populous city, but western Scholars like Professor Jacobi call it 'a misrepresentation of the matter in overrating the real state of things.' According to him Kundalpura or Kundaggama (Kundagrama) is the same as the Kotiggama of the Buddhists, where Buddha had sojourned and was visited by the famous courtesan Ambapali. He calls it a halting place of caravans, an insignificant place and an outlying village and a suburb of Vaisali, the capital of Videha. Consequently, Siddhartha was only a petty chief, a baron, no king, nor even the head of his clan, but only a land-owner and exercised only the degree of authority which in the East usually falls to the share of one belonging to the recognized aristocracy of the country. "For," says he, "he is frequently called merely Kshatriya has wife Trisala is, so far as I remember, never styled Devi, queen, but always Kshatriyani. Whenever the Gnatrika Kahatriyas are mentioned, they are never spoken of as Siddhartha's Samantas or dependents, but are treated as his equal," Now, we can say that it is this slip of memory which makes him disregard Siddhartha's claim to a powerful monarchy; for we know that his wife is frequently styled Devi in the Digambara Granthas, and Siddhartha is said to be a wise virtuous, industrious, and a powerful king. Moreover, Chetaka, the powerful king of Videha, would not condescend to marry his daughter or sister, as the case may be, Trisala, to Siddhartha, a mere land-owner, as Professor Jacobi supposes him to be, this being against the popular custom among the Kshatriyas of those times. Siddhartha, too, would not give his choice to such a match. Neither it was a love-match. All these remarks go to show that, Siddhartha, if not a powerful monarch, exercised, at least, a kingly authority equal, if not more, to that of Chetaka.

Anyhow this seems to be undeniable the Mahavira's father

was a king and a ruler, no matter how far his rule and power extended.

As to the birth place of Mahavira, it is probable but not certain, as Dr. Hoernle suggests, that the Jaina tradition, which represents Kundalpura as a large town, may be correct, inasmuch as Kundalpura is taken as equivalent toVesali (Sanskrit Vaishali). He puts his birth place at Kollaga, another suburb of Vesali, of which the Natha or Naya (Gnatri?) Kshatriyas were the chief inhabitants, and after whom Mahavira is called a Nathabansi or a Naya Kulin. He supposes that the city commonly called Vesali occupied a very extended area, which included within its circuit, (at the time of Hwen Thsang) of about 12 miles, (see *Cunningham's Archaeological Reports*, Vol. I, p. 56), besides Vesali proper (now Besarh), several other places. Among these were Vaniyagrama spoken of in the Uvasagdasao, and Kundalpura. These two together with Kollaga make the three suburbs of Vesali spoken of as three districs in a Buddhist tradition quoted by Rockhill in his life of Buddha. Now as to his first supposition that Kollaga and not Kundalpura was the birth place of Mahavira, we can say that it is quite unnecessary and without ground; for both the Digambaras and the Shvetambaras assert that Kundalpura was the place where he was born. There is no mention of this place in either of the authorities. Had it been the actual birth place of Mahavira, the Jainas, careful writers as they were, would have never left it unmentioned. There does not seem to be any good reason to prefer the unauthentic traditionary evidence of the Buddhists to that of the Jainas themselves. His second supposition though based on traditionary evidence, seems, in all probability, a reasonable one; and we may rest assured that Kundalpura, a suburb of Vesali, as really it was, was the birth place of Mahavira. It may be added that what led Jacobi to call it a halting-place was the wrong explanation of the word Sannives which means a religious establishment. Siddhartha had one younger brother too, who was called Suparsva about whom we know nothing from either the Shvetambaras or the Digambaras except that he was living with his elder brother in his palace.

Trisala or Priyakarini, the mother of Mahavira, was a beautiful, meritorious, a loving and a virtuous lady, who is said to have possessed all the good qualities of the head and the heart. In the Shvetambara Shastras she is spoken of as sister to Ketaka (Chetaka) the powerful ruler of Videha who belonged to the Vashistha gotra. For this also she is called Vedehadatta. In the Digambara Shastras she is called as daughter of Chetaka, the king of Siddhadesha. It is not known whether these two Chetakas are the same or different persons. She was an affectionate mother and would not allow her son to become a *Sanyasi*, when he was a boy.

The Shvetambara Granthas also say that Mahavira had an elder brother, Nandivardhana, with whom Mahavira is said to have lived in his boyhood. They also assert that he had one elder sister known by the name of Sudarsana. On the other hand we find no mention of them in the Digambara Shastras.

Mahavira's parents were both fortunate men, inasmuch as they lived to see their son a grown up man of thirty-two. The *Mahavira Purana* says nothing in connection with this.

It has been stated by both that Mahavira was born on the thirteenth day of the later half of Chaitra about 72 years before the end of the fourth *Kal* in the Dushama-sushama period. On this occasion great performances and rejoicings took place in the king's palace which lasted for ten days. Streets were illuminated, charitable deeds were performed, and prisoners were liberated. It is in such circumstances that our Lord Mahavira was born.

IV

Mahavira's life may be divided into three periods. The first discovers him in the enjoyment of the royal grandeur of his father and leading a pious life of a Shravaka or a house-holder. In the second he is deeply immersed in the religious meditation, *Dhyana*, and severe bodily mortification, of which *Yoga* is but a form, in order to prepare himself for the great work of a religious preacher which has given a lasting permanency to his name. In the beginning of this period we find him disgusted with the worldly pleasures and determined to know the truth by meditation. At the end of it we find him the master of the truth, a Kevalin. In the third period we find him preaching his gospel to his pupils and the men of the world and bearing all the hardships that a religious preacher has to suffer, thus realising his doctrines in his right conduct, Samyak-charitra. His birth and *Nirvana* being added to these make the five great points of his life described so beautifully in the Jaina Shastras, and known as the five Kalyanakas.

Then we begin with the early life of Mahavira. As a matter of fact, the early lives of great men, great in the real sense of the word, are always wrapped up in mystery. Superstitious men as we are, we are likely to invent by our conjectures, myths and miracles, and connect them with the early epochs of the lives of great men. Common people are easily led to believe any thing that is said by the more refined among them. It is how the lives of great men grow mysterious. Mahavira's early life is also looked upon as a sort of mysterious thing, but the spell is easily broken if we subject it to a little scrutinizing and comparative study of the Jaina Shastras. Thus we see that both the Digambaras and the Shvetambaras assert that Mahavira led the life of a Shravaka, a layman, for thirty years living with his father and mother in Kundalpura. The difference is only in the detais. The *kalpa-sutra* is silent about this. It only says that "the Venerable Ascetic Mahavira had lived thirty years in Videha when his parents went to the world of the gods. (*i.e.,* died), and he with the permission of his elder brother and the authorities of the kingdom fulfilled has promise, *i.e.* became a *Sanyasi.*" This does not throw any light upon the kind of life that he led during these thirty years. The *Acharanga-sutra,* another Shvetambara work like the *Kalpa-sutra,* however, clears, this to some extent. It says that "the Venerable Ascetic Mahavira, after his intellect had developed and the chilhood had passed away, lived in the enjoyment of the allowed, noble, five-fold joys and pleasures : (consisting in) sound, touch, taste, colour and smell." This, too, does not satisfy our curiosity, and we learn from it only that he had developed his intellect in his childhood and nothing more than this. The latter half of the above quotation asserts that Mahavira, in the very prime of his youth, passed his time in the enjoyment of senses and not in the spiritual study of his Self and thus preparing himself for the great mission of his life. Of course this does not mean that he was addicted to, or a slave of, these pleasures : (consisting in) sound, touch, taste, colour and smell; otherwise it would not be reasonable to expect from him the performance of the great mission of his life, of reviving the decayed frame of the religion of the *Tirthankaras* by promulgating their doctrines throughout the whole of Northern India. He lived in the enjoyment of these pleasures only as far as it is allowed. But the Digambara Acharyas do not allow him the enjoyment of any worldly pleasures at all. From them we learn that in his very eighth year he had taken the vow of observing the *Twelve Pratimas* or the rules of conduct of a Shravaka or a layman. He was pious from his very childhood, and never deviated from the paths of integrity and virtue. His very mission of life was to give an example of an ideally noble life and thus teach the world to become good, by practically showing them how to lead it and not by mere precepts.

It has been just remarked that the life of a man to a great extent depends upon the kind of instruction given in childhood. The nurse is the first educator of men, hence the importance of having good nurses for the nourishing and the educating of children. "Give your child to be educated by a slave," said an ancient Greek, "and instead of one slave, you will then have two." King Siddhartha knew the necessity of providing children with good nurses, and he, therefore, employed the services of the best nurses in the country. From the Shvetambara Shastras we learn that he was attended by five nurses : a wet nurse, a nurse to clean him, one to dress him, one to play with him, one to carry him. The Digambaras hold that he was attended by the Chhappan Kumarikas of the Ruchakadwipa. Who these nurses were and where this island Ruchaka is, cannot by ascertained now. But we can say that great care was taken of his nursery and early education.

From his childhood we pass to his boyhood, and about this we learn from both the authorities that, in addition to his leading the life of a strict Shravaka, he took great interest in out-door games and martial exercises.

He used to go the royal gardens of his father with his play-mates and with the sons of his father's ministers and amuse himself there with several kinds of feats of strength and physical exercises. He had a handsome and symmetrical body and a magnetic personality. He was a man of great courages and supreme valour. He is never said to have lost his courage even on the occasions requiring great strength of body and the mind.The Digambara Shastras tell us an anecdote illustrating his supreme valour and perseverance. It runs thus :

"One day, while playing with his friends in the garden of his father, Mahavira saw an elephant, *mad-mad*, ferocious on account of the juice issuing from his temples, coming towards him. All his companions, boys and they were, being wonder-struck and afraid of the impending danger deserted him and ran off. Without losing a moment, Mahavira—went near the elephant, caught hold of his trunk with his strong hand and ascended his back at once."

This looks somewhat like a miracle and an impossibility. "Miracles," says Paul Carus, "have ceased to be a religious test; yet the belief in the miraculous power of the master still bears witness to the holy awe of the first disciples and reflects their religious enthusiasm." Thus we see that every sect has some miracle—connected with its founder to illustrate the great might and valour of the man. It is possible, then, that the Jinas, too, following the popular custom, might have invented this story to illustrate the unlimited valour (*Ananta veerya*) of the last of their twenty-four *Tirthankaras.* But we cannot call it entirely an invented miracle. It is possible in all probability.

From this we come to his education, the real part of a man's life. Curious enough to remark that both the Digambaras and the Shvetambaras say nothing about it. They assert that

Mahavira had brought with him 'a highly (though not fully) developed spiritual nature from his previous births, and, therefore, he was wiser than the wisemen of his age. The Digambara Shastras say that from his very childhood he possessed the *mati, shruti* and *avadhi gyan* or three of the five kinds of knowledge.

In the *Kalpa-sutra* we read that 'he possessed supreme, unlimited, unimpeded knowledge and intuition,' Thus we see that both the authorities assert the same thing with only this difference that one says him to possess the *Avadhigyan* and the other says that he was in possession of the *Abhogika gyan* which is inferior to the Avadhi knowledge. But all this does not satisfy us. We want to know if education was imparted to him in the modern way. We would know if he could read and write. We wish to be informed of his skill in learning. But perhaps, the Acharyas did not think it necessary to educate Mahavira who was a born instaurator of all knowledge. However, this may not convince the modern readers, and we have to assume that Mahavira was really educated in the palace of his father.

In the preceding pages much has been said about the childhood, the boyhood, the education and the bodily valour of Mahavira. We see that there is not much difference in the description of these as given by the two sects. The facts differ a little, but the kind of life that he led is the same in both. However, when we come to his youth, we find that there is a real and wide difference between the opinions of the two sects. The Digambaras hold that Mahavira was never married and led the life of a Brahmachari in his youth and was disgusted with the world from his very boyhood. On the other hand the Shvetambaras assert that he was married to a charming princess Yashoda belonging to the Kaundinya gotra, but they say nothing about the parents and the relations of this princess. They further say that Mahavira had a daughter Anojja or Priyadarshana. She was married to Jamali, a pupil of Mahavira, and had a daughter called Seshavati or Yashovati. Upon this authority Professor Jacobi constructs the following genealogical table of Mahavira showing his other relations :

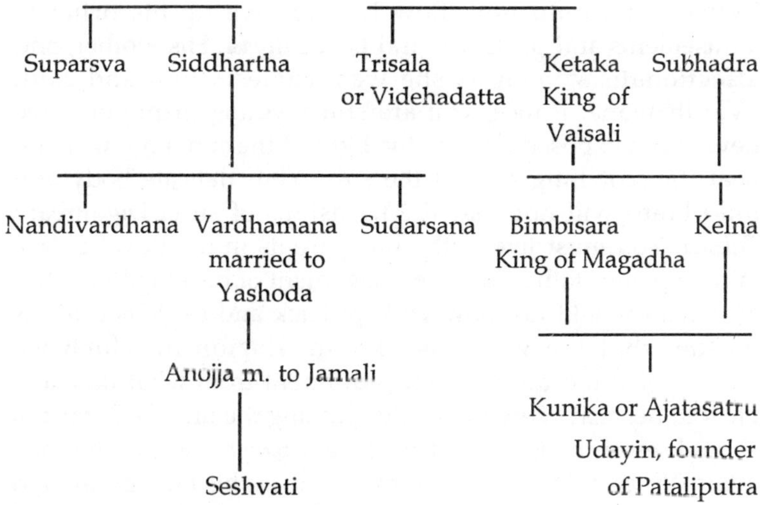

As to his having an uncle, an elder brother, and a sister, the Digambaras do not admit it. As to his parents both assert the same. As to his posterity the Digambaras say nothing about it. As to his other relations and his connection with the ruling dynasties of Magadha, we will see later on.

V

It has been said above that Mahavira was disgusted with the world and had a mind to become a *Sanyasi* from his very boyhood; but he was kept from doing so by the remonstrances of his parents. We have no testimony to show whether or not he was brooding upon his early idea of renouncing the world all along. According to the Digambara Acharyas it was in his thirtieth year that one day, while meditating upon his Self, all of a sudden he reflected upon his age which he knew through his three-fold knowledge to be of only seventy-two years, and this reflection reminded him of his long cherished wish of becoming a *Muni.* This shows that the idea of renunciation was out of his mind at least for sometime, but he had not totally given it up and when still on the verge of manhood he determined to leave the world and become a *Nirgrantha Muni.* The same authority further says that his parents were still living and would not allow him to give up his princely amusements and pleasures and be a *Sanyasi*. His mother, and affectionate woman as she was, came to him and said, "Vardhamana, Prince, you are still a young man; you have never been exposed even to the light of the sun; how will you bear the scorching rays of the sun? Your delicate body and mild limbs will not bear the hardships of strict Digambara *Diksha*; You must live with your parents in the Royal Palace and help your father in the management of his kingdom." But Mahavira would not now be kept back and explained to his mother that the world is like an illusion in which we shortsighted mortals see things different from what they are. He told her that every man, after passing the life of a Shravaka should leave the Raga and become a *Sanyasi* so that he may attain *Nirvana*. Through his remonstrances his mother, though with some reluctance, gave her consent, and Mahavira became a *Muni* in his thirtieth year.

From the Shvetambara point of view, as we have already remarked, he had thought of renouncing the world several times, but his devotion to his old parents and the love of his young wife stood in his way. In his twenty-eighth year his parents died and he 'perceived with his supreme unlimited knowledge that the time of his Renunciation had come.' But his elder brother would not allow him to do so. "Vira," said he, "the deaths of our parents are still fresh in our memories; you are leaving us this time would simply render our bereavement more unbearable and painful." Mahavira lived for two years more in the palace with his brother and after that time "with the consent of those in power entered the spiritual career and thus fulfilled his promise in his thirtieth year."

Now from both these sources we learn that Mahavira became a *Muni* in his thirtieth year only with this difference that from the Digambara point of view his parents were living at that time and the idea of Renunciation came suddenly to him, while from the Shvetambara point of view his parents were dead and he was brooding upon the idea all along.

Further they agree in asserting that this took place on the tenth day of the latter half of Marga-shirha (*Magsir*). When he determined to renounce the world, he began to distribute his wealth according to the Acharanga-sutra, amounted to three hundred and eighty-eight *krores* and eighty *lacs* of gold. This appears to be somewhat exaggerated. However, it is possible that he might have distributed his wealth among his subjects. The authority quoted above further says that he fasted for two days and a half before leaving his home. On the tenth day of the latter half of *Magsir* in the afternoon he left his palace and "marched to a place outside the Kshatriya part of his capital Kundalpura, being carried on his palanquin, Chandraprabha, which only a thousand men can carry, and being followed on his way by a train of all kinds of men raising a shout to victory and praising him with swift and soft words." The place to which he was carried and where he performed his first penance was a park known as the Sarthi Khanda according to the Digambaras and Gnatri Shanda or the Shandavana of the Gnatris according to the Shvetambaras. There he had his palanquin stopped. A special throne, known as the Pandushila or the five daises placed one over the other, each of the upper one being somewhat smaller than the lower one so as to make one able to climb above, was erected there. This was ornamented, surrounded on all sides by garlands and had a sandal or an Asoka tree over it. Mahavira took his seat upon this dais below the sandal tree, took off his ornaments, garlands and finery & c., and entered the state of houselessness. He then renounced the twenty-four Parigrahas or the attachments and assumed the twenty-eight Mul-gunas† or the chief qualities of a monk. Thus he adopted the holy conduct of Jaina Nirgrantha Muni. Then followed a very bold and a trying ceremony known as the Keshalochana ceremony which, as is the custom, requires a man who wishes to enter the spiritual order of the Jaina Munis, to "pluck out with his right and left (hands) on the right and left (sides of his head) his hair in five handfuls." The process is not of cutting or shaving the hair of the head as is the custom with the Hindu *Sanyasis,* but it is of plucking it out in handfuls. No doubt it requires a great courage and a strong will to do it and only those can do it who have no love with their flesh and bones, who are really disgusted with the world and who have completely mastered their passions. It is said that if a man hesitates from dong so at the time of the ceremony, he is disqualified to enter the sacred order. Obviously the custom is a trial of a man's courage and fortitude, and Mahavira is said to have passed it very successfully. He tore out the hair of his head without shrinking from the severe trial.

It is also said that Mahavira possessed the Manha paryaya Gyan at this time. Then he paid obeisance to all the Siddhas who had attained *Nirvana* before him, and then formed the following resolution : "I shall for twelve years neglect my body and abandon the care of it; I shall with equanimity bear, undergo, and suffer all calamities arising from divine powers, men or animals."

Notes and References

1. The knowledge of thing which having come into existence, are not destroyed, acquired through the senses and the mind.
2. The knowledge of things acquired in addition to the mati-gyan through reasoning and study of the Jaina scriptures. It deals with all things now existing and also with those that were in the past or may be in the future.
3. The knowledge of facts going on the different places without going to those places at all.

   The other two kinds of knowledge are : *Manahparyaya,* capacity to read the thoughts of others; and *Kevalgyan,* full knowledge, *i.e.,* a knowledge of all things, in all their modifications. (See *Tattvarthahigama sutra,* Shlokas 13-30).

2 JAINISM BEFORE LORD MAHAVIRA

The history of Jainism before Lord Mahavira is shrouded in considerable obscurity. Materials which can reconstruct it are scanty, dubious and capable of different interpretations. Scholars have, therefore, come to widely divergent conclusions. The Jainas themselves believe that their religion is eternal and that before Mahavira (C. 600 B.C.), there lived twenty-three Tirthankaras who appeared at certain intervals to propagate true religion for the salvation of the world. Some scholars hold that there are traces of the existence of *Sramana* culture even in pre-Vedic times. H. Jacob tried to prove, both from the Buddhist and the Jaina records, that Parsvanatha, the immediate predecessor of Mahavira, who is said to have flourished some 250 years before him, is a historical personality.

Jaina Religion as Eternal

According to the traditions preserved in the scriptures, Jaina religion is eternal, and it has been revealed again and again in every cyclic period of the world by innumerable Tirthankaras. The whole span of time is divided into two equal cycles, *Utsarpini Kala* and *Avasarpini Kala*. Each *Utsarpini* and *Avasarpini Kala* extends over ten *Kota-Koti Sagaropama* years which are subdivided into six parts known as aras. The six divisions of *Avasarpini* are known as *Sushama-Sushama, Sushama, Sushama Duhshama, Duhshama Sushama, Duhshama and Duhshami-Duhshama*. The six divisions of *Utsarpini* are *Duhshama Duhshama, Duhshama, Duhshama-Sushama, Sushama-Duhshama, Sushama and Sushama-Sushama*. During each successive ara of *Avasarpini Kala*, the age, height,strength and happiness of the *Yugalikas* gradually declined. In all, fourteen *Kulakaras* (*Manus*) are said to have flourished during this period.

After the *Kulakaras*, twenty-four Tirthankaras appeared at certain intervals and preached the true religion for the salvation of the world. Their names are : (1) Rishabha, (2) Ajita, (3)Sambhava, (4) Abhinandana,(5) Sumati, (6) Padmaprabha, (7) Suparsva, (8) Chandraprabha, (9) Suvidhi or Pushpa, (10) Sitala, (11) Sreyamsa, (12) Vasapujya, (13) Vimala, (14) Ananta, (15) Dharma, (16) Santi, (17) Kunthu, (18) Ara, (19) Malli, (20) Munisuvrata, (21) Nami, (22) Nemi, (23) Parsva, and (24) Vardhamana or Mahavira.

All Tirthankaras were Kshatriyas; Munisuvrata and Nami belonged to Harivamsa, and the remaining twenty-two to the Ikshvaku race. Malli, according to the Svetambaras, was as woman, but this the Digambaras deny, for according to them no female can attain liberation. The interval in years between one Tirthankara and the other has been calculated. Parsva's predecessor, Arishtanemi, is stated to have died 84,000 years before Mahavira's *Nirvana*. Nami died 500,000 years before Arishta Nemi, Munisuvrata 11,00,000 years before Nami; the next intervals are 65,00,000 and 10,00,000 or a *crore*; the following intervals cannot be expressed in definite number of years, but are given in *Palyopamas* and *Sagaropamas*, the last interval being one *crore* of *crores* of *sagaropamas*. The length of the life and height of the Tirthankaras are in proportion to the length of the interval.

Besides twelve Universal monarchs (Chakravartis), nine *Vasudevas*, nine *Baladevas* and nine *Prativasudeva* lived within the period ranging from the first to the twenty-second Tirthankara. Together with the twenty-four Tirthankaras, there are sixty-three great personages (*Trishashtisalakapurushacharita*) of Jain history.

From such statements and descriptions of the blissful state of the world at its initial stages, it is evident that the Jainas, like the Hindus, attributed to the first race of man a longer life and greater strength and happiness than what fall to the share of his offspring in the present age. We know that the Greeks and Romans also held similar views. The world has grown worse and worse, and the life of man of shorter and shorter, so that the twenty-third Tirthankara, Parsva, is said to have lived only for a hundred years and died 250 years before his more celebrated successor, Mahavira, who lived only for seventy-two years.

Archaeological Evidence to Ascertain the Truthfulness of the Legends

This legendary account of the existence of Jainism in such an early period on the basis of Jaina scriptures is not reliable, as it is not consistent with archaeological facts. The archaeologists tell a different story. The earliest man of Early Paleolithic Culture lived in India in the Middle Pleistocene Period, *i.e.*, some 200,000 years ago. Economically, man was then a savage and a hunter, and with the help of stone tools, he subsisted largely on fruits, roots and grubs, and on the chase with the help of his bow and arrow. The Middle Stone Age Culture is assigned to the later half of the Pleistocene (25,000 years before), and the tools are of typical flake nature, smaller than those of Early Stone Age Culture. Up to the Mesolithic stage of culture of the Early Holocene Age, man was still a hunter and used tiny stone tools called microliths, which are non-geometric. Pottery did not come into existence till then.

If the evidence of the lowest levels of Langhraj in Gujarat is taken to be a general feature, the geometric element seems to have made its appearance in the microlithic industry. It was followed by the appearance of pottery. There is also some evidence, though inconclusive, regarding agriculture and domestication of animals at this stage. A picture of people using pottery and geometric microliths is also afforded by the cave-shelters of Madhya Pradesh. None of these stages has been dated with reasonable approximation.

The carbon-14 datings for the pre-pottery village culture of Kili Ghul Mohammad, near Quetta in Pakistan, confined to the Baluchi hill (Period I *viz.* 3600 ± 85 B.C. and 3510 ± 515

B.C.), are of great value. They provide evidence for the domestication of animals and for agriculture but not for the use of pottery. Kili Ghul Mohmmad III marks the infiltration of copper. Kalibangan and Kotdiji cultures (3000 B.C.) are famous for pre-Harappan deposits, such as pottery, and structures. The Harappan civilization with many metropolitan centers, such as Rupar in the East Punjab, Kalibangan in North Rajasthan, Alamgirpur in Uttar Pradesh and Rangpur, Lothal, and Somanatha in Gujarat, is the last and most elaborate phase of long cultural evolution (2500-1800 B.C.). It was followed by the various Chalcolithic cultures (1800-600 B.C.) – the Painted Grey Ware Culture of the Ganga-Yamuna basin, the Chalcolithic Cultures of Madhya Pradesh and the Deccan, the Neolithic Cultures of the North West, etc. It is in the light of the material furnished by these different cultures that we should study Jainism before Mahavira. The archaeological evidence does not prove such an antiquity of Jainism as is revealed by the Jaina scriptures.

The Theory of Twenty-four Tirthankaras

The *Kalpasutra* ascribed to Bhadrabahu (3rd century B.C.) shows the early stages of the development of Jainism when the tradition of four Tirthankaras or Jinas was cherished by the Jaina community. The four Jinas, whose life history is presented in the *Kalapasutra*, are Rishabhadatta, Arishtanemi, Parsva and Mahavira. The conception of the former Buddhas was current even in Buddhism as early as the third century B.C. because some of them were worshiped in their own *stupas*. Both in Jainism and Buddhism, the number gradually increased from four to seven, and from seven to twenty-four Tirthankaras. The tradition of twenty-four Tirthankaras became well established among the Jainas in about the first or second century A.D. It might have risen earlier in Jainism, as the Nirgranthas were never spoken of, in Buddhist writings, as a newly risen sect nor was Nataputta referred to as their founder. Accordingly, the Nirgranthas were, probably, an old sect at the time of Buddha, and Nataputta only a reformer of the Jaina Church which might have been founded earlier by

Parsvanatha.

Rishabha as Founder of Jainism

According to the Jaina tradition, Rishabha, who belonged to the Ikshvaku family of Ayodhya, was the founder of Jainism. His parents were Nabhiraja and Marudevi. The son's name was Bharata after whom India is said to be named. He was the first Jina and the first Tirthankara who was born in an age when people, primitive and illiterate, did not know any art. He is said to have taught the arts of cooking, writing, pottery, painting and sculpture for the first time. It was during his time that the institution of marriage, the ceremony of cremation the dead, building of the mounds and the festivals in honour of Indra and the Nagas came into existence. We may, thus, look upon him as a great pioneer in the history of human progress.

It is often said that there is a reference to Lord Rishabha in the Vedic literature. Some Vedic preceptors paid reverence to Lord Rishabha, and regarded him as the Lord of Lords. In the Rigveda, and in the *Taittirtya Arnayaka*, Vatarasanas have been used in the sense of *Sramanas*. Vatarasana has also been mentioned, and in the same context an excellent tribute has been paid to Kesi. This Kesi alludes to Rishabha because in Jaina literature, there is tradition that Lord Rishabha was called Kesi. Even on the ancient images of Lord Rishabha, locks of hair are noticed. In the Rigveda, Kesi has been mentioned along with Vrishabha. It is more probable that the reference to Lord Rishabha in *Vratyakhanda* of the *Atharvaveda* is only metaphorical. From this it is argued that Vrishabha lived before the Vedic times and was the first fountain head of *Sramana* culture. It is from the context of the *Rigveda* that Lord Rishabha has been depicted as one who sponsored Vatarasana Sramanas in the *Bhagavata Purana* of the eighth century A.D.

Against this, it may be argued that though in the *Rigveda* and in other Vedic writings, 'Rishabha' has been mentioned many times, its meaning has been controversial and susceptible of different interpretations. There is no evidence of Rishabha being mentioned as the founder of Jainism in Vedic literature.

Even in the days of Mahavira, Rishabha was not known as the founder Nirgrantha sect from any contemporary source. From about the fourth or third century B.C., it seems that Rishabha became popular as the first Jina, the first Tirthankara, and the founder of Jainism. Like the imaginary Manu of Brahmanical literature, he has been described as the first ruler and founder of the new Social Order.

Arishtanemi or Neminatha as Tirthankara

Besides Rishabhadeva, Arishtanemi or Neminatha has also been mentioned as the Tirthankara of the Jainas in the *Kalpasutra*. He is said to be the twenty-second Tirthankara. He was the son of a king named Samudravijaya of Sauripura, a big town on the bank of the Yamuna. His mother's name was Sivadevi. He was named Arishtanemi because his mother saw in a dream a *nemi*, the outer rim of a wheel, which consisted of *rishta* stones flying up to the sky. Giranara or Raivataka hill is considered to be his nirvana-place.

Neminatha is connected with the legend of Srikrishna as his relative. According to the *Trishashtisalakapurushacharita*, he was a cousin of Lord Krishna who negotiated his marriage with Rajamati, daughter of Ugrasena, ruler of Dvarika, but Neminatha, taking compassion on the animals which were to be slaughtered in connection with the marriage feast, left the marriage procession suddenly and renounced the world. He then left Dvarika and proceeded to a garden called Sahasamabhavana on the mount Raivataka, where he practiced asceticism and attained salvation. According to the *Kalpasutra*, he lived up to the age of 1,000 years.

The *Chhandogya Upanishad* refers to Krishna, son of Devaki, as a disciple of Ghora Angirasa who instructed him about *tapas* (asceticism), *dana* (charity), arjava(simplicity or piety), *ahimsa* (non-injury) and *satyavachana* (truthfulness)—virtues which are extolled by Krishna in the *Gita*. As Jaina tradition makes Vasudeva-Krishna a contemporary of Tirthankara Arishtanemi who preceded Parsvanatha, some scholars identify Ghora Angirasa with Neminatha. Neminatha is also known to have instructed Srikrishna, but his identification with Ghora Angirasa is by no means correct as he is not known by this name in Jaina literature.

The age when Vasudeva-Krishna flourished cannot be determined with certainty. The reference in the Chhandogya *Upanishad* seems to point to a date in the sixth or seventh century B.C. The *Mahabharata* war, in which Krishna is known to have participated, was according H.C. Ray Chaudhuri, fought either in the 14th century B.C. or in the 9th century B.C.

The curious Jaina version of Krishna legend along with that of Arishtanemi having some points of similarity between itself on the one hand and the Brahmanical and Buddhistic versions on the other, was invented with the obvious purpose of gaining popularity for the Jaina faith in Western India by making the local people believe that the whole of the Yadava race attained salvation under the influence and guidance of the 22nd Tirthankara, Neminatha. Actually, Neminatha is not a historical figure at all and the same is probably the case with Lord Krishna also.

Jainism as a pre-Vedic Religion

It has been pointed out by some scholars that Jainism is a pre-Vedic religion. G.G. Pandey has tried to show that the anti-ritualistic tendency, within the Vedic fold, is itself due to the impact of an asceticism which antedates the *Vedas*. Jainism represents a continuation of this pre-Vedic stream. Some of the relics, recovered from the excavations at Mohenjodaro and Harappa, are related to *Sramana* or Jaina tradition. The nude images in *Kayotsarga, i.e.,* the standing posture lost in meditation, closely resemble the Jaina images of the Kushana period. *Kayotsarga* is generally supposed to belong to the Jaina tradition. There are some idols even in *Padmasana* pose. A few others, found at Mohenjodaro, have heads of serpents. They probably belonged to pre-Vedic Naga tribe. The image of the seventh Tirthankara, Lord Suparsva, has a canopy of serpent-heads.

Even after the destruction of the Indus civilization, the straggling culture of the *Sramanas*, most probably going back to pre-Vedic and pre-Aryan times, continued even during the Vedic period as is indicated by some such terms as *Vatarasana, Muni, Yati, Sramana, Kesi, Vratya, Arhan* and *Sisnadeva*. The *Kesi Sukta* of the Rigveda delineates the strange figure of the Muni who is described as long-haired, clad in dirty, tawny-coloured garments, walking in the air, drinking poison, delirious with *Mauneya* and inspired. There can hardly be any doubt that the *Muni* was to the Rigvedic Culture an alien figure. The *Taittirtya-Aranyaka* speaks of *Sramanas* who were called *Vatarasanah*. They led a celibate life and could disappear at will and teach the Brahmanas the way of righteousness.

The word *Sramana* occurs in the *Upanishads*, although the *Mundakopanished* has various references to the shaven-headed ascetics who revile the *Vedas*. All the passages of Vedic literature, taken together, suggested that the *Yatis* were the people who had incurred the hostility of Indra the patron of the Aryas, and whose bodies were, therefore, thrown to the wolves.

The *Panchavimsa Brahmana* describes some peculiarities of the Vratyas. They did not study the *Vedas*; they did not observe the rules regulating the Brahmanical order of life. They called an expression difficult to pronounce when it was not difficult to pronounce at all and spoke the tongue of the consecrated though they themselves were not consecrated. This proves that they has some Prakritic form of speech. (The Prakrit language is especially the language of the canonical works of the Jainas.) K.P. Jayaswal states that they had traditions of the Jainas current among them.

In the *Rigveda, Arhan* has been used for a *Sramana* leader : 'Oh Arhan you fed compassion for this useless world.' The mention of *Sisnadevas* (naked gods) in the *Rigveda* is also noteworthy.

As a matter of fact, however, there is no definite evidence for the existence of Jainism in pre-Vedic times. The images representing *Kayatsarga* excavated at Mohenjodaro, cannot be ascribed to Jainism unless there is some evidence for it. Even from the various terms mentioned in the *Rigveda*, no definite conclusion can be drawn regarding the existence of Jainism in those days.

Jainism it appears, was not extant in so early a period, but the primitive currents of religious and philosophical speculation of the pre-Vedic period along with Sankya-Yoga and Buddhism considerably influenced this religion. All the three shared a kind of pessimism, a conclusion that human life is full of misery. No trace of this attitude is to be found in the optimistic outlook of the Vedic Aryans. The doctrine of transmigration, unknown to the early Brahmanas, suddenly emerges in the *Upnishads* and forms an essential element in these three systems. What is more important is the fact that this doctrine assumes its peculiarly Indian form by its association with the doctrine of *Karman*, and we know that some of the most primitive ideas of *Karman* are found in Jaina Metaphysics as well. An atheistic attitude and a kind of dualism between spirit and matter characterize all the three systems of thought. To the same primitive influence of pre-Vedic times may also be attributed the introduction of the practice of image-worship. From early times, the cult of symbols and images seems to have been current among the Jainas who continued the traditional religious practices of the pre-Aryan settlors of the Sindhu Valley region.

H. Jacob noticed some marks of antiquity in the character of Jaina philosophy. Such a mark is the animistic belief that nearly everything is possessed of a soul; not only have plants their own souls, but particles of earth, cold water, fire and wind too. This theory of primitive animism in Jaina philosophy indicates that this religion originated at a very early time when higher forms of religious beliefs and cults had not taken hold of the Indian mind. Another mark of antiquity in Jainism is that in the development of metaphysics, the category of quality is not yet clearly and distinctly conceived, but it is just evolving, as it were, out of the category of substance.

In the Vedic period, there existed two distinct religious cultural traditions – the strictly orthodox and Aryan tradition of the Brahmanas and the straggling culture of the *Munis* and

Sramans, most probably going back to pre-Vedic and pre-Aryan times. During the later Vedic period, the two streams tended to mingle, and the result was the great religious ferment from which Jainism appears to have originated. Jainism and other Sramika religious sects grew up among the imperfectly Aryanised Communities of the East in response to the cultural atmosphere and social needs. These sects spread out, flourished and became highly popular there. On the other hand, Brahmanical religion had its stronghold in the North and the West.

Parsvanatha as an Historical Figure

H. Jacob and others have tried to prove on the authority of both the Jaina and the Buddhist records that Parsva was a historical personage. Their arguments are as follows :

1. In the Buddhist scriptures, there is a reference to the four vows (*Chaturyama Dharma*) of Parsva in contradiction to the five vows of Mahavira. The Buddhist could not have used the term *Chaturyama Dharma* for the Nirgranthas unless they had heard it from the followers of Parsva. This proves the correctness of the Jaina tradition that the followers of Parsva, in fact, existed at the time of Mahavira.

2. The Nirgranthas were an important sect at the time of the rise of Buddhism, as may be inferred from the fact that they are frequently mentioned in the *Pitakas* as opponents of Buddha and his disciples. This is further supported by another fact. Mankhali Gosala, a contemporary of Buddha and Mahavira, divided mankind into six classes, and of these, the third class contained the *Nirgranthas*. Gosala, probably, would not have ranked them as a separate class of mankind if they had recently come into existence. He must have regarded as members of a very important and at the same time an old sect.

3. The *Majjhima Nikaya* records a dispute between Buddha and Sakadal, the son of Nirgrantha. Sakdal was not himself a Nirgrantha. Now, when a famous controversialist, whose father was a Nirgrantha, was a contemporary of Buddha, the Nirgrantha sect could scarcely have been founded during

Buddha's life-time.

4. The existence of Parsva's Order in Mahavira's time is proved by the reported disputes between the followers of Parsva and those of Mahavira. The followers of Parsva, who did not fully recognize Mahavira as their spiritual guide, existed during Mahavira's life-time. A sort of compromise was effected between the two sections of the Jaina Church.

These arguments clearly show that Parsvanatha was a real historical figure. Very few facts of his life are, however, known. The *Kalpasutra* informs us that Parsva was the son of king Asvasena of Varanasi (Banaras) and queen Vama, belonging to the Ikshvaku race of the Kshatriyas. No such person as Asvesena is known, from Brahmana records, to have existed. The only individual of that name, mentioned in epic literature, was a king of the snakes (Nagas), and he cannot in any way be connected with the father of the Jaina prophet 'Parsva'. Parsva is said to have been born in 877 B.C. It is evidently impossible to prove the correctness of this date as we do not have single definite date in Indian history before the time of Buddha.

Many legends have gathered round Parsva. Throughout his life he was connected with snakes in one way or the other. In his childhood, for instance, while he lay by the side of his mother, a serpent was seen crawling about there. When he grew up, he saved a serpent from the grave danger it was in. He also saved a poor terrified snake which had taken shelter in a log of wood to which a Brahman ascetic, Kamatha, was setting fire. After its death, the snake became God Dharanendra who spread a serpent's hood over Parsva.

Parsva was married to Prabhavati, the daughter of Prasenajit the king of Kusahthala. He must have been a man of genial nature, as he is always given the epithet *Purishadaniya*, 'beloved of men'. He lived for thirty years in great splendour and happiness as a householder, and then, forsaking all his wealth, became an ascetic. After 84 days of intense meditaiton, he attained the perfect knowledge of a prophet, and from that time, he lived for about seventy years in the state of most exalted perfection and sainthood. At last, he attained *Nirvana* (liberation) in 777 B.C. on the summit of Mount *Sammedasikhara*, now named Parsvanatha hill after him.

A man of practical nature, Parsva was remarkable for his organizing capacity. He organized the *Samgha* (Organization) efficiently for the propagation of Jainism. He had eight *ganas* and eight *gandharas*, namely, Subha and Aryaghosha, Vasishtha and Brahmacharin, Saumya and Sridhara, Virabhadra and Yasas. He had an excellent community of 16,000 *Sramanas* with Aryadatta at their head; 38,000 nuns with Pushpachula at their head; 164,000 lay votaries with Suvrata at their head; 372,000 female lay votaries with Sunanda at their head; 350 sages who knew the four *Purvas;* 1,400 sages who were possessed of the *avadhi* knowledge; 1,000 kevalins; 1,100 sages who could transform themselves; 600 sages possessing correct knowledge; 1,000 male and 2,000 female disciples who had reached perfection; 750 sages, each gifted with a mighty intellect; 600 professors and 1,200 sages in their last birth. Here the Digambara texts differ. According to them there were ten *ganas* and ten *ganadharas* among whom Svayambhu was the chief apostle. They also differ in giving the number of nuns layman and female lay votaries which, according to them, was twenty-six thousand, one lac and three lacs respectively. The numbers given above seem to have been exaggerated, but the division of Jaina *Samgha* in different branches proves the great organizing capacity of Parsava. He is said to have visited many cities, the most important of which for the dissemination of Jainism are Ahichchhatra, Amalakappa, Savatthi, Kampillapura, Sageya, Rayagiha, and Kosambi.

According to the Jain tradition, the sacred literature descending from the time of Parsva was known as *Puvvas* (*Purvas*). These 'Earlier' compositions were called *Puvvas* (*Purvas*) evidently because they existed prior to the *Angas*. They are said to have formed a common basis of Jaina and Ajivika canon. It is form these *Purvas* that Gosala Mankhaliputta, the leader of the Ajivikas drew inspiration. It is said that the Ajivika canon, consisting of eight *Mahanimittas* and two *Margas,* was atleast partially based upon these *Purvas.*

The fourteen *Purvas* were reckoned as constituting a twelfth *Anga* called *Drishtivada.* The knowledge of the fourteen *Purvas* remained up to *Sthulabhadra,* the eight patriarch after Mahavira. For some time, only ten *Purvas* were known and then the remaining *Purvas* were gradually lost. H.L. Jain thinks that in the *Shatkhandagama* of Pushpadanta and Bhutabali, we have not only an important canonical book of the Digambaras but also a later representation of the *Drishtivada* which contained the original fourteen Purvas.

The Jaina *Sutras* and the early Buddhist texts enlighten us about the doctrines and followers of Parsva who was merely an ascetic of the ancient hermit type, and not a philosopher like Mahavira. The religious order founded by him had a reputation for a high and rigid standard of conduct. He made four moral precepts binding upon his followers, precepts which were later enforced by Mahavira and Buddha among their followers. His rules were not confined only to these four precepts but they embraced many other rules laid down for the practical guidance of the fraternity and laity. All the fundamental rules of the Nigantha community were due to Parsva and his followers. B.M. Barua points out that Parsva, the philosophic predecessor of Mahavira, had rules of conduct which demanded a philosophic justification in order that they might not appear arbitrary or be confused with social conventions.

The *Uttaradhyayana Sutra* furnished a dialogue which sheds abundant light on his obscure point. The interlocutors are the two leading representatives of the Nigantha Orders of the time. Kesi, a follower of Parsva's rule, asks Guatama, who was one of the chief disciples of Mahavira : "When the four precepts promulgated by the great sage Parsva are held equally binding upon the two orders, what is the cause of difference between us?" "Wisdom" replies Gautama, "recognizes the truth of the law and the ascertainment of true things. The first saints were simple but slow of understanding, the last saints, prevaricating and slow of understanding, those between the two, simple and wise; hence there are two forms of the Law. The first could only with difficulty understand the precepts of the Law, and the last could only with difficulty observe them, but those between them easily understood and observed them." Here the purport of Gautama's reply is that Parsva's was mere religious order while Mahavira's was not only a religious order, but also a distinct school of thought.

About the teachings of Parsva, it must be admitted, we have no exact knowledge. His religion was, however, meant for one and all without any distinction of caste or creed. He allowed women to enter his Order. He laid stress on the doctrine of *ahimsa*. Ac ording to him, strict asceticism was the only way to the attainment of salvation. Fundamentally, the doctrines of Parsva and Mahavira were the same. The only points of difference concerned vows and garments. Parsva preached four vows instead of five and allowed an under and upper garment. It is interesting to find the monks of the Order of Parsva practicing *Tinakappa*. Parsva's doctrine of the six classes of living beings served as the basis of Mahavira's doctrine of six *lesyas*. According to H. Jacob, the Order of Parsva seems to have undergone some changes in the period between the death of Parsva and the advent of Mahavira.

Parsva enjoined on his followers four great vows : (1) Abstinence from killing living beings; (2) Avoidance of falsehood; (3) Avoidance of theft, and (4) Freedom from possessions. H. Jacob has clearly perceived that a doctrine attributed to Mahavira in the Buddhist *Samannaphala Sutta* properly belonged to his predecessor, Parsva, insofar as the expression *Chatuyama Samvara* is concerned. The doctrine is that, according to Mahavira, the way to self-possession, self-command, and imperturbability consists of a 'four-fold self-restraint', such as restraint in regard to all water, restraint in regarding to all evil, and restraints imposed for the purification of sin and feeling a sense of ease on that account.

The Jaina writers tell us that Nagnajit, king of Gandhara, Nimi, king of Videha, Durmukha, king of Panchala, Bhima, king of Vidarbha, and Karakandu, king of Kalinga adopted the faith of the Jainas. As Parsva was probably the first historical Jina, these rulers, if they really became converts to his doctrines, have to be placed between 842 B.C. and 600 B.C. They are known to have ruled over their respective kingdoms before the sixth century B.C.

Parsva had a large number of followers round about Magadha even in the days of Mahavira's parents, who belonged to the Jnatr-Kshatriyas, were worshippers of Parsva. Following the teaching of Parsva, they peacefully died practicing the slow starvation of their senses. The *Uttaradhyayana* relates a meeting between Kesi and Gautama as representatives of the two Jaina Orders, the old and the new. The *Bhagavati Sutra* refers to a dispute between Kalasavesiyaputta, a follower of Parsva, and a disciple of Mahavira. The *Nayadhammakahao* says that Kalt, an old maiden joined Parsva's order and was entrusted to Pupphachulla, the head of the nuns. The two sisters of Uppala joined the order of Parsva, but being unable to lead the rigid life of the order, they became Brahmin *parivrajikas* (female wanderers). Munichanda, a follower of Parsva, lived in a potter's shop in *Kumaraya-Sannivesa* in the company of his disciples. Vijaya and Pagabbha, two female disciples of Parsva, saved Mahavira and Gosala in *Kuviya-sannivesa*. The *Bhagavati Sutra* refers to Gangeya, a follower of Parsva in Vaniyagama. He gave up the four vows of Parsva and adopted the five Mahavratas of Mahvira. The *Nayadhammakahao* mentions Pundariya who accepted the four vows of Parsva. The followers of Parsva moved in the company of five hundred monks into the city of Tungiya. A number of laywomen joined Parsva's Order. The *Rayapasenaiyasuya* refers to a follower of Parsva named Kesi who visited Seyaviya where a discussion between him and Paesi took place regarding the identity of the soul and body. A follower of Parsva named Udaka met Gautama, the famous disciple of Mahavira. Gautama was successful in winning over Udaka to his side. From the dialogue between Udaka and Gautama, it appears that the followers of Parsva and the disciples of Mahavira were respectively known as the Nigantha Kumaraputtas and the Nigantha Nathaputtas.

3 TEACHINGS OF MAHAVIRA

Mahavira was not the founder but only a reformer of the existing faith of Jainism. His teachings are partly based on the religion of his predecessor, Parsvanatha, and partly independent. He appears to be a religious philosopher who gave a philosophic justification for the rules of conduct propounded by Parsvanatha. He was responsible for the codification of an unsystematic mass of beliefs inhering the earlier religion of his predecessor into a set of rigid rules of conduct for monks and laymen. Besides, he had to introduce changes in the existing religion in order to meet the needs of the time. There were several orthodox and heretical sects with their well-known teachers going strong during his time. He understood and mastered the doctrines of the current philosophical systems such as the Kriyavadins, the Akriavadins, the Vinayavadins and the Ajnanavadins. Sometimes he borrowed certain ideas from others in order to bring them into harmony with his own system. He also formulated his own doctrines under the influence of the controversies endlessly going on with his religious contemporaries. Some of his teachings also arose as a natural reaction against corrupt practices current in the society of this period.

No direct evidence regarding the teachings of Mahavira has been preserved. Originally, they are supposed to have been embodied in the Fourteen *Purvas* and the Eleven *Angas*. These original texts are, however, according to the Digambaras, lost without a trace, but the Svetambaras do not subscribe to this view. According to them, an attempt was made for the compilation of the Eleven *Angas* at the Council of Pataliputra after a famine of twelve year's duration in about the third century B.C., and the *Purvas* were considered to be the twelfth *Anga* under the name of Drstivada. This type of *Agama* literature grew up by stages during the ten centuries following the death of Mahavira. The final reaction of this Agamika literature with several alterations took place at the council of Valabhi under the presidency of Arya Devarddhi in 454 (or 467 A.D.).

It seems that the teachings of the Jainism underwent some changes in the interval between the time of Mahavira and the final composition of the Jaina canon. Older parts of the *Acharanga* and the *Sutrakitanga* may well claim to preserve much original matter, and the same way be true to some extent of some portion of the *Bhagavati Sutra* and the *Uttaradhyayana Sutra*. The earliest Buddhist texts, known as the Pali Nikayas, also refer to the beliefs and teaching of Mahavira. Though we cannot expect them to give a fair and honest exposition of the tenets of their opponents, they somehow corroborate the evidence of the Jaina texts. In the light of both these evidences, an estimate of the teachings of Mahavira should be made.

The teachings of Mahavira were simple, practical and ethical, but gradually they developed into a complicated system with considerable emphasis on details. Because of conservatism, the evolution was more or less in a straight line, and there are no dissensions on fundamentals in Jainism. Mahavira and his disciples propounded not only the doctrinal side of Jainism relating to the nature of the truth and the ideal but also mapped out the practical and disciplinary path leading to the realization of both. It was chiefly in and through the life of monks or mendicants that the ideal of conduct was sought to be fulfilled.

Nirvana

The ultimate object of Jainism as taught by Mahavira is *Nirvana* which consists in the attainment of peace and infinite bliss. *Nirvana* is just another name for *Moksa* or liberation, *Mukti* or deliverance, salvation or beatitude, Gautama, a disciple of

Mahavira, explained *Nirvana* to Kesi, a disciple of Parsva : "It is a safe, happy, quiet and eternal place in view of all but difficult of approach where there is no old age, nor death, nor sorrow, nor pain, nor disease. It is a state of perfection which is obtained by putting an end to the stream of existence." It is liberation from a state of bondage brought on by *karman*. It is deliverance from old age, disease, death, and all that constitutes the self.

This highest goal is to be attained through annihilating the old *Kramans* (*Nirjara*) lying heavy on the soul by the practice of austerities (*Tapas*), and to stop the influx (*Asrava*) of new *Karmans* by the practice of self-restraint, called *Samvara,* with regard to the body, speech and mind.

Even in a Pali *Sutta,* the main aim of Mahavira's teaching has been mentioned as Sukha or infinite bliss which is not reachable through the finite happiness of even so fortunate among men as the reigning monarches; it is reachable only through *dudkkha* or pain of foregoing and forsaking all finite happiness. Had it been possible to attain beatitude through mundane happiness, king Srenika Bimbisara of Magadha would certainly have attained it. It the Pali *Sutta, Dukkha* or painful and difficult path meant *Dukkarakarika,* or a rigorous practice of penances. It was to be resorted to by us as a means of wearing out and ultimately destroying the effects of sinful deeds (*papakamma*) committed in a former existence. The practice of the three-fold self-restraint was to be taken recourse to by the aspirant as a means of not giving effect to a new *karman.*

Right Faith (Darsana), Right Knowledge (Jnana), and Right Conduct (Caritra)

Right Faith, Right Knowledge, and Right Conduct are the three essential points in Mahavira's teachings which lead to perfection by the destruction of *Kramans.* Without Right Faith, there is no Right Knowledge; without Right Knowledge there is no Virtuous Conduct; without virtues, there is no deliverance and without deliverance (*Moksha*), there is no perfection.

The excellence of one's faith depends on the following points : that one has no doubts about the truth of the tenets; that one has no preference for the tenets of others; that one does not doubt the saving qualities of one's own faith; that one is not shaken in the right belief; that one practices piety, that one encourages the weak; that one supports and loves the confessors of the law, and that one endeavours to exalt one's own faith.

Faith is produced by nature (*Nisarga*), instruction (*Upadesa*), command (*Ajna*), study of the *Sutras*, suggestion (*Bija*), comprehension of the meaning of the sacred lore (*Abhigama*), complete course of study (*Vistàra*), religious exercise (*Kriya*), brief exposition (*samkshepa*), and law (*Dharma*).

He who truly understands by a spontaneous effort of his mind the nature of soul, inanimate things, merit and demerit, and who puts an end to sins (*Asramasamvara*), believes by nature. He who believes the four truths taught by the Jinas believes by nature. He who believes by these truths having learnt them from somebody else believes by instructions. He who had got rid of love, hatred, delusion and ignorance believes by command. He who obtained righteousness by the study of the *Sutras* believes by the study of *Sutras*. He who knows the sacred lore believes by the comprehension of the sacred lore. He who understands the true nature of all substances believes by a complete course of study. He who sincerely performs all duties by Right Knowledge, Faith, etc. believes by religious exercise. He who is not versed in the sacred doctrines believes by brief exposition. He who believes in the truth of the realities, believes by the law. There is no right conduct without right belief; it must be cultivated for obtaining Right Faith; righteousness and right conduct originate together of righteousness precedes right conduct.

There are different kinds of obstruction right faith, such as sleep, activity, very deep sleep, a high degree of activity, and a state of deep-rooted greed. *Vedantya* is two-fold : pleasure and pain, *Mohaniya* is two fold : faith and conduct. The three kinds of *Mohaniya* concerning faith are right faith, wrong faith, and faith, partly right and partly wrong.

The *Uttaradhyayana Sutra* speaks of five kinds of knowledge : (1) *Sruta* of Knowledge derived from the study of sacred books; (2) *Abinibodhika* or knowledge obtained from one's own experience, thought, or understanding; (3) Avadhi or supernatural knowledge; (4) *Manahparyaya* or knowledge of the thoughts of other people; and (5) *Kevala*, the highest knowledge.

The *Avadhi-Jnana* is also employed in the sense of knowledge co-extensive with the object. The *Kalpa-Sutra*, for instance, says : "He viewed the whole *Jambudvipa* with his knowledge called *Avadhi*." Here Avadhi means that which is limited by the object, that which is just sufficient to survey the field of observation.

The *Manahparyaya-janan* is defied in the *Acharanga Sutra* as a knowledge of the thoughts of all sentient beings. The *Kevala-jnana* according to the same text, is omniscience enabling a person to comprehend all objects, to know all conditions of the world of gods, men, and demons : whence they come, where they go, where they are born, etc.

The first kind of knowledge in Jainism corresponds to the Buddhist *Sutamaya panna*; the second kind to *Chintamaya panna*; and the third kind to *Vilokana*; the fourth kind to *Chetopariyanana*; and the fifth kind to *Sabbannuta* or omniscience involving the three faculties. One of the Buddhist texts refers to limited knowledge (*Antavanta Jnana*) as propounded by Mahavira. Knowledge which is confined to the limited world is itself limited in its character. The Pali *Antavanta Jnana* is evidently the same term as the Jaina *Avadhi Jnana*.

Knowledge of substances, qualities and all developments (*Dravya, Guna* and *Paryaya*) has also been imparted by the Jinas. Substance is the substratum of qualities; qualities are inherent in a substance, but a characteristic feature of developments is that they inhere in substances of qualities. *Dharma, Adharma*, space, time, matter, and souls are the six kinds of substances. Insofar as *Dharma, Adharma*, and space are concerned, each of them is a substance, but time, matter, and souls form an infinite number of substances. The distinctive feature of *Dharma* is motion, that of *Adharma* is immobility, and that of space (*Akasa*) is room. The distinguishing mark of time is duration, that of the soul the realization of knowledge, faith, conduct, austerities, energy and its manifestations. The characteristic mark of matter is sound, darkness, luster, etc., that of development is singleness.

Right conduct, which destroys *Karma*, is the avoidance of everything sinful (*Samayika*), the initiation of the novice (*Khedopasthapaṅa*), purity produced by peculiar austerities (*Pariharavisuddhiku*), reduction of desire (*Sukshma samparaya*), and annihilation of sinfulness (*Akashaya yathakhyala*).

Virtue consists in right conduct. But there is no right conduct without right belief, and no right belief without the right perception of truth. Right conduct is achieved by threefold restraint, the restraint of the body, the restraint of speech and the restraint of mind. The first step towards virtue lies in the avoidance of sins. There are various ways of committing sins, directly and indirectly, through physical acts or through spoken words or even through thoughts. Thus to avoid sins, one must guard oneself by the *Samitis* or *Guptis*.

Not to kill anything, to live according to the rules of conduct and without greed, to take care of the highest good, to control oneself always while walking, sitting and lying down, and in the matter of food and drink, to shake off pride, wrath, deceit and greed, to possess the *Samitis*, to be protected by the five *Samvaras*, and to attain perfection by remaining unfettered among the fettered - these, in short, are the cardinal principles of *Garitra* as taught by Mahavira.

Austerities

The road to final deliverance also depends on austerities which destroy the bad *karmans*. These austerities are of two kinds : external and internal. The external austerities are of six kinds – (1) fasting (*Anasanu*), (2) abstinence (*Avamodrika*) (3) collecting alms (*Bhikshacharya*), (4) abstention from dainty food

(*Rasaparityaga*), (5) mortification of the flesh (*Kayaklesa*), and (6) taking care of one's limb (*Samlinata*).

Fasting is of two kinds (1) temporary (*Itvara*) and (b) fasting which precedes and ends with death (*Maranakala*), Temporary fasting is either that in which a desire (for food) is present, or that in which no such desire exists. Temporary fasting is briefly of six kinds : (1) in the form of a line, (2) in the form of a square, (3) in the form of a cube, (4) of a sixth power, (5) of a twelfth power, and (6) of any arrangement. Fasting, which is to precede death, is of two kinds with regard to the motions of the body : with change (of position) and without change. And, again, it is of two-fold : admitting relief or not admitting relief : one may either leave the place (which one has chosen to die in) or not leave it; in both cases one may not take any food.

Abstinence is briefly of five kinds : with regard to *(a)* substance, *(b)* place *(c)* time and *(d)* state of mind, and *(e)* development. He who takes less food than he usually does performs abstinence with regard to substance. Place signifies a village, a capital, a mine, settlement of a wild tribe, a poor town, a town with a harbour, a large town, an isolated town, a hermitage, a halting place, a resting place, a garden, a house, etc. Abstinence with regard to time is observed by him who goes about in a part of the four *Paurushis* (3 hours) of the day. If he collects alms in a part of the third *Paurushis* or in its last quarter, he observes abstinence with reference to time. Abstinence with regard to the state of mind is observed by him who accepts alms from a man or a woman, from a person richly ornamented or plain, if that person does not change his disposition or condition. A monk who observes abstinence according to the particulars which have been enumerated with regard to the substance, place, time, and state of mind, observes abstinence with regard to development too.

With regard to collecting alms, there are eight principal ways of collecting them : the seven *Eshanas* (or modes of begging) and other self-imposed restrictions. Abstention from dainty food means abstention from such highly nourishing food and drink as milk, curd, *ghee*, etc. Mortification of the flesh consists in such different postures as *Virasana*, etc. which benefit the soul, and which are difficult in living and sleeping in separate and unfrequented places where there are neither women nor cattle.

Internal austerities are of six types—(1) *Prayaschitta* or expiration of sins, (2) *Vinaya* or politeness, (3) *Vaiyavrtya* or serving the *Guru*, (4) *Svadhyaya* or study, (5) *Dhyana* or meditation, and (6) *Vyutsarga* or abandoning the body. Expiration of sins is ten-fold, what must be confessed, etc. This is to be strictly observed by a monk and is called expiration of sins. Politeness consists in rising (from one's seat), folding of the hands, offering a seat, loving the *Guru*, and cordial obedience. There are ten kinds of service, such as serving *Acarya*, etc., doing service, consists in giving one's assistance as well as one is able to give. Study is five-fold : (1) learning one's lesson, (2) questioning the teacher about it, (3) repetition, (4) pondering, and (5) religious discourse. To abstain from meditation is to abstain from meditation on painful and sinful things; one should, rather, meditate on the Law with a collected mind. If a monk remains motionless while lying down, sitting or standing upright, this is called abandonment of the body, which is one of the internal austerities.

Five Vows (Vratas) for the Ascetics

While *Parsva* taught only four vows for the realization of absolute happiness, Mahavira taught five in all, making chastity a separate vows altogether. These five vows are *Ahimsa* (not to kill), *Satya* (not to lie), *Asteya* (not to steal), *Brahmacarya* (to abstain from sexual intercourse), and *Apratigraha* (to renounce all interest in worldly things, especially in property).

The first great vow of the Jaina is abstinence from killing living beings. In thoughts, words and acts, he should do nothing injurious to beings who people the world, whether they move or not. A Jaina is wary in his walk. He searches into his mind and speech. He is careful in laying down his utensils. He eats and drinks after proper inspection.

The visible effect of *Ahimsa* was sought to be proved by a practical demonstration. Already in Mahavira's time, the righteous kings of India made it a point of duty to vouchsafe lawful protection to all forms of life within the sacred precincts of a religious establishment. This principle of causing no harm to any being had a salutary effect in man's habitual diet. Those who came under the influence of Mahavira's personality and teaching gave to the eating of meat and fish for good, and adhered to a strictly vegetarian diet.

The second great vow is the avoidance of falsehood. A Jaina speaks after deliberation. He comprehends and renounces anger, greed, fear, and mirth. The third great vow is the avoidance of theft. A Jaina begs after deliberation for a limited space. He consumes his food and drink with the permission of his superiors. A Jaina who has taken possession of some space should always take possession of limited part of it and for a fixed time. He should constantly have his grant renewed. He may beg for a limited ground for his co-religionists after deliberation.

The next vow is the avoidance of sexual pleasure. A Jaina should desist from continually discussing topics relating to women. He should not regard and contemplate the lovely forms of women. He should not recall to his mind the pleasures and amusements he formally had with women. He should not eat and drink too much. He should not drink liquor of eat highly seasoned food. He should not occupy a bed or a couch belonging to women.

The last great vow is freedom from possessions. If a living being with his ears open hears agreeable or disagreeable sounds, he should not be attached to them. If he with his eyes sees agreeable or disagreeable forms, he should not be attached to them. If he with his nose smells agreeable or disagreeable smells, he should not be attached to them. If he with his tongue tastes agreeable or disagreeable things, he should not be attached to them. If he with his organs of feeling feels agreeable of disagreeable things, he should not be attached to them.

The explanation offered by the Jaina texts in support of the addition of the vow of celibacy is as follows. The *Uttarddhyayana* says that "the first saints were simple but slow of understanding, the last saints prevaricating and slow of understanding, those between the two, simple and wise : hence there are two forms of the Law. The first could but with difficulty understand the precepts of the Law, and the last could only with difficulty observe them, but those between them easily understood and observed them."

It is however wrong to suppose that Parsva did not advocate celibacy. What he did was that in the vow of *Aparigraha* (non-possession) he included the vow of celibacy. This indirect implication of non-possession could easily be understood by the followers of Parsva who were 'simple and wise'. Mahavira's disciples, on the other hand, being prevaricating and slow of understanding could only with difficulty observe 'the vow of non-possession'. He had therefore to add the fifth vow of abstinence from all sexual acts in clear terms.

On this H. Jacobi remarks, "As the vow of chastity is not explicitly mentioned among Parsva's four vows, but was understood to be implicitly enjoined by them (i.e. Parsva's followers), it follows that only such men as were of an upright disposition and quick understanding would not go astray by observing the four vows literally, *i.e.*, by not abstaining from sexual intercourse, as it was not expressly forbidden. The argumentation in the monastic order to have occurred between Parsva and Mahavira, and this is possible only on the assumption of a sufficient interval of time having elapsed between the last two Tirthankaras. And this perfectly agrees with the common tradition that Mahavira came 250 years after Parsva."

It is on the basis of the number of vows observed that the sect of Parsva was known as *Caturyama* and that of Mahavira as *Panchayama*. These vows were strictly observed by monks who took them on entering the order. In their case, the vows were called the five great vows (Mahavira). Lay people, however, observed these vows as far as their worldly situation permitted. The five vows of the lay people were, of course, *anuvrata* or small vows.

A correct representation of the 'four-fold self-restraint', even in the sense of which the followers of Parsva understood it, is not wanting in Buddhist literature. Just then a separate vow of chastity was added to the 'four-fold self-restraint' to complete the list of five great vows (*Pancamahavratasa*) promulgated by Mahavira. These have been enumerated as abstinence from the idea of killing, the idea of theft, the idea of unchastity, the idea of lying, and some such tapoguna or virtue of an ascetic. It is interesting indeed to note that even some of the Jaina phrases have been reproduced in the Buddhist text.

As celibacy and nudity are closely related from the point of view of controlling the senses and the non-attachment to bodily pleasures and external needs, Mahavira also introduced the practice of nudity among the monks. His predecessor, Parsva, is said to have allowed an under and an upper garment to his followers.

Doctrine of the Nine Categories or Truths (Nava Tattva)

It was in opposing to Gosala's deterministic theory based on his biological researches that Mahavira is said to have gradually formulated his theory of the nine categories as well as his theory of *Karma*. His doctrine of the nine categories was meant to explain how the bondage of the soul arises by way of karmic effects upon it and how these effects are got rid off and the liberation of the soul is obtained. The categories are as follows : (1) *Jiva* (soul), (2)*Ajiva* (inanimate things), (3) *Bandha* (the binding of the soul by *Karma*), (4) *Punya* (merit), (5) *Papa* (demerit), (6) *Asrava* (that which causes the soul to be affected by (demerit), (7) *Samvara* (the prevention of *Asrava* by watchfulness), (8) *Nirjara* (the annihilation of *Karma*), and (9) *Moksha* (final deliverance). He who verily believes in the true teaching of the above nine fundamental truths possesses righteousness.

As corollaries to these terms, the theory of the categories

came to include two groups of terms. The *Pancastikayas* (five substances) comprehending and characterizing the world of existences are : (1) *Dharma* (medium of motion), *Adharma* (medium of rest), *Akasa* (space), *Jiva* (soul) and *Pudgala* (matter). The three terms of substance (*Dravya*), qualities (Guna) and *Paryaya* (Development) comprehend and characterize the five *Astikayas*.

The first pair of terms , *Jiva* and *Ajiva*, comprehends the world of existence as known and experienced. The *Jiva* signifies all that has life while *Ajiva* indicates those that are without life. The world of life is represented by six classes of living things and beings, three of which are immovable and three movable. Earth-lives, water-lives, and plants are immovable beings, while movable beings include all fire-lives, wind-lives, and those with an organic body. Living things are either subtle or gross, and living beings are either those still belonging to *Samsara* or those whose souls are perfected. Through the gradation of living things and beings, one can trace the evolution of the senses. The lowest form of being is provided with only one sense of touch.

It is only in relation to the six classes of beings that the process of *Karma* sets in and the nature of man's conduct is determined. "Know and understand," taught Mahavira, "that they all desire happiness; by hurting these beings, men do harm to their own souls, and will again and again be born as one of them. Every being born high or low in the scale of the living creation, among movable and immovable beings, will meet with its death. Whatever sins the evil-doer commits in every birth, for them he must die."

Things without life are either formed or formless. The formed are compound things and atoms constituting the world of matter. The world of the formless is represented by four *Astikayas, viz., Dharma, Adharma, Akasa* (space) and time. *Dharma* and *Adharma* explain motion and absence of motion respectively; *Akasa* (space) provides habitation for all living and non-living beings, and time explains their duration of existence. *Dharma, Adarma,* and space are each one substance only; but time, matter and souls are in infinite number of substances. Thus the category of *Ajiva* helps us complete the study of the world of life and existence.

The third term or category is *Bandha* or bondage of soul. *Bandha* is the subjection of the soul to the laws of the birth and death, of youth and age, of pleasure and pain, and other vicissitudes of life brought about by the effect of *Karma*.

The soul, which on one of the *Astikayas*, represents the principle of intelligence. The characteristic of the soul is knowledge, faith, conduct, austerities, energy, and realization of its developments. *Buddhaghosha* in his commentary on the *Brahmajala Sutta, Digha Nikaya* 1, 2, 381, mentions the Niganthas as holding the opinion that the soul has no colour, and it continues to exist after death and is free from ailments. This description is consonant with the opinion of the Jainas about the nature of the soul.

The categories of Merit (*Punya*) and Demerit (*Papa*) comprehend all acts or deeds, pious and sinful, which keep the soul bound to the circle of the births and deaths.

Airava is that which causes the soul to be affected by sins, and *Samavara* is the principle of self-control by which the influx of sins is checked or stopped. The category of *Samavara* comprehends the whole sphere of right conduct.

Nirjara or *Karmakshaya* consists in the wearing out of the accumulated effects of *Karma* on the soul by the practice of austerities, and *Moksha,* which logically follows from *Nirjara,* signifies the final deliverance of the soul from the bondage of *Karma. Siddhi* or perfection is just another aspect of liberation.

Theory of Karma

Mahavira'a theory of *Karma* is known as Dynamistic philosophy of notion of the freedom of the will. According to it, pleasure and pain, and happiness and misery of the individual depend upon his free will, exertion and manly strength. *Karma* is the deed of the soul. It is material forming a subtle bond of extremely refined Karmic matter which keeps the soul confined to its place of origin or the natural abode of full knowledge and everlasting peace.

Mahavira's great message to mankind is that birth is nothing, caste is nothing. *Karma* is everything, and that on the destruction of *Karma*, all future happiness depends. The theory of *Karma* represents all the most ancient and original feature of Jaina thought. According to H. Jacobi, "This *Karma* theory, if not in all details, certainly in the main outlines, is acknowledged in the oldest parts of the canon and presupposed by expressions and technical terms occurring in them. Some of the passages concerning the theory of *Karma* found in the old texts of Jainism are as follows :

"The painful condition of the self is brought about by one's own action, it is not brought about by any other cause (fate, creator, chance or the like)."

"Individually a man is born, individually he dies, individually he falls (from this state of existence), individually he rises (to another). His passions, consciousness, intellect, perceptions, and impressions belong to the individual exclusively. Here, indeed, the bonds of relationship are not able to help nor save one."

"All living beings owe their present from of existence to their own *Karma;* timid wicked, suffering latent misery, they err about (in the circle of births), subject to birth, old age, and death."

"The sinners cannot annihilate works by new works; the pious annihilate their works by abstention from works; the wise and happy men, who got rid of the effects of greed, do not commit sins."

"Pleasant things are not produced from pleasant things."

"He who intends (to kill) a living being but does not do it by his body, and he who unknowingly kills one, both are affected by that through a slight contact (with it) only, but the demerit (in their case) is not fully developed."

"He who knows himself and the world; who knows where (the creature) go, and whence they will not return; who knows what is eternal and what is transient; birth and death, and the future existence of men."

"He who knows the torture of being below (in hell); who knows the influx of sin and its stoppage; who knows misery and its annihialtion,—he is entitled to expound the Kriyavada."

"A perfect saint believes in the soul, believes in the world, believes in reward and believes in action. I did it I shall cause another to do it; I shall allow another to do it."

The passages cited above are sufficient to prove that *Kriyavada* expounded by Mahavira is in its essential feature only a theory of soul and *Karma*. According to this theory, there are as many souls as living individuals, and *Karma* consists of acts, intentional and unintentional, that produce effects on the nature of the soul. Thus the soul is not passive in the sense that it remains untouched or unaffected by what a person does, but is susceptible to the influences of *Karma*.

Even in some early Buddhist texts, we find the traces of *Kriyavada* as expounded in Jainism. In *Anguttara Nikaya*, III, 74, for instance, a learned Lichchavi prince of Vaisali, Abhaya, gives the following account of some Nigantha doctrines : "The Nigantha Nataputta teaches the annihilation by austerities of the old *Karma*, and the prevention by inactivity of new *Karma*. When *Karma* ceases, misery ceases; when misery ceases, perception ceases; when perception cease, every misery will come to an end. In the way, a man is saved by pure annihilation of sin (*nijjara*) which is really effective."

Another piece of information about Nigantha doctrines may be gathered from the *Mahavagga*. There a story is told of Siha who wanted to pay the Buddha a visit, but Nataputta tried to dissuade him from it simply because the Niganthas held to *Kriyavada* while the Buddha's beliefs were grounded in *Akriyavada*.

These passages throw light on the doctrine of *Karma* expounded by Mahavira. The theory of *Karma* has special significance if we consider it along with the views of Mahavira's contemporary religious thinkers. The Vedic thinkers thought that the world has been created and is governed by the gods. Purana Kassapa maintained that when a man acts or causes other to act, it is not his soul which acts or causes to act. Katayana advocated that whether a man buys or causes to buy, kill or causes to kill, he does not thereby commit any sin. Kesakambain explained that life ends here, and there is no world beyond. Denying the hereafter and the efficacy of all social institutions founded upon beliefs in the future existence of man, he cannot inform us whether an action is good or bad, virtuous or vicious, well done or otherwise, whether it is in man's power to reach perfection or not, or whether there is heaven and a hell. Gosala denies that our happiness and misery, weal and ill, are caused by us individually or determined by any other cause than what we term fate or necessity.

Karma is believed, according to Mahavira, to be the result of actions arising out of four sources : (1) the first source of *Karma* is attachmetn to worldly things such as food, raiment, dwelling place, women, etc.; (2) it is produced by uniting one's body, mind, and sppech to worldly things; (3) it is also engendered by giving the reins to anger, pride, deceit or greed; and, (4) lastly by false belief which is a fruitful source of it. *Karma* accumulates energy and automatically works it off without any outside intervention.

Karma is divided according to its nature, duration, essence, and content. It is intimately bound up with the soul. There are eight kinds of *Karmans* : (1) *Jnanavaraniya* acts as an obstruction to right knowledge; (2) *Darsanavaraniya* prevents one from beholding the true faith; (3) *Vedaniya* leads to the experience of pain or pleasure; (4) *Mohaniya* leads to delusion; (5) *Ayukarma* determines the length of life; (6)

Nama determines the name or individually of the embodied soul; (7) *Gotra* determines his Gotra; and (8) *Antarya* prevent one's entrance into the path that leads to eternal bliss.

While it is on the first step (*Mithyattvagunasthanaka*) the soul is completely under the influence of *Karma* and knows nothing of the truth. Whirling round in the cycle of rebirth, it loses some of its crudeness and attains to a state which enables it to distinguish between what is false and what is true. A soul remains in an uncertain condition, one moment knowing the truth and the next doubting it. Either through the influence of his past good deeds or through the teachings of his *Guru*, man comes to acquire what is true faith. He then realizes the great importance of conduct and finds himself quite capable of taking the twelve vows. As soon as he reaches the state of an *Ayogikevaligunashanaka*, all his *Karma* is purged away, and he proceeds at once to *Moksa* as a *Siddha*.

There are four kinds of destructive *Karma* (*Khatiyakarma*) which keep the soul tethered to mundane existence. They are as follows: (1) Knowledge-obscuring *Karma*, (2) faith-obscuring *karma*, (3) *Karma* which obstructs the progress of the soul, and (4) *Karma* which deludes the soul. Indeed *Karma* plays an important part in Jaina metaphysics. Jainism as a practical religion teaches us to purge ourselves of impurities arising from *Karma*.

Six Lesyas

The *Lesyas* are different conditions produced in the soul by the influence of different *Karmans*. They are, therefore, not dependent on the nature of the soul, but on the *Karma* which accompanies the soul, and are, as it were, the reflection of the *Karmans* on the soul. The *Lesya* is, according to the Sutrakritanga, a term signifying, 'colour'.

The *Ajivika* expression *Chalabhijatiyo* as explained by Buddhaghosha implies the same method of classification of men in terms of six colours. According to H. Jacobi, Mahavira borrowed the idea of the six *Lesyas* from the Ajivikas and altered it to bring it into harmony with the rest of his own doctrines. This view is not correct because the idea of the six *Lesyas* was prevalent in Jainism earlier than *Mahavira*. The classification of living beings in terms of six colours may be traced back to Parsva's doctrine of six *Jivanikayas*.

The *Mahabharata* expression *Jiva-Shatvarna* hardly leaves room for doubt that *Lesya* is a term indicative of colour. The

Buddhist idea of the contamination of mind by the influx of impurities from outside, illustrated by the simile of a piece of cloth dyed blue, red, yellow, or the like would seem to have some bearing on the Jaina doctrine of the *Lesyas*.

The Jaina religious efforts are directed towards the acquisition of pure *lesya*. This doctrine of the six *Lesyas* is merely hinted at here and there in the *Sutrakrtanga* and fully explained in the *Uttaradhyayana*. They are named in the following order: black, blue, gray, red, yellow, and white. The black *Lesya* has the colour of a rain-cloud, a buffaloes' horn. The blue *Lesya* has the colour of the blue Asoka having red flowers. The gray *Lesya* has the colour of *Atasi* having blue flowers. The red *Lesya* has the colour of vermilion. The yellow *Lesya* has the colour of orpiment. The white *Lesya* has the colour of a conch-shell. The taste of the black *Lesya* is more bitter than that of *Tumbaka*. The taste of the blue *Lesya* is infinitely more pungent than that of *Trikatuka* (black pepper and dry ginger). The taste of the gray *Lesya* is infinitely sourer that of unripe mango. The taste of the yellow *Lesya* is infinitely better than of excellent wine and various liquors. The taste of the white *Lesya* is infinitely better than that of dates, grapes, and milk.

The smell of the bad *Lesyas* (*viz.*, of the first three) is infinitely worse than that of a dead cow, dog, or snake. The smell of the three good *Lesyas* is infinitely more pleasant than that of fragrant flowers and of perfumes when they are pounded. The touch of the bad *Lesyas* is infinitely worse than that of a saw, the tongue of a cow, or the leaf of the teak tree. The touch of the three good *Lesyas* is infinitely more pleasant than that of cotton, butter or *Sirisha* flowers.

The degrees of the *Lesyas* are three, or nine, or twenty-seven, or eighty-one, or two hundred and forty-three. Each of these degrees is three-fold : low, middle, and high. He who acts on the impulse of the five sins, who commits cruel acts, and who is wicked and mischievous, is described as one fostering the black *Lesya*. He who nourishes anger, ignorance, hatred, wickedness, deceit, greed, carelessness, love of enjoyment, etc., develops the blue *Lesya*. He who is dishonest in words and acts, who is a heretic, a deceiver, a thief, etc. develops the gray *Lesya*. He who is humble, well-disciplined, restrained, free from deceit, who loves the law, develops the red *Lesya*. He who controls himself and is attentive to his study and duties, develops the yellow *Lesya*. He who controls himself, who abstains from constant thinking about his misery, who is free from passion, who is calm and who subdues his senses, develops the white *Lesya*. The black, blue, and grey *Lesyas* are the lowest *Lesyas*; through them, the soul is dragged into certain miserable courses of life. The red, yellow, and white *Lesyas* are the good *Lesyas*, for through them the soul is brought into a state of happiness. In the first and last moment of all these *Lesyas*, when they are joined with the soul, the latter is not born into a new existence.

Doctrine of Nayas

Sanjaya is an important landmark in the development of Mahavira's philosophy. H. Jacobi assumes that in opposition to the agnosticism (*Ajnanarada*) of Sanjaya, Mahavira propounded his doctrine of *Naya*. The canonical text just mention *Nayas* without fixing up their number four or seven. It is true that the *Bhagavati* and the *Pannavana* refer to the seven-fold *Naya*, but these texts contain a good deal of later material. In the post canonical works, the doctrine of *Nayas* was called *Syadvada* (*Saptabhanginyaya*), according to which there can be seven alternatives to a decisive conclusion. *Nayas* were actually the ways of expressing the nature of things from different points of view; they were the ways of escaping from the tendencies of insensitivity and dogmatism which Mahavira disliked. They appealed to the masses because they encouraged a tolerant attitude towards different religions.

The question with regard to which Sanjaya suspended judgment were in fact the questions to be excluded from the problems of knowledge. Is the world eternal, or is it non-eternal? Is it both eternal and non-eternal, or is it neither eternal nor non-eternal? Is the world finite of infinite? Is there any individual existence of man after death, or is there not? Is the absolute truth seen face of face by a seer, comprehended by a philosopher, part of real tangible existence,or not? It was with regard to these and similar questions that Sanjaya refused to submit any affirmative answer. To avoid error, he contented himself with the four famous negative propositions : A is not B; A is not not-B; A is not both B and not-B, A is not neither B nor not-B.

It is with regard to these questions that Mahavira declared : "From these alternative, to you cannot arrive at truth; from these alternatives, your are certainly led to error." The world is eternal as far as that part is concerned which is the substratum of the (*dravya*) "world"; it is not eternal as far as its ever-changing state is concerned. In regard to such questions, Mahavira's advice to his disciples was neither to support those who maintained that the world is eternal nor those who advocated that it is not eternal. He would have said the same thing regarding such propositions as the world exists and it does not exist; the world is unchangeable; the world is in constant flux; the world has a beginning; the world has no beginning; the world has an end; the world has no end, etc. Those who are not well-instructed differ in their opinions and hold fast to their dogmas without reason. And these were precisely the questions which Buddha regarded as unthinkable on the ground that those who will think about them are sure to go mad, without ever being able to find a final answer, or to reach apodeictic certainty.

If one has to answer such question, one should answer them by saying, contrary to both a dogmatist and a sceptic, "It may me that in one sense, looking from one point of view, A is B. It may be that in another sense, looking from another point of view, A is not-B. It may again be that looking from a third point of view, A is and B and not-B. It may equally be that when viewed from a fourth point of view, A is neither B nor not-B."

Exertion of Righteousness

Mahavira has given instructions regarding exertion of righteousness. Those who believe in it, accept it, practice it, comply with it, study it, and understand it, have obtained perfection, enlightenment, deliverance and final beatitude. He has dealt with the following subjects :

1. Longing for liberation (Samvega)

By longing for liberation, the soul obtains an intense desire for the Law. Impelled by an intense desire for the Law, he quickly arrives at an increased longing for liberation. He destroys anger, pride, deceit and greed. He becomes possessed of right faith and by the purity of faith, he will reach perfection after one birth.

2. Disregard of Wordly Objects (Nirveda)

By disregarding worldly objects, the soul quickly feels disgust for pleasures enjoyed by men, gods and animals. He becomes indifferent to all ceases thereby to engage himself in any undertaking, with the result that he enters the road to perfection.

3. Desire for the Law (Dharmasraddha)

Through his desire for the Law, the soul becomes indifferent to pleasures. He abandons the life of householders and as a houseless monk, puts an end to all sufferings, mental and physical.

4. Obedience to the Co-religionists (Gurusadharmikasusrushana)

Through obedience to them, the soul obtains discipline. Through discipline and avoidance of misconduct, he avoids being born as a denizen of hell; through his devotion to the Guru, he obtains truth as a good man and gains perfection and beatitude.

5. Confession of Sins before Guru (Alokana)

By this act, the soul gets rid of the thorns of deceit, wrong belief, etc. He obtains simplicity and annihilates *Karma.*

6. Repenting of one's Sins to Oneself (Ninda)

By this act, the soul obtains repentance, and becoming indifferent by repentance, he prepares for himself an ascending scale of virtues, by which he destroys the *karmans* resulting from delusion.

7. Repenting of one's sins before the Guru (Garha)

By this act, the soul obtains humbleness. He will leave off all blamable occupations and apply himself only to the praiseworthy ones.

8. Moral and intellectual purity of the soul (Samayika)

This purity enables the soul to refrain from all sinful occupations.

9. Adoration of the twenty-four Jinas (Caturvimsatistava)

Through this adoration the soul arrives at the purity of faith.

10. Paying Reverence to the Guru (Vandana)

It enables the soul to destroy such *Karma* as leads to birth in low families. He wins the affection of the people and brings about general good-will.

11. Expiation of Sins (Pratikramana)

Through expiration of sins the soul obviates transgressions of the vows and thus stops the *Asravas* or sins.

12. A Particular Position of the Body (Kayotsarga)

Kayotsarga helps the soul get rid of the past and present transgressions which require *prayaschitta* (expiatory rites).

13. Self-denial (Pratyakhyana)

Self-denial enables the soul to close the door against *Asravas* and to prevent desires from arising in him.

14. Praises and Hymns (Stavastutimangala)

Through praises and hymns he obtains wisdom consisting in knowledge, faith, and conduct.

15. Keeping the Right Time (Kalasya pratyupekshana)

By keeping the right time, he destroys *Karma* which obstructs right knowledge.

16. Practicing Penance (Prayascittakarana)

By practicing penance, he gets rid of sins and commits no transgressions.

17. Begging Forgiveness (Kshamapana)

By begging forgiveness, he obtains happiness of mind.

18. Study (Svadhyaya)

Study helps him destroy the *Karma* which obstruct right knowledge.

19. Recital of the Sacred Texts (Vacana)

By the recital of the sacred texts, he obtains destruction of *Karma* and preserves the sacred lore.

20. Questioning the Teacher (Paripricehana)

By questioning the teacher, he arrives at a correct comprehension of the Sutra and its meaning.

21. Repetition (Paravartana)

By repetition, he reproduces the sounds or syllables and commits them to memory.

22. Pondering (Anupredsha)

By pondering on what he has learnt, he loosens the firm hold which the seven kinds of *Karma* have upon the soul; he shortens their duration and mitigates their power.

23. Religious Discourse (Dharmakatha)

Through religious discourses he destroys his Karma and exalts the creed, and by exalting the creed, he acquires Karma for the future bliss.

24. Acquisition of Sacred Knowledge (Srutasyaradhana)

By the acquisition of sacred knowledge, he destroys ignorance.

25. Concentration of Thoughts (Ekagramanahsannivesana)

By concentration of his thoughts, he obtains stability of the mind.

26. Control (Samyama)

By control, he achieves freedom from sins.

27. Austerities (Tapas)

Austerities help him cut off *Karma*.

28. Cutting off Karma (Vyavadana)

By cutting off *Karma*, he obtains freedom from action.

29. Renouncing Pleasure (Sukhasata)

By renouncing pleasures, he obtains freedom from false longing.

30. Metal Independence (Apratibaddhata)

Through mental Independence he gets rid of attachment.

31. Using Unfrequented Lodging and Beds (Vicitrasayanasanasevana)

By using unfrequented lodgings and beds, he obtains *Gupti* or conduct. He will be steady in his conduct.

32. Turning Uway the Uorld (Vinivartana)

By turning away from the world, he will strive not to perform any bad action.

33. Renouncing Collection of Alms in One District Only (Sambhogapratyakhyana)

By doing so, he overcomes obstacles and unhindered by them, exerts himself to attain liberation; he is content with the alms he gets, and does not hope for, care for, or covet those of a fellow-monk. Not envying other monks, he takes up a separate, agreeable lodging.

34. Renouncing Articles of Use (Upadhipratyakhyana)

By renouncing the articles of use, he studies successfully; in the absence of the articles of use, he becomes exempt from desires, and does not suffer misery.

35. Renouncing Food (Aharapratyakhyana)

By renouncing (forbidden) food, he ceases to act for the sustenance of the life; ceasing to act for the sustenance of his life, he does not suffer misery when without food.

36. Conquering the Passion (Kashayapratyakhyana)

By conquering his passions, he becomes free from passions; thereby he becomes indifferent to both happiness and pain.

37. Renouncing Activity (Yogapratyakhyana)

By renouncing activity, he obtains inactivity; by ceasing to act, he acquires no new *Karman,* and destroys the one he had acquired before.

38. Renouncing the body (Sarirapratyakhyana)

By renouncing his body, he acquires he pre-eminent virtues of the *Siddhas,* by the possession of which he goes to the highest region of the universe, and becomes absolutely happy.

39. Renouncing Company

By renouncing company, he obtains singleness and avoids disputes, quarrels, passions, etc.

40. Renouncing All Food (Bhaktapratyakhyana)

By renouncing all food, he prevents his birth many times.

41. Perfect Renunciation (Sadbhavapratyakhyana)

Through perfect renunciation, he enters the final stage of pure meditation where there is no return.

42. Confirming to the Standard (Pratirupata)

By conforming to he standard of monks, he obtains ease and will be careful. He will inspire all beings with confidence and practice austerities.

43. Doing Service (Vaiyavritya)

By doing service, he acquires Karma which get for him the name and family name of Tirthankara.

44. Fulfilling All Virtues (Sarvagunasampurnata)

By fulfilling all virtues, the boon he receives is that he will not be born again; he will thus be exempt from the pains of the body and mind.

45. Freedom from Passion (Vitaragata)

Freedom from passion enables him to cut off the ties of attachment and desire, making him indifferent to all agreeable and disagreeable sensations of sound, touch, colour, and smell.

46. Patience (Kshanti)

Patience enables him to overcome troubles.

47. Freedom from Greed (Mukti)

Freedom from greed helps him welcome voluntary poverty and free him from the desire for material prosperity.

48. Simplicity (Arjava)

Through simplicity, he will become upright in action, thought and speech, and will become veracious and a true practitioner of the law.

49. Humility (Mardava)

Through humility he will acquire freedom from self-conceit; he will become a man of kind and meek disposition, and avoid the eight kinds of pride.

50. Sincerity of Mind (Bhavasatya)

Sincerity of mind will help him obtain the purity of mind, which will induce him to exert himself for the fulfilment of the Law; and he will practice the Law in the next world too.

51. Sincerity of Religious Practice (Karanasatya)

Through sincerity in religious practice, he obtains proficiency in it; being proficient in it he will act up to his words.

52. Sincerity in Acting (Yogasatya)

Through sincerity in acting, he will become pure in his actions.

53. Watchfulness of the Mind (Manoguptata)

Through the watchfulness of the mind, he concentrates his thought, thereby practicing true control.

54. Watchfulness of Speech (Vag-guptata)

Watchfulness of speech ensures freedom from prevarication and enables one's mind to act properly.

55. Watchfulness of the Body (Kayaguptata)

Through the watchfulness of the body, he obtains restraint (*Samvara*) and prevents sinful *Asravas*.

56. Discipline of the Mind (Manahsamadharana)

By disciplining his mind, he obtains concentration of his thoughts and obtains development of knowledge, which produces righteousness and annihilates wrong belief.

57. Discipline of the Speech (Vaksamadharana)

By disciplining his speech, he obtains development of faith and acquires facility in becoming enlightened, destroying all preventing causes.

58. Discipline of the Body (Kayssamadharana)

Through the discipline of the body he facilitates the developments of his conduct. He may also obtain perfection, enlightenment, and deliverance.

59. Possession of Knowledge (Jnanasampannata)

Through his possession of knowledge, he acquires an understanding of words and their meanings.

60. Possession of Faith (Darsanasampannata)

Through his possession of faith, he destroys wrong belief, which is the cause of worldly existence, and he will not lose his inner light; but he endues his self with the highest knowledge and faith, and purifies it.

61. Possession of Conduct (Caritrasampannata)

Possession of conduct helps him obtain stability, with which a houseless monk destroys the four remnants of *Karma* which even a *Kevalin* possesses; after that he obtains perfection, enlightenment, deliverance and final beatitude, and puts an end to all misery.

62. Subduing the Ear (Srotrendriyanigraha)

By subduing the organ of hearing, he overcomes his delight in all pleasant or unpleasant sounds and acquires no new *Karma* while destroying the old one.

63-66. Subduing the Eye, the Organ of Smell, Tongue and the Organ of Touch (Cakshurindriyanigraha, Ghranendriyanigraha, Jihvendriyanigraha and Sparsaṇendriyanigraha)

This applies also to his subduing the organs of sight, smell, taste and touch with regard to pleasant colours, smells, tastes, and touches.

67. Conquering Anger (Krodhavijaya)

By conquering anger he obtains patience; he acquires no *Karma* productive of anger, and destroys the Karma he had acquired before.

68. Conquering Pride (Manavijaya)

By conquering pride he obtains simplicity.

69. Conquering Deceit (Mayavijaya)

By conquering deceit he obtains humility.

70. Conquering Greed (Lobhavijaya)

By conquering greed he obtains contentment.

71. Conquering Love, Hate and Wrong belief (Premadveshamithyadarisanavijaya)

By conquering love, hatred and wrong belief, he exerts himself for right knowledge, faith and conduct. After destroying various kinds of *Karma,* he obtains absolute and complete knowledge and faith.

72. Stability (Saileshi)

He first stops the functions of his mind, then the functions of his speech, then those of the body, and at last he ceases to breathe. During the short interval required and pronouncing five short syllables, he is engaged in the final pure meditation in which all the functions of his bodily organs cease and the four remnants of his *Karma* are at the same time destroyed.

73. Freedom from Karma (Akarmata)

After getting rid of his *Avdarika Karmana* (and *Taijasa*) bodies the soul takes the form of a straight line, goes in a moment, without touching anything and taking up no space, (upwards to the highest *Akasa*), and then develops into his natural form and obtains perfection.

The Four Requisites

It is difficult for a living being to obtain these four things of great value : (1) Human birth, (2) Instructions in the Law, (3) Belief in it, and (4) Power of self-control. The universe is filled with innumerable creatures born in the world in different families and castes for having done various actions. Sometimes they go to the world of gods and sometimes to hell and sometimes they become Asuras (demons) in accordance with their actions; sometimes they become *Kshatriyas* or *Chandalas* or worms or ants. Living beings will reach ants. Living beings of sinful actions, who are born again and again, are not disgusted with this *Samsara*. Through the destruction of their *Karma*, living beings will reach in time a pure state and will be born as men. Though born as human beings, it would be difficult for them to hear the law; having heard it, they will do penances, combat their passions, and abstain from killing living beings. It will be difficult for them to believe in the law though indeed they will hear it. Many who are shown the right way are led astray.

The pious obtain purity and the pure stand firmly in the law. Having enjoyed in due time the unrivalled pleasures of human life, they will obtain true knowledge through their pure religious merit acquired in a former birth; knowing full well that the four requisites are difficult to obtain, they will apply themselves to self-control and will be eternal *Siddhas* (perfected ones) when they will be able to shake off the remnant of *Karma* by their penances.

Impurity

Since one cannot prolong life, one should not on that account be careless. Those who acquire wealth by evil deeds and by adhering to wrong principles, will lose it. People in this world and in the next cannot escape the effect of their own actions. Wealth will never protect a careless man in this world. Like a wise man, trust nobody but be always wary and on the alert.

One cannot quickly arrive at discernment; therefore one

should exert oneself, abstain from pleasures, understand the world, guard oneself, and be impartial like a sage. External things weaken the intellect and allure many; therefore keep them out of mind. Remove pride, delusion, greed and deceit. Heretics, who are impure and proud, are always subject to love and hatred, and they are wholly under the influence of their passions. Despising them as unholy men, one should desire virtue till the end of one's life.

Death Against (and with) One's Will

There can be two ways of dying : (1) Death with one's will, and (2) death against one's will. Death against one's will is the death of an ignorant man, and it happens to him several times. Death with one's will is the death of a wise man, and it happens only once as, for instance, in the case of a *Kelalin*. A fool being attached to pleasure does cruel actions. He who is attached to pleasures and amusements will be caught in the trap of deceit. The pleasures of this life are within the reach of your hand but the future pleasures are uncertain. It is doubted whether there is any world other than our own. An ignorant man kills, lies, deceives, drinks wine and eats meat, thinking that there is nothing wrong in doing what he does. A man desirous of possessing wealth and woman accumulates sins by his act thought. Fools, who do cruel deeds, will suffer violently. When death really comes, the fool trembles in fear. He dies against his will. Some householders are indeed superior to some monks of self-control. But the saints are verily superior to all householders in self-control. A faithful man should practice the rules of conduct meant for householders. He should never neglect the fast. Those who are trained in self-control and penance, whether monks or householders, and those who have obtained liberation by the absence of passions, go straight to the highest regions. The virtuous and the learned do not tremble in the hour of death. A wise man will become calm through patience and will have an undisturbed mind at the time of death. When the right time for death has come, a faithful monk should in the presence of his teacher suppress all emotions or fear of joy, and wait for his end. When the time for quitting the body comes the sage dies willingly.

On Discipline

A wise man should not be angry if reprimanded. He should rather, be a man of forbearing temperament. Nor should he associate with mean persons and be guilty of doing anything mean (*chandaliya*) or evil. He should meditate by himself after having learnt his lessons. He should never refuse to confess if he does anything mean. He should not speak unasked for. He should not tell a lie when asked. If the self is subdued, a person will be happy. It is better to subdue one's own self by self-control and penance than be subdued by others with fetters and corporal punishment. He should never do anything disagreeable to his superiors either in words or deeds, openly or secretly. He should never remain silent if spoken to by his superiors. He should always approach his teacher politely. An intelligent pupil will rise from his seat and answer the teacher's call modestly and attentively. A good pupil has the best opinion of his teacher, for he thinks that his teacher treats him like his own son or brother. He should not provoke his teacher's anger, nor should he himself lose his temper. If the teacher is angry, he should pacify him by kindness and appease him with folded hands. An intelligent man, who has learnt the sacred texts, takes his duties upon himself. When a worthy teacher is satisfied with a pupil, he will transmit to him his vast knowledge of the sacred texts, and the pupil will gladden the heart of his teacher by his good deeds.

Egoism, delusion, carelessness, illness, and idleness are the five causes which render good discipline impossible. Discipline calls upon the practitioner : (1) not to be fond of mirth, (2) to control himself, (3) not to speak evil of others, (4) not to be without discipline, (5) not to be of wrong discipline, (6) not to be covetous, (7) not to be choleric, and (8) to love truth.

Actions of Ignorant and Wise Men

All men, who are ignorant of truth, are subject to pain. A wise man who considers well the way that lead to bondage and birth should search for the truth. A man of pure faith should realize the truth that he will have to suffer for his own deeds.

Clever talking will not bring salvation. Even while sinking lower and lower through their sins, fools believe themselves to be wise men. One should move about carefully in the endless *Samsara*. One should never desire worldly objects but sustain one's body only to be able to annihilate one's *Karma*. Recognising the cause of *Karma*, one should move about waiting for one's death.

It is an ignorant man who kills, tells lies, robs on the highway, steals goods, and deceives others. He will go to the world of the *Asuras* (demons) against his will. Those men who, through the exercise of various virtues, become pious householders, will surely reap the fruit of their actions. A virtuous man cheerfully ascends to the state of gods. He who has not given up pleasures will not be able to reach the true end of his soul. He will go astray again and again though he has been taught the right way. A sinner will be born in hell and a virtuous man will be born in heaven.

The best of the sages who are free from delusion and possess perfect knowledge and faith, speaks for the benefit, eternal welfare, and the final liberation of all beings.

It is difficult to satisfy anybody. The more one gets the more one wants. Man's desire increases with his means. One should not desire women who continually changes their minds, who entice men, and then make a sport of them as of slaves.

Vanity of Worldly Pleasures

Karma is produced by sinful thoughts, and it is by the influence of his *Karma* that Chitra and Sambhuta were separated. All singing is but prattle, all dancing is but mocking, all ornaments are but a burden, all pleasures produce but pain. Pleasures, which are liked by the ignorant and which produce pain, do not delight pious monks who do not care for pleasures but are intent on the virtue of right conduct. He who has not done good deeds in this life and who has not practiced the

Law, repents of it in the next world or even when he has become a prey to death which leads off a man in his last hour. He alone will have to endure his sufferings, neither his kinsmen, nor his friends, nor his sons, nor his relations, for *Karma* follows the doer. Life drags on towards death continuously, and old age carries off the vigour of man. Time runs out and the days quickly pass. Pleasures which men enjoy are not permanent. They leave them as soon as they come just as a bird leaves a tree devoid of fruits. If one is unable to give up pleasures, then one must do noble deeds, follow the Law and have compassion on all creatures.

Man's life is transitory and precarious. He finds no delight in domestic life. Pleasures bring him only a moment's happiness. But suffering for a long time brings intense suffering and no happiness. Pleasures are an obstacle to the liberation from existence, and are a mine of evils. The soul cannot be apprehended by the senses because it possesses no corporeal form; and, since it has no corporeal from, it is eternal. The fetter of the soul born of our evil deeds is called the cause of worldly existence. Being ignorant of the law, human beings formerly did sinful actions, and through their wrong-mindedness, they could not enter the order. Mankind is harassed by death. He who has acquired righteousness may look upon death as his friend. Faith will enable him to put aside attachment. The pleasures he enjoys cause the continuance of his wordly existence. One should be cautious in this matter. He should learn the law thoroughly, practice severe penance, and never dissipate his energy.

The Causes of Carelessness

Through the possession of true knowledge, through the avoidance of ignorance and delusion, and through the destruction of love and hatred, one arrives at deliverance which is nothing but bliss. One should serve the *Guru* and the old teachers, avoid foolish people, apply oneself earnestly to study, and to ponder over the meaning of the *Sutra*. A *sramana* who engaged in austerities longs for righteousness should eat only the quantity of food allowed, should select a companion of right understanding and should live in a solitary. If he does not meet with a suitable companion, he should live by himself, abstaining from sins and not devoted to pleasures. Love and hatred are caused by *Karma* which has its origin in delusion. *Karma* is the root of birth and death. Misery ceases with the absence of delusion, delusion with the absence of desire, desire with the absence of greed, and greed with the absence of property. Rich and delicious food should not particularly be preferred, for it generally makes men overstrong, and desires rush upon the strong. The mind of those who always live in unfrequented lodgings, who eat poor food, and who subdue their senses, will not be attached by passions which are vanquished as disease is by medicine.

A monk engaged in penance should not allow himself to watch the shape, beauty, coquetry, laughter, prattle, gestures and glances of women nor retain a recollection of them in his mind. Not to look at women, nor to long for praise, and think of them, is the high ideal of all noble souls and is always wholesome to those who delight in chastity. Those who possess the three *Guptis* cannot be disturbed by the well-adorned goddesses. To a man who longs for liberation, who is afraid of *Samsara* and lives according to the law, nothing in the world offers so many difficulties as women who delight the mind of the ignorant. To those who have overcome the attachment of women all other attachments will offer no difficulties. From the desire for pleasure arises the misery of the whole world. The dispassionate will put an end to whatever misery of the mind and body there is. A monk who is engaged in austerities and who longs for righteousness should not fix his thought on the pleasant objects of the senses.

He who is passionately fond of colours will come to untimely ruin. He who passionately hates a colour will, at the same moment, suffer pain. He who is very fond of a lovely colour hates all others, hence a fool suffers misery. He who has a passion for colour will kill many moveble and immovable beings. A passionate fool intent on serving his own personal end torments those beings in many ways. When he is not satisfied with these colours and when his craving for them grows stronger and stronger, he will become discontented. Misled by greed, he will grab another man's property. When overcome by a violent desire, he grabs another man's property and when he is not satisfied with those colours, then his deceit and falsehood increase in proportion to his greed; yet he will not get rid of his misery. He who is indifferent to true colours is free from sorrows. All such passions as anger, pride, deceit, disgust, aversion to self-control, delight in sexual things, mirth, fear, sorrow, carnal desire for women, arise in him who is attached to pleasures. When he ceases to desire the objects of his senses his desire for pleasure also becomes extinct. A dispassionate man, who performs all duties, will quickly remove the obstacles to right knowledge and right faith. Then he knows and sees all things. He is free from delusions, hindrances, and sins. He is proficient in meditation and being pure attains beatitude. He gets rid of all misery which afflicts mankind. He becomes infinitely happy and obtains the final aim.

Sinful and Wicked Deeds

There are three ways of committing sins : by one's own action, by commission, and by approval of the deed. A learned or a virtuous man will generally be punished for his deed when he is given to actions of deceit. Men who are drowned in lust and addicted to pleasures will be deluded for want of self-control. Heroes of faith, who do not commit sin, and who exert themselves as they should, who subdue anger and fear, will never kill living beings. The wicked suffering latent misery wander about in the circle of births, subject to old age and death. One should not kill living beings in the three-fold way (in thought, act and speech) if one is intent on spiritual welfare and abstention from sins. A sinner does not confess himself to be wrong; instead he boasts of his sin when reprimanded. The adulterers are severely punished. The feet bound together with the fetters of sensuality, will be subject to delusion again and again.

Those who kill other for the sake of their own pleasure

are wicked. Reckless men who cut down the sprouts for their own sport destroy many living beings. Sprouts are beings capable of natural development. People who destroy seeds for their own pleasure are wicked. All creatures who have committed sins will suffer. A miserable man who becomes a monk in order to get food from others and a flatterer in order to fill his belly will come to grief. Wrong beliefs and bad conduct are worthless. Servile man should not desire pleasant sounds and colours; he should rather conquer his longing for all kinds of pleasures.

Sinners, subject to love and hatred and wrong-doing, acquire *Karma* arising from passions and commit many sins. The careless commit sins in their thought, act and speech. A cruel man does cruel things and is thereby involved in other cruelties. Sinful undertakings will in the end entail suffering. A pious monk, free from bonds and fetters, annihilates his bad *Karma* and removes the thorn of sin. Following the rules of right conduct, he exerts himself.

Sentient beings engage themselves in the following kinds of activities : sinning for one's own interest, sinning without a personal interest, sinning by staying, through accident, by error or sight, by lying, by taking what is not freely given, by mere conceit, through pride, through greed, through deceit, through bed treatment of one's friends and actions concerning a religious life.

Hells

In hell there is suffering from heat and cold. The sinners are cut, pierced, and hacked to pieces with swords and daggers, with darts and javelins. They undergo sharp, horrible, and acute pain. The imprudent sinners, who injure many beings without relenting, will go to hell and cross the river Vaitarani, the waves of which cut like sharp rajors. They are pierced with long pikes and tridents. They roll about and are roasted in the Kadamba Bahula river. They come to the great impassable hell called Asurya, where the Sun does not shine. Here also they are roasted. The sinners are hewn with axes like piece of timber. They are stewed in iron caldrons filled with their own blood. They are not reduced to ashes. They undergo this kind of punishment for their misdeeds. In hells sinners suffer on account of their sinful deeds done by them while on earth. The noses, ears, and lips of the sinners are cut off with razors and their tongues are pulled out with sharp pikes. They are thrown into large caldrons and boiled there. They are compelled to drink molten lead and copper when they are thirsty. In hell there is a terrible towering mountain called the Vaitalika where evil-doers are long tortured. Thus the sinners are tortured day and night. They cry at the top of their voices in a dreadful hell which contains various implements of torture.

Hells are round inside, square outside, their floor thickly set with rajor-like arrows. They are filled with perpetual darkness. Their floor is slippery with a coat of marrow fat, flesh, blood, and matter, and besmeared with grease. They are very rugged, difficult to pass and horrid. Those who are condemned to live in these hells do not sleep, nor do they get any consolation or comfort or recreation. The denizens of hell suffer intolerable agonies.

A Gloomy View of the World

Mahavira presents a gloomy picture of the world. According to him, the soul has to undergo births and deaths, and all their concomitant experiences. The senses and mental faculties become manifest in varying degrees in the varying forms of beings. Because of affection, passion, and attachment, man finds himself in an awful situation. The world presents a constant scene of quarrel and strife, death and carnage, and of all mad pursuits of life, the ultimate end of which is disappointment. For the sake of food and drink, lodging and comfort, woman and wealth, man is involved in various difficulties that lead the soul from sin to sin. Because of their attachment to seductive pleasures of the senses like sounds and colours, tastes and smells, and touches and perception, living beings suffer and find no escape from pain. The path to these pleasures is the path to birth, disease, decay, and death. Looking at the miserable condition of the world, man craves for liberation, deliverance and perfection.

Real Brahmana

He who has no worldly attachment after entering the order, who does not repent of having become a monk, and who takes delight in noble words is called a Brahmana. He who is free from love, hatred, and fear is called a Brahmana. A lean, self-subduing ascetic, who reduces his flesh and blood, who is pious, and who has reached *Nirvana,* is a Brahmana. He who thoroughly knows living beings and does not injure them in any of the three ways (by his thought, word, and deed), is a Brahmana. He who does not speak untruth from anger, or from greed, or from fear is a Brahmana. He who does not take anything which is not given to him is a Brahmana. He who does not carnally love divine, human, and animal beings in thoughts words, and deeds is a Brahmana. He who is not defied by pleasures is a Brahmana. He who is not greedy, who lives unknown, who has no house, and who has no friendship with householders, is a Brahmana. He who has given up his former connections with his relations and parents and who is not given to pleasures is a Brahmana. One does not become a *Sramana* by the tonsure, nor a Brahmana by pronouncing the sacred syllable *Om*, nor a *Muni* by living in the forest, nor a *Tapasa* by wearing clothes of *Kusa*-grass. One becomes a *Sramana* by equanimity, a Brahmana by chastity, a *Muni* by knowledge, and a *Tapasa* by penance. One becomes a Brahmana or a *Kshatriya* or *Vaisya* or a *Sudra* by one's actions. He is a Brahmana, who is exempt from all *Karma*. The most excellent Brahmanas, who possess good qualities, are able to save themselves and others.

Code of Conduct for Ascetics

Mahavira also prescribed certain rules of conduct for ascetics. These rules are classified under such general heads as begging, walking, modes of speech, entry into other's possessions, postures, place of study, and attending to the calls of nature. Here begging includes begging food and drink, begging a bowl, begging clothes, and begging a residence or a couch. Under these subheads are to be found the rules governing the modes of eating, drinking, and lying down. Walking includes travelling, crossing, swimming and other forms of movement. The postures are those that are involved in religious exercises.

The reasons why these rules have been laid down are grounded in such general principles as the avoidance of situations in which the monk or nun may be guilty of hurting or killing all forms of life, or of inconveniencing others, or of wounding the social, moral, or religious scruples of others, the avoidance of situation in which the monk or nun may run the risk of endangering his own position or of receiving bodily injuries, or of feeling discomfort, or of being found guilty of theft or trespass, or of moral degradation, or of mental perturbation, and the avoidance of all situations in which the monk or nun may be found acting under the slightest influence of greed, ill-will, evil intention, discontent, delusion, inconsideration, haughtiness, and the like.

Discipline

A monk on receiving an order from his superiors goes to him, watching the movement of his head and motions. He is will-behaved. He who desires his own welfare should adhere to the rules of good conduct. He who desire liberation will be received everywhere. He should acquire valuable knowledge and avoid what is worthless. He should rather be meek than talkative in the presence of the wise. A monk should avoid untruth and never tell anything sinful or meaningless or hurtful. On the highway or in a barber's shop, a monk, who is all alone, should not stand with a single woman, nor should he talk to her. A monk should sally forth at the right time and return at the right time. He should not approach dining people sitting in a row; he should collect alms that are freely given. He should eat moderately at the right time. He should wait for his alms alone, not too far from other monks, nor too near them.

On Troubles

There are twenty-two troubles which a monk must learn and know, bear, and conquer in order not to be vanquished by them. They are as follows : hunger, thirst, cold, heat, gadflies and gnats (all biting or stinging insects like lice), nakedness, women, to be discontented with the objects of control, erratic life, place for study, lodging abuse, corporal punishment, asking for something, to be refused, illness, the pricking of grass, dirt, kind and respectful treatment, understanding, ignorance and righteousness. A monk, who is strong in self-control and does penance, should not cut or cause another to cut anything to be eaten, nor cook it or cause another to cook it, even though his body is weakened by hunger. He should know the measure of food and drink permitted and wander about with a cheerful mind. Though troubled by thirst, he should drink distilled, not cold, water. Wandering about in deserts and feeling thirsty, he should bear the suffering caused by thirst. If a retrained monk occasionally suffers from cold on his wanderings, he should not walk beyond the prescribed time, remembering the teachings of the Master. A monk should not entertain such a thought : 'I have no shelter and nothing to cover my skin, therefore I shall kindle a fire to warm myself.' If a monk suffers from the heat of things hot or from the heat of the body, he should not lament the loss of comfort.

A monk should remain undisturbed even if bitten by insect. He should not scare them away nor keep them off. He should not kill living beings. Nor should he entertain such thoughts : "My clothes are torn, I shall go naked or else I shall get a new suit. "A houseless and poor monk, who wanders from village to village, should endure the hardships of an ascetic life. He should wander about free from sins and perfectly passionless. He knows that worldly men have a natural liking for women. Knowing this, he renounces women and easily performs his duties as a perfect monk.

A monk should acquire no property. He should sit down above in a burial place, or in a deserted town, or under a tree. Sitting there, he should brave all dangers. A monk, who does penances and is strong in self-control, will not be effected beyond measure by good or bad lodgings. If a layman abuses a monk, he should not be angry with him. If a monk hears bad words, he should silently overlook them and should not take them to heart. He should not be angry if beaten. He should not entertain sinful thoughts. He should meditate on the law. He should beg food from a householder when his dinner is ready. A monk who thinks thus, "I get nothing today, perhaps I shall get something tomorrow" will not be grieved by his want of success.

If a monk suffers pain or falls sick, he should cheerfully make his mind steady and bear the evils that attack him. He will be a true monk if he continues to search for the welfare of his soul. If a naked ascetic lies on the grass, his body will be hurt. Even then he will not use clothes. A wise monk should not lament the loss of comfort. He should overcome all difficulties while waiting for the destruction of his *Karma*. By practicing the noble and excellent Law, he should carry the filth on his body till he expires. He should not evince any predilection for one who salutes him or rises from his seat on his approach or invites him to accept alms in his house. He should not think thus : "There is no life to come nor an exalted state to be acquired by penances."

A monk should know what alms may be accepted and beg food only for the sustenance of life. Those who explain the marks of the body and who knew its imminent changes are not to be called novices.

The Leaf of the Tree

Just as the yellow leaf of a tree falls to the ground when its days are done, so does the life on man come to its close. As life is so fleeting and existence so precarious, one should wipe off the sins ever committed. A rare chance is human birth for living beings and hard are the consequences of actions. The soul which suffers from it carelessness is driven about in the *Samsara* by its good and bad *Karmans*. It is a chance rare enough to become an elect. If one believes in the law, one will surely practice it when the human body grows old and the hair turns white, when the power of ears, eyes and the tactile nerves diminishes—when, in short, all human power begins to decline. One should cast aside all attachments and give up wealth. The enlightened and liberated monk should control himself and should show all the road to peace.

The True Monk

If a monk is dogmatic in his assertions, if he is malicious, egotistical, greedy, and without self-discipline, if he is always unkind, if he does not share what he has with others, then he is ill-behaved. If he is always humble, steady, free from deceit, if he is not proud of his learning, if he listens to friendly advice, if he does not speak ill of his friend behind his back, if he is enlightened, polite, decent and quiet, then he is will-behaved. Monks will go to the highest place only after their *Karma* has been annihilated.

He who adopts the law with a view to living as a monk should live in company of other monks, upright and free from desires. Free from love, he should live as a model of righteousness, abstaining from sins and versed in the sacred law. Ignorant of abuse and iniquity a steadfast monk should be a model of righteousness, always protecting his soul from sins; neither rash nor passionate, he should endure everything. He controls himself, keeps the vows, practices austerities and meditates on his soul. A true monk does not care for his life, abandons every delusion, avoids men and women, and does not betray any curiosity. He does not progress and live on divinations. He also abstains himself from spells, roots, every kind of medical treatment, purgatives, emetics, fumigation, anointing of the eye, etc. A Jaina monk is forbidden to take beds, lodgings, drinks, food, dainties and spaces from the householders. He who understands all religious disputations, who practices self-discipline, who dedicates on his soul, who is wise, hardy, and observes everything, who is calm, and does not hurt anybody – he who does all this is a true monk. He who does not live by any art, who is without house and without friend, who subdues his senses, who is free from all bondages and sins and who eats little and lives single – he, too, is a true monk.

The Ten Conditions of Perfect Chastity

There are ten conditions for the realization of celibacy. By hearing and knowing them, the monk will reach the highest degree of self-discipline, of contemplation, of stopping sins by means of *Samitis* and Guptis, will guard his senses and chastity. The ten conditions are the following :

(*i*) A monk may occupy various places for sleep or rest, but he should not occupy such places frequented by women, cattle, or eunuches. If he occupies such places for sleep or rest as are frequented by women, cattle or eunuches his chastity will be suspected or he will acquire a dangerous illness of long duration or he will become a slave to passion.

(*ii*) He should not talk about women.

(*iii*) He should not sit together with women on the same seat.

(*iv*) He should not look at or think of the charms or beauties of women.

(*v*) He should not eavesdrop behind a screen or wall and listen to the singing or laughing or crying or women.

(*vi*) He should not remember the pleasures and amusements which he enjoyed in the past in the company of women.

(*vii*) He should not eat well-dressed food.

(*viii*) He should not eat or drink to excess.

(*ix*) He should not wear ornaments.

(*x*) He should avoid sounds, colours, tastes, smells and sensations of touch.

Bad Monks

A bad monk is one who despises learning and discipline which his preceptors and teachers have taught him. He is disrespectful to his teachers and preceptors. He does not control himself though he believes himself to be well controlled. He hurts living beings and walks with great haste and without care. He is fierce and overbearing. It is the duty of a monk to examine very closely everything which he uses in order to avoid hurting living beings. He always slights his teachers and is deceitful, talkative, arrogant, greedy and rough. He delights in quarrels and perverts truth. He is not careful in sitting down. He is careless about his bed. He does not practice austerities. He eats after sunset, and when admonished, he makes and angry reply. Leaving his own teacher, he follows a heretical one. He is a man of bad disposition and frequently changes his school (*Gana*). He lives by fortunetelling, not by alms, and eats the food given by his relations. A pious monk is one who avoids sins, who is welcomed in this world, and who is the conqueror of the world.

Duties of a Monk

One should adopt the Law of the monks as well as their vows, virtues, and their endurance of the calamities, an endurance which enables him to abandon the great distress and the great delusion. He should keep the five great vows, *viz*. not to kill, to speak the truth, not to steal, to be chaste, and to have no property at all. A wise man should follow the law taught by the Jains. A monk should be of a forbearing nature, restrained, and chaste. He should live with his senses under control. He should wake about in utter indifference and bear everything, pleasant and unpleasant. He should not approve of everything everywhere nor care for respectful treatment or blame. A monk, who encounters dangerous and dreadful calamities, is not afraid of them. He should endure with equal equanimity both cold and heat, unpleasant feelings and physical disorders which attack the human body. An ascetic will by means of his simplicity enter the path of *Nirvana*. He is neither grieved nor pleased. He is intent on the benefit of his soul and strives for the highest good. A merciful monk should use beds far from those which have not been prepared for him.

The Samitis and Guptis

There are five *Samitis* and three *Guptis* which constitute eight articles of the Jaina creed. The *Samitis* are the following : (1) going by paths trodden by men, beasts, carts, etc. and looking carefully so as not to cause the death of any living beings; (2) gentle, sweet, and religious speech; (3) receiving alms in so nice a manner that the forty-two faults are avoided; (4) receiving and keeping things necessary for religious exercises; and (5) answering the call of nature in an unfrequented place.

The three *Guptis* are the following : (1) preventing the mind from sensual pleasures by engaging it in contemplation, study, etc., (2) preventing the tongue from saying bad things through a vow of silence, and (3) putting the body in an immovable posture.

A well-disciplined monk should have only such walks as are pure with regard to their cause, time, road, and effort. Knowledge, faith, and right conduct are included in the 'cause', the 'time' is daytime, the 'road' excludes bad ways, and the 'effort' is four-fold as regards substance, place, time, and condition of the mind. He should work diligently and avoid agner, pride, deceit, greed, laughter, fear, loquacity, and slander. He should use blameless and concise words at the appropriate time and avoid while begging faults in the search, in the receiving, and in the use of food, lodging, and the articles of daily consumption. There are sixteen *Udgama doshas* by which food becomes unfit for a Jaina monk : the undesirability for instance inherent in the food prepared by a layman for religious mendicants, the undesirability of the food which a layman has prepared for a particular monk, which has been prepared for festivities or which has been reserved for a monk when he has to open locks before he gets the food or when a monk calls while the dinner is being cooked, and for his sake more food is put in the pot which is on the fire, etc.

There are ten faults of receiving, e.g. when a monk accepts alms from a frightened layman (*Sankita*), when the food is soiled by animate or inanimate matter (*Mrakshita*), when a layman mixes up pure with impure food (*Unmisrita*), etc. A zealous monk should wipe the thing after having inspected it with his eyes; then he should take it up or put it down. Excrements, urine, saliva, mucus, and uncleanliness of the body should be disposed of in the way prescribed. In a place neither frequented or seen by others, which offer no obstacles to self-control, which is not covered with grass or leaves, which is spacious, in such a place he should leave his excrements, etc.

There are (1) truth, (2) untruth, (3) mixture of truth and untruth, and (4) a mixture of what is not true and what is not untrue. A zealous monk should not harbour any desire for the misfortune of others, nor should he think of causing misery to living beings or their destruction. In standing, sitting, living down, jumping, going and in the use of his organs, a zealous monk should prevent his mind cherishing evil desires, etc. These are the *Samitis* for the practice of the religious life and *Guptis* for the prevention of everything sinful.

The Correct Behaviour of Monks during the Several Parts of Day and Night

The correct behaviour of monks consists of the following : *Auasyika* is required when a monk leaves a room; *Naishedhiki* on entering a place; *Aprichchhana* or asking the Superior's permission for what he is to do himself *Pratiprichchhana*, for what somebody else is to do; *Chhandana* or placing at the disposal of other monks the things one has got; *Ichchhakara* in the execution of one's intention by oneself or somebody else; *Mithyakara* in blaming oneself for sins committed; *Tathakara* in assenting to make a promise; *Abhyutthana* in serving those who deserve respect, and *Upasampad* in placing oneself under another teacher.

After sunrise during the first quarter of the first *Paurushi* (the forth part of a day or a night), a monk should inspect and clean his things and pay his respects to his superior. He should ask him with folded hands : what shall I do now? If he is ordered to do some work, he should do it ungrudgingly. A clever monk should divide a day into four equal parts, and fulfil his duties in all the four parts. In the first *Paurushi*, he should study; in the second he should meditate; in the third, he should go on his begging-tour; and in the fourth, he should study again. The *Paurushi* increases or decreases a digit (equal to five minutes) every week, two digit every fortnight, and four digits every month. A clever monk should divide the night into four parts and do his duties in all the four parts. In the first *Paurushi*, he should study; in the second, he should meditate; in the third, he should sleep and in the fourth, he should study again. When a small part of the quarter is left in which the leading star is seen, a monk should watch.

In the first quarter of the first *Paurushi*, he should inspect his things, pay his respect to his superior, then begin his study not allowing himself to be affected by any pain. In the last quarter of the first *Paurushi*, after paying his respect to the *Guru* a monk should inspect his alms-bowl without performing the expiation of sins concerning time. He should inspect his mouth, cloth, then his broom; and, taking the broom in his hand, he should inspect his cloth. Standing upright, he should hold his cloth firmly and inspect it leisurely. Then he should spread it and at last wipe it. He should spread the cloth without shaking or crushing it in such a way as to make the folds disappear; he should fold it up six times in length and nine times in breadth, and .hen he should remove whatever living organisms that are there with his hands. He must avoid inattentiveness in commanding his work, in taking up the corners of the cloth, in folding it up, in removing the dust, in putting it down on some other piece of cloth, and in sitting upon the hunches (*Vedika*). One must not hold the cloth loosely or at one corner. If he who is engaged in inspection, a thing talks with anybody, renounces something, receives his lessons from another, he obviously neglects his inspection. One who is careful in his inspection, protects the six kinds of living beings *e.g.* the earth bodies, the water bodies, the fire bodies, the wind bodies, and animals.

In the third *Paurushi*, he should beg food and drink for any of the following six reasons : (1) to prevent illness, (2) to serve the *Guru*, (3) to comply with the rules of walking, (4) to comply with the rules of self-control (5) to save one's life, and (6) to meditate on the law. A zealous Jaina monk should not beg food for the following reasons : (1) in the case of illness (2) in the case of disaster, (3) to preserve one's chastity, and the *Guptis*, (4) out of compassion for living beings, (5) in the interest of penance, and (6) to put an end to one's life.

In the forth *Paurushi*, a monk should put away his alms-bowl, and then he should begin to study. In the last quarter of the fourth Paurushi he should pay his respects to the *Guru*, and having performed *kalapratikramana*, he should inspect his lodging. A true monk should find a suitable place where to discharge his excrements and urine. He should reflect on the transgressions he has committed during the day with regard to knowledge, faith, and conduct. Having finished Kayotsarga and paid his respect to the Guru, he should confess the sins committed during the day. Then, having recited the *Pratikramana Sutra* and having destroyed his sins, he should pay his respect to the *Guru*. Having finished *Kayotsarga*, he should pronounce the customary prayers. A monk should do the same thing in the first *Paurushi* during the night, in the fourth *Paurushi*, and in the last quarter of the fourth *Paurushi*. Then he should reflect on all the sins committed during the night with regard to knowledge, faith, and conduct. Then he should confess the sins committed during the night. Having finished *Kayotsarga* and paid his respect to the *Guru*, he should practice those austerities which he has undertaken, and praise the saints who have attained perfection.

Mode of Life

A monk will not be subject to transmigration if he practices self-control in the different spheres of life. Love and hate are two evils which produce bad *Karma*. A monk should always keep away from hurtful, conceited and delusive acts. Hurtful acts (*danda*) are three-fold since they refer to thoughts, words, and acts. Conceited acts are pride in riches, in taste and in pleasure of fashion. Delusive acts are *Maya, Nidana* and false belief (*Mithyadarsana*). A monk endures calamities and does his best to escape from the four different kinds of praises, passions, expressions of the emotions, and of the four meditations. He always exerts himself with regard to the five vows, the five objects of the senses, the five *Samitis*, and the five actions. He also exerts himself with regard to the six *Lesyas*, the six kinds of bodies, and the six regular functions as eating. He always exerts himself with regard to the seven rules of accepting alms and the seven causes of danger to others.

A monk guards himself against the eight objects of pride while following the ten-fold Law of the monks. The eight objects of pride are : caste, family, beauty, etc. The monk devotes himself to the eleven duties of the *Upasaka* (lay-disciples) and to the twelve duties of the *Bhikkhus*. He always exerts himself with regard to the thirteen actions productive of *Karma*, fourteen kinds of living beings, and the fifteen places of punishment of the wicked. He is always aware of the sixteen *gathas*, eighteen kinds of continence, and nineteen *Jnatadhyayanas* (Naya), twenty-one forbidden actions, and twenty-two troubles. He always exerts himself with regard to the twenty-three lectures of the *Sutrakritanga*, the twenty-five clauses, and the twenty-six chapters of the *dasas*. He always exerts himself with regard to the twenty-seven virtues of the laity and the twenty-eight lectures of the *Prakalpa*, the twenty-nine causes of wrong knowledge, the thirty causes of delusion, the thirty-one qualifications of the perfected one, the thirty-two pure operations of the mind, speech, and body, and the thirty-three articles regulating the intercourse between monks, especially pupils and teachers.

The Houseless Monk

Renouncing his wife, a sage should know and give up those attachments which enslave men. A monk possessing self-restraint should abstain from killing, stealing, dying, physical intercourse, and greed. He should not long for a pleasant dwelling house. He should happily live in a burial place, in a deserted-house, beneath a tree, in solitude, etc. A well-controlled monk should live in a place which is not much too crowded and where no women live. He should abstain from building a house. Full of compassion for living beings he should neither cook nor cause others to cook. He should cause nobody to cook because beings, living in water, corn, wood, etc., are destroyed in the process. A monk should not light a fire. He should not in his thoughts long for gold and silver. He is not to engage in buying and selling. He who is to live on alms should beg, not buy. He should collect his alms in parts and contentedly go at his begging hour, whether he gets alms or not. A sage should not eat for the sake of the delicious taste of the food but for the sustenance of his life. He should meditate on true things only, committing no sins and owning no property. He should walk about careless about his body till his end comes. Only such a sage obtains absolute knowledge and reaches eternal beatitude, free from passions and sins, and without property and without egoism.

Begging Food

A monk or a nun on a begging tour should not accept as alms whatever herbs he or she recognizes. Only such things should by accepted as are pure and acceptable. None should accept food which has been prepared for Brahmanas, guests, beggars, etc. Nor should one accept food which does not belong to the giver. The monk and nun may accept food from noble families, distinguished families, and royal families. They should not, however, attend any festive entertainment. Nor should they accept food about which they have some doubts in their mind. A monk or a nun desirous of entering the abode of a householder should not do so when it is found 'that the milch cows are being mulched, or the food is being cooked, and that it is not yet distributed.'

A monk or a nun on a begging tour should not accept flattened grains, grains containing much chaff. He or she should not accept fossil salt or sea salt which is impure and unacceptable. He or she should not accept food which has been prepared over the fire, for such food is impure and unacceptable. He or she should not accept food which has been placed on a post or on a roof or on a platform or some such elevated place. He or she should not accept food which is kept in an earthen ware. He or she should not accept food placed on the earth body, wind body or fire body, for such food is impure and unacceptable. He or she should not accept food which is placed on vegetable or animals matter. He or she should not accept such water as has been taken from the bare ground. He or she should not accept juice of mangoes, pomegranates, coconuts, temarinds, etc. He or she should not accept raw things, such as mustard seeds, raw powdered fruits, unripe wild rice, honey, liquor, etc. He or she should not accept raw plants, vegetables, raw substances, etc. He or she should not accept any part of a sugarcane, as it is impure and unacceptable, meat or fish containing many bones; but food which is offered on the hands of the giver is dried up. A monk or a nun should not use for religious postures a lodging used by a householder, in which there are workmen, children, cattle, food, and drink.

A mendicant should not stay in halting places, garden houses, family houses, monasteries much frequented by fellow ascetics. It is difficult to obtain pure and acceptable alms. A monk or a nun should not use for religious postures a lodging where the householder and his wife go about naked or hide themselves, or talk about sexual pleasures. He or she should not use for religious postures a lodging which is a common playground.

A monk shall not beg pointing at the householder with a finger or goading, the threatening, or scratching him with a finger praising or cursing him.

Modes of Speech

He or she should speak with precision, employing his language with moderation and restraint, a language which is grammatically correct and whose true import, he fully understands. A monk or a nun should not use speech if it be sinful, blamable, rough, coarse and hard. Seeing a diseased personal, he or she should not talk thus : "He has got boils or leprosy. His hand, foot, nose, ear, or lip is affected." A monk or a nun seeing a man should speak about him thus : 'His body is well grown, well compacted, his flesh and blood are abundant.'

Walking

When a monk or a nun knows that in a village or a town, there is no large place for religious practices or for study, he or she should not remain there during the cold season. He or she may circumspectly wander from village to village. When on a pilgrimage, he or she should not choose a road passing through a forest. If there is some water-way on the way which must be crossed in a boat, he or she should not get into a boat which plies up or down or across the river. A monk or a nun entering a boat should not choose the stern or the prow or the middle of the boat. If a monk or a nun finds water entering through a leak in the boat which becomes dirty all over he or she should not approach the boatman and inform him about it. While swimming in the water, he or she should not touch another person's foot, hand, or body with his or her own hand; he or she should not dive up and down, lest water should enter into his or her eyes, ears, nose, or mouth. If while swimming in the water he or she is overcome by weakness, he or she should throw off his or her clothes, either all or a part of them. A monk or a man should not wipe or rub or brush or dry or warm or heat his or her body. If while going on a pilgrimage he or she comes across shallow water, he or she should first wipe his or her body from head to feet. He or she should wade through the shallow water in a straight line. A monk or a nun wading through the shallow water must not plunge into deeper water for the sake of pleasure.

If a monk or a nun perceives wagons, carts, a friendly or hostile army, he or she should not walk straight on. A monk or a nun, wandering from village to village together with a master or a teacher, should not touch the hand of the master or the teacher with his or her own.

Begging Clothes

A monk or a nun wanting clothes may beg for clothes made of wool, silk, hemp, palm leaves, cotton, etc. He or she should not accept clothes which a layman has bought, washed, dyed, rubbed, cleaned, or perfumed. A monk or a nun should not accept clothes made of fur or clothes that are fine or beautiful, etc. He or she should not accept plaids of fur or other materials. He or she may ask a householder or his wife for clothes which have been well inspected. He or she should not accept clothes which are full of eggs or living organisms, for they are impure. He or she may accept clothes which are strong, lasting, and are fit for a mendicant.

If a mendicant borrows for a short time a robe from another mendicant, the owner of it should not take back such a robe for himself nor should he give it to somebody else. A monk or a nun should not make coloured clothes colourless, he or she should not, that is, colour colourless clothes. If a monk sees thieves on his way, he should not leave the robe out fear to save his clothes.

Begging for a Bowl

Monk, and nuns should not accept a bowl bought by a layman. They should not accept expansive bowls or bowls containing precious materials. They may accept a bowl from a householder or his wife after having it thoroughly inspected. They may beg for a bowl used by a former owner or by many people. Entering into the abode of a householder for the sake of alms, they should circumspectly leave it after examining their alms-bowls and removing all living beings from it if there be any. They should not wipe or rub a wet or moist alms-bowl.

Spot where one can ease oneself

They should not empty their bowls of excrement on the bare ground or on wet ground or on dusty ground or on a rock or clay containing life or a timber inhabited by worms. They should not ease themselves at a place where the householders or their sons have sown or will sow rice, beans, pulse, or barley. They should not ease themselves at a place where there are heaps of refuse, mud etc. They should not sit in fireplaces or at a place where suicide is committed, or in gardens, parks, woods, temples, or wells. They should not sit on cross-roads or on town-gates or on pathways or at a place where charcoal is produced or the dead are burnt. They should not empty their bowls at sacred places near rivers, marshes or ponds. They should not ease themselves in fresh clay-pits, fresh pasture-grounds for cattle or in a field of vegetables. Monks and nuns should take their own chamber-pot and ease themselves in a secluded place where no people pass or see them, and leave the excrement on a heap of ashes.

Other Miscellaneous Acts

A monk is holy through his innocence. He allows no trouble to influence his words, thoughts and acts. He should take no notice of seductive pleasures and endeavour to shake off delusion. Knowing the highest Law, he should perform his religious duties. He should be free from attachment and earnest in the performance of austerities.

Begging is a hard task. It is painful to take anything but what is freely given. Some weak men, who are unable to preserve their chastity, will become disheartened. Some fools take a pious monk for spy, bind him and insult him. Some low people, who lead a life of iniquity and who are subject to love and hatred, injure a monk.

There are some tender affections which monks cannot easily overcome. A monk should renounce attachment, for every attachment is a cause of sin. A holy monk may find many inducements and seductions in this world, but he should not break down like weak bullocks carrying a heavy burden uphill. A monk should snap off the ties that bind him to his house; he should wander about for the welfare of his soul. A wise and thoroughly restrained monk should bear all hardships and wander about till he attains his final liberation. The Buddhists hold that pleasant things are produced from pleasant things. Those who exert themselves at the proper time feel no remorse afterwards. The heroes, who get rid of their fetters, do not long for their life. A monk should strive for the attainment of *Nirvana* which consists in peace.

Considering the consequences a worthy monk should have no intercourse with women. He should avoid them. Those who have intercourse with women have ceased to practice meditation. When a monk breaks the Law, doles on women and is absorbed by that passion, they afterwards scold him, lift their foot up, and trample down his head. One should not mind the entreaties of women, but abstain from their friendship and company. The pleasures which are derived therefrom are causes of blamable actions. A monk should abstain from women and commit no unnatural crime. A wise and learned monk, whose soul is uncontaminated, will abstain from doing work for others; he will endure all hardships with all his might.

A virtuous monk should never keep company, with the wicked. He should not stay in the house of a householder except under compulsion. He should obey and serve a wise and pious teacher. If beaten, he should not be angry. With a placid mind he should bear everything.

A true monk should not say that this is meritorious and that is not meritorious. He should guard his soul, bring his senses under his control, and put a stop to the current of the *Samsara.* Free from sins, he is entitled to expound the pure, complete, and unparalleled Law. He should try to attain beatitude.

If a poor monk, subsisting on the meanest food, clings to vanities and makes his monkshood a means of sustenance, he will suffer again and again. An eloquent monk gifted with bright ideas and possessed of a high intellect and pure soul, should combat pride of genius, pride of sanctity, pride of birth, and pride of good living. A monk having conquered aversion to self-control and delight in sensual objects, should silently repeat to himself, "A man must come and go according to his *Karma* alone." The pious are not given to blamable sinful practices. Avoiding all evils, monks should without embarrassment and passion preach the Law.

Making manifest the conduct of the virtuous, an intelligent monk should not leave the company of his teacher. A monk who complies with rules for the *Yatis* regarding postures, lying down, sitting and exertion, who is thoroughly acquainted with the *Samitis* and *Guptis,* should explain each single point of conduct. He should not allow himself to be influenced by pleasant sounds. He should preserve in self-control. A novice, who has not mastered the law, does not know the law, but he will know it afterwards through the words of the Jainas. A monk possessed of a sound conduct will explain the moral nature of the virtuous. A monk, by hearing the desired truth, gets bright ideas and becomes a clever teacher; by desiring the highest good and practicing austerity, he obtains his final liberation. Such virtuous men do not conceal the truth of falsify it. Nor do they cherish any desire for fame. Indeed, a monk should be honest and fearless in his exposition of the *Syadvada*. He should use words appropriate to a monk and should be impartial and wise. He should utter pure speech in accordance with the creed of the Jinas and should learn the sacred text thoroughly. While his endeavour should be to teach the creed and not to speak unduly long, he should also do his utmost to deliver faithfully what he has learnt. He should not prevent the truth from coming to light nor render it obscure.

A monk, who does not act nor kill, who is free from anger, pride, deceit and greed, who is calm and happy, will never entertain the wish that after his departure from the world he will become a god or a perfected saint. He does nothing that arises from a sinful cause, nor does he get such things done by another person. A monk should not take food or drink when he knows that a householder, to satisfy him or a co-religionist, has brought it. One should eat when it is time for eating, seek cover when it is time for seeking cover, and sleep when it is time for sleeping. When a monk preaches the law, he should preach it not for the sake of food or drink, but he should preach it indefatigably for no other motive that the annihilation of *Karma*. Such a monk searches the law, knows the law, and endeavours to gain liberation. He renounces action and worldly occupation, he is free from passions, possesses the *Samitis*, is wise, virtuous and liberated, lives on simple food, desires to get across the shore of the *Samsara* and never departs from general and particular virtues.

A monk abstains from the five cardinal sins, from the slaughter of living beings, etc. He does not clean his teeth with a tooth brush; he does not accept perfumes, emetics, and collyrium. Such a monk does not act nor kill; he is free from anger, pride, deceit, and greed; he is calm and happy. He is well controlled and restrained, avoids and renounces sins, is not active but careful and thoroughly wise.

The wrongly instructed *Sramanas* do not comprehend the soul's bondage through *Karma* (*Karmabandha*). A wise monk should improve his chances for final liberation. He should conform himself to the rules laid down by the Jinas and wander patiently about till he attains final liberation.

A monk, who has achieved his religious perfection through the instruction of the Awakened one and stands firm in it, who guards himself in the three-fold way with regard to thoughts, words and acts , and who possesses the things requisite for crossing the immense Ocean of existence, may preach the law.

If a mendicant thinks that on account of his illness, he has become weak and is unable to wander from house to house, on his thus complaining the householder may bring food and give it to him. By practising monastic rules, one becomes tranquil, free from sin, and guards himself against the allurements of the senses. Entering a village or a town, a monk should beg for straw. After getting the straw, he should retire with it to a secluded spot. After having examined and cleaned the ground, he should spread the straw on it. A naked monk thinks thus : 'I can bear the pricking of the grass, the influence of cold and heat, the stinging of flies and mosquitoes. I can sustain all those painful feelings but cannot abandon the covering of the privities.' Knowing the two obstacles relating to the body and mind, a wise man who has thoroughly learnt the law, can get rid of his *Karma.* Subduing the passions and living on little food, he should endure hardships. If a mendicant becomes unattached internally and externally, he should strive after absolute purity. If crawling animals feed on his flesh and blood, he should neither kill them nor rub the wounds; even if these animals destroy the body, he should not stir from his position. A well-controlled monk should give up all motives except his own in thrice three-fold way (of body, speech, and mind). He should not lie on sprouts or grass, but inspecting the bare ground, he could lie on it. Without any food or comfort, he should bear pain. If a sage becomes weak, he should strive after calmness, that is to say, he should not give way to melancholy thoughts. He should move about on the ground, and stretch his limbs for the benefit of the whole body. He should walk about when tired of lying and sit down when tired of standing.

4 THE GREAT SCRIPTURES OF JAINS

Importance

The study of Jain scriptures is important in many respects :

1. They represent one of the oldest religions of India which has contributed a lot towards Indian culture as it stands today.
2. While Brahmanism and Buddhism, the two great currents of Indian culture, have changed considerably from time to time, Jainism has been able to preserve, to a great extent, its original form. Thus, Jain scriptures provide faithful picture of ancient civilization.
3. Soon after the death of Mahavira, Jainism lost contact with royal families. Even in the time of Mahavira, in spite of a number of princes following him, royal support for the propagation of his mission was negligible. Jain monks, going on foot from place to place and door to door, established their contact with the masses. Consequently, Jain literature reflects the common life of that period.
4. Jain literature represents all phases of linguistic development beginning from 600 B.C. up to the modern period. Thus, it is very important for linguistic study as well.
5. Jains, though small in number, have their hold all over India. They are a progressive community guided mostly by ascetics. A strange synthesis of wealth and

devotion to asceticism can be discovered in the Jain laity.

General Attitude

Indian systems of philosophy go from one extreme to the other regarding the authority of scriptures. On the one side there is the school of Mimamsakas giving supreme authority to the *Vedas* and admitting no interference by perception or inference in that sphere. On the other extreme is Carvaka who relies on perception only. The Buddhist also does not admit the authority of scriptures. Jainism stands in the middle. It admits scriptures as an independent source of knowledge, and at the same time holds that they are based on experience. Of course, the experience of a layman, whose judgment is always biased, cannot be accepted as the final truth, but that of one possessing full knowledge of the subject and at the same time rising above all pride and prejudice can be safely accepted as the final authority. The scriptures get their validity from persons of that type.

Authorship

According to Jainism the scriptures are neither eternal nor the words of God or a person deputed by God. As a matter of fact Jainism disagrees with the very idea of God or His messenger. It holds that every soul, when liberated from the bondage of *Karma* becomes *Paramatman*, the great soul. Scriptures are the records of the experience of those noble souls. There is one difference between the Vedic and Jaina traditions. The latter holds that Scriptures are not the very words of enlightened souls but convey their spirit only. Their authorship goes to the chief disciples who have heard from them.

Tradition

Mahavira is known as the founder of the present order of Jainism. As a matter of fact he did not found any new institution but reformed and rearranged the older one, which he himself inherited. According to the Jain tradition Risabhadeva was the first to found this tradition. He is accepted as God incarnate in Vedic tradition as well. He was born in a hoary past and both the traditions attribute antiquity to his date. After Rishbhadeva there were twenty-three more *Tirthankaras*. The twenty-third was Parsvanath, whose historically has got general acceptance. He was born in Benaras 250 years before Mahavira.

Regarding the tradition of scriptures it is held that the tradition of Risabhadeva continued up to the eighth *Tirthankara*. Then, there was a break. Again the tradition continued during the last eighth *Tirthankaras*. If this account is accepted the present canon goes back to Kunthunatha, the 17th *Tirthankara*. But, nothing can be said about his date too. So, we have to satisfy ourselves with Parsvanatha only though it can be said on definite grounds that the tradition is older.

Purvas

In the time of Parsvanath and earlier *Tirthankaras* Jain canon was divided into *Purvas* as the name itself suggests. This literature existed for a time side by side with the 12 *Angas*, the new canon compiled by the disciples of Mahavira. Gradually 'he *Purvas* were lost along with the twelfth *Anga Drstivada* which included a gist of them.

The *Nandi Sutra* provides a list of the 14 *Purvas* along with their contents. It shows that the *Purvas* consisted mainly of philosophical discussion. The word *Pravada* with the name of every *Purva* suggests the same thing. It is also said that they were in Sanskrit, and not Ardha Magadhi. *Visesavasyaka Bhasya* says that the twelve *Angas* were composed out of the *Purvas* for the ordinary people. It shows that before Mahavira Jain religion also took interest in intellectualism and little attention was paid towards practical life. Mahavira gave his sermons in local dialect and laid more stress on practical side of religion, which is a common factor about every saint of India.

Authorship of the Present Agamas

The present Jaina canon is divided into tow main divisions of *Angapavitta, i.e.,* included into the limbs of the personified scriptural knowledge. (*Sruta Purusa*) and that which is not included. Authorship of the fist group goes to Sudharman, fifth of the chief disciples of Mahavira. The second group is the contribution of later sages. Till one thousand years after the death of Mahavira many new works were composed and got a position in the canon.

Three Councils

Like three *Sangitis* in the Buddhist tradition Jainas also held three councils for arrangement of the canon. These councils are known as *Vachanans*. The first *Vachana* was held at Patna 170 years after the death of Mahavira. The second at Mathura after 609 years. The third at Valabhi in Gujarat after 992 years. These *Vachanas* also show how the center of Jainism shifted from Magadha to Western U.P. and from U.P. to Gujarat. Even now Gujarat and Rajasthan are the biggest centers of Jainism. These are the provinces where Jainism has greatly influenced the life of masses and contributed a lot in shaping their regional culture.

The third council convened by *Devardhi Ganin* brought the Angas into final form. Though all the works, as given by Devardhi Ganin in his list in the *Nandi-Sutra*, are not extant, he includes all the works as Agamas. No work, composed after that, was recognized as canon. Devardhi Ganin also provides a classification of the canon. But, it is not in conformity with the prevalent tradition. Instead of going into a critical examination of the list I would present only the prevalent classification. At present, generally, 45 works are regarded as the canon. They are classified as follows : 11 Angas, 12 Upangas, 6 Chheda Sutras, 4 Mula Sutra, 2 supplementaries and 10 miscellaneous works.

Division According to the Subject Matter

As Buddhism has divided its canon into there *Pitakas* of Sutta, Vinaya and Abhidhamma, Jainism divides its canon into the following four classes :

1. Dravyanuyoga – Metaphysics.
2. Ganitanuyoga – Mathematics.

3. Carana-karananuyoga – Ethics.
4. Dharma-katnanuyoga – Biographical and didactic tales.

All the four types of literature are useful for culture and discipline of mind. Shrimad Raja Chandra, a Jain Yogin whom Gandhiji held as his *Guru*, explains the utility of the above as follows :

1. In case of doubt one is advised to deliberate on metaphysics.
2. In case of sloth on ethics.
3. In case of the mind led astray by passions one should study biographies of the virtuous.
4. In case of dullness one should deliberate on the problems of mathematics.

Agmas According to Digambara Tradition

According to the tradition of Digambaras the present Agamas are not original. They are the works not only edited but altogether composed a new by Devardhi Ganin.

On the other hand they accept two works, namely, *Satkhandagama* and *Kasayaprabhrta* as the direct remnants of canonical literature. Dr. Hira Lal gives the following account of them being reduced to writing : "The teachings of Lord Mahavira were arranged into twelve *Angas* by his pupil Indra Bhuti Gautama, and they were handed down from preceptor to pupil by word of mouth till gradually they fell into oblivion. Only a fraction of them was known to Dharasena who practiced penances in Chandra Guha of Girinagara, in the country of Saurashtra (modern Kathiawar). He felt the necessity of preserving the knowledge and so he called two sages who afterwards became famous as Puspadanta and Bhutabli and taught to them portions of the fifth Anga *Vivahapannati* and the twelfth *Anga Ditlivada*. These were subsequently reduced to writing in *Sutra* from by the two eminent pupils. Puspadanta composed the first 177 *Sutras* and his colleague Bhutabali wrote the rest, the total being 6000 *Sutras*."

Eleven Angas

The *Angas*, as has been already said, from the main body of *sruta*. Both, the traditions of Svetamdaras as well as Digambaras' are one in this respect. Originally, the number of *Angas* was twelve. The twelfth *Drstivada* has been lost in course of time. The name suggests that it contained philosophical discussions with heretical systems. The loss of *Purva* literature as well as of this *Anga* suggests that the traditions of Mahavira did not encourage discussion with opposite systems. Jain ascetics paid more attention towards practical side. Before the advent of Siddhasena and Samantabhadra in the fifth century A.D. we do not find any work attempting to refute opposite systems. The *Sutrakrtanga*, which refers to many heretics, leaves them with the remarks that followers of the wrong path cannot attain salvation and they will suffer the tortures in hell.

The *Angas* are also known as *Gani Pitakas*, the box of a group leader. The word *pitaka* suggests two things. Firstly, it may be borrowed from the Buddhist who divides his canon into three *pitakas*. Secondly, the word came into use when the canon was reduced to writing. The written books were placed into small boxes which were again fastened by a cloth. The custom prevails even now. It appears that every group leader was provided with one set of *Agamas*, which he carried with him in his wanderings.

Names and Contents of the Angas

1. *Ayaranga* (Sanskrit *Acaranga*) is the first of *Angas* and deals with *Acara, i.e.*, the way of life. It has sections known as *Sruta Skandhas*. The first section which makes a very archaic impression, is decidedly earlier than the second. It records in short and pithy sentences the message of Mahavira, most probably in his own words. It is not a systematic treatment of a particular subject but a collection of wise sayings.

The *Ayaranga* begins with the fundamental question of Indian philosophy, i.e., the eternity of soul. "Many people do not know about their existence before birth and after death."

These lines remind us of the questions of Naciketas in the *Kathopanisad*. The people who know their relation in the next life believe in (1) the existence of soul, (2) in the existence of this universe, (3) in the existence of action, and (4) in the existence of the fruit of action. These are the four fundamentals on which the ethics and philosophy of Jains are founded.

Non-violence or the principal of non-killing and non-injury to any being is the essence of Jainism. Mahavira declares :— I speak thus, all saints (Arhats) and Lords (Bhagavats) in the past, in the present and in the future, they all say thus, speak thus, announce thus and declare thus; one may not kill, nor ill use, nor insult, nor torment, nor persecute, any kind of human being, any kind of creature, any kind of thing having a soul, any kind of beings. That is the pure, eternal, enduring commandment of religion, which has been proclaimed by the sages who comprehend the world."

Again he exhorts, " You yourself are the being which you intend to kill, you yourself are the being which you intend to ill-use, you yourself are the being which you intend to insult, you yourself are the being which you intend to torment, you yourself are the being which you intend to torment, You yourself are the being which you intend to persecute. Therefore, the righteous one, who has awakened to this knowledge, and lives according to it, will neither kill nor cause to kill.

"All beings long for life, like comfort, dislike pain, fear death, desire life, are anxious to be alike, life is dear to all." This note of respect for life rings throughout the first section of *Ayardanga*.

Similarly, Mahavira wanted to impress upon man that he himself and none else is his redeemer. "O man! thou art thy friend, why seekest thou for a friend outside?" "Control your own-self thus, you will get rid of all miseries."

He wanted that a man should realize the infinite power possessed by him. Instead of entreating gods for their pleasure and trembling from their wrath he should recognize his inner strength and stand on his own feet. Thus Mahavira taught humanity to worship man in place of deities. He brought deities to touch the feet of the virtuous.

Mahavira was dead against the obnoxious system of caste. He preached, "Frequently, I have been born in a high family, frequently in a low one; I am not mean nor noble, nor do I desire social preferent."

The famous line "That who knows one, knows all; that who knows all, knows one" gives a logical interpretation to the Jaina theory of Omniscience. According to the principal of relative existence everything is related to the other. Thus the complete knowledge of one thing presupposes the knowledge of entirety.

In the second lecture known as "Conquest of the World", he says that the apparent qualities of things are the root of sin. Beings are attracted by them, get attachment and suffer all sorts of miseries. This stanza reminds us of the *Kathopanisad* making a distinction between good and pleasant.

He further says that the social relations of father, mother, wife, sister, son, daughter, daughter-in-law etc., ensnare a person and distract him from the path of salvation. The first lecture taught men to rise above hatred and the second to be away from attachment. These are the two main factors which obstruct the progress of soul.

In the sixth lecture of the fifth chapter, we have a beautiful description of the state of liberation. "There, a being is freed from the cycle of birth and death and purified from the dust for *Karmans*. The nature of such a state cannot be described in words. All words, fall short and return back without approaching it. Logic cannot reach it, Intellect cannot grasp it." We see here a clear tinge of the *Upanisads*, which is the general tone of the path of spiritualism.

The *Ayaranga* lays much stress on severe asceticism. If a monk suffers from cold, he should rather freeze to death then break his vow. However ill and weak he may be, he should rather die than break his vow of fasting. He is to go naked, so as to expose himself to the pricking of the blades of grass, to the inclemency of weather and the bites of flies and mosquitoes. A Jain monk is exhorted to have the following as his motto : "He should not long for life, nor wish for death, he should yearn after neither life, nor death. He, who is indifferent and wishes for the destruction of *Karman,* should continue his contemplation. Becoming unattached internally and externally, he should strive after absolute purity."

"He wandered naked and homeless. People struck him and mocked at him. Unconcerned, he continued on his meditation. In Ladha the inhabitants persecuted him and set the dogs on him. They beat him with sticks and with their fists, and threw fruits, clods of earth and potsherds at him. They tried to disturb him in his meditations by all sorts of torments. But, like a hero in the forefront of the battle, Mahavira withstood it all. Whether he was wounded or not, he never sought medical aid. In winter he meditated in the shade, in the heat of summer he seated himself in the scorching sun.

The second book provides the rules of conduct for a monk in detail.

The first book of *Ayaranga* decidedly possesses a universal appeal and provides formula for solution of the eternal problems of life. It deserves a high place among the great scriptures of the world.

2. The second *Anga* is *Suyagada*. It is important for the study of heretic systems prevalent at that time. This is also divided into two sections. The second is probable only an appendix, added later on to the old *Anga* which we have in the first section. The explicit purpose of the book is to keep young monks away from the heretical doctrines of other teaches to warn them of all dangers and temptations, to confirm them in their faith and thus lead them to the highest goal. There is a graphic description of the cares and dangers with which the monastic life is fraught, but, which the novice should not allow himself to be repelled. His friends and

relatives seek to hold him back and paint the joys of family life to him in attractive colours. Kings and minsters, Brahmins and warriors endeavour to entice him to return to the world, but he is to withstand all these temptations. Critics and heretics attack him, and he should stand up to them courageously. Most especially, however, the young monk should beware of the blandishments of women, who use their utmost endeavours to fascinate him in every description full of honour of the plight of men who have been caught in the web of women.

3. The third *Anga* is Thananga. Like *Anguttara Nikaya* of the Buddhist it deals with various themes of religion in numerical order from 1 to 10.

4. The fourth Anga *Samavaya* also deals with the same subject-matter in the same style. It does not stop at the number 10 but goes further as far as million. These two Anga gives a number of themes related to the later period. It is more appropriate to accept them as later interpolation rather than to fix a later date of the entire works.

Many parables describing the nature of human beings in their various station's are highly interesting.

5. The fifth *Anga* is *Bhagvati-Viyaha-pannati*, known as *Bhagvati* in short. It is a big volume dealing with the entire field of Jainism. It is partly in the form of questions and answers, Mahavira replying to the questions of his principal disciple Goyana Indrabhuti, and partly in the form of dialogue legends. This work gives a more vivid picture than any other work of the life and work of Mahavira, his relationship to his disciple and contemporaries, and his whole personality.

The legendary portion of the work also gives an account of the predecessors of Mahavira, and of pious ascetics who attained great divine dignity through their severe castigation. The legends of the disciples of Parsva, and of Jamali and Gosala are specially important to which the whole XV chapter is devoted.

The Bhagvati gives a true insight about the method of

teaching and the society in the time of Lord Mahavira.

6. The sixth *Anga* is *Naya Dhamma Kahao, i.e.*, examples and religious narratives. It has many interesting stories peculiar to Jainism originally or recast into that fashion.

7. The seventh *Anga* is *Uvasagadasao* describing the life and duties of ten lay adherents. Their life gives a picture of the social status enjoyed by the lay devotees of Mahavira.

8. & 9. The eighth *Anga* is *Antagada-dasao* and the ninth *Anuttarovayaiya-dosao*. Both of them are biographies of saints and nuns attaining salvation or the highest place in heavenly abode, through severe penances. The former is generally preached during the eight days of the Annual Festival known as *Paryusana*. It gives an example how princes and queens gave up all attachments with their bodies and emaciated themselves through severe penances. The legend of Krishna, recast according to the Jain, tradition, is important for a comparative study of the cult.

10. The tenth *Anga* is *Panha Vagaranam*. It is a didactic treatment of the five ways of sin and five of virtue, known as the ten gates. Its contents correspond neither with the list given in the *Nandi* nor that in the *Thananga*. It appears that a later work has got the place of the old *Anga* which is extinct.

11. The eleventh *Anga* is *Vivagasuyam, i.e.*, the text of the ripening (of actions). It contains legends on the retribution of good and evil deeds after the manner of the *Buddhist Karman* stories in the *Avadana sataka* and *Karma sataka*.

12. The twelfth *Anga* is lost. Its contents are given in the *Nandi* and *Samavaya*.

Twelve Upangas

Corresponding to the twelve *Angas* there are twelve *Upangas*. One *Upanga* is ascribed to every *Anga*. As a matter of fact the term *Upanga* has no connection with the *Anga*. *Upangas* are rather independent works treating of independent subjects. The *Nandi* terms them as *Angavairitta* (extra-limbs) in places of *Upanga* (sub-limbs).

The first *Upanga* is *Uvavai* and deals with the various types of births into the regions of heaven and hell, the theme which was so dominant in Indian religion at that time.

The second *Upanga Rayapaseniya* is important. It begins with a long story of the pilgrimage of the God Suryabha to Mahavira. The dramatic performance of the God in honour of Lord Mahavira is a valuable document in the history of ancient drama. The nucleus of the work is really in the dialogue between king *Paesi* and the monk *Kesi*. This is a splendid lively dialogue, in which *Kesi* endeavours to prove to Paesi that there is a soul independent of the body, while Paesi narrates his experiments leadings to the contrary.

The third *Upanga, Jivabhigama* is a treatise in 20 sections describing in detail the varieties of living being and their habitations.

The fourth *Upanga Pannavana* is a work of Syamacarya. In its 36 chapters it describes almost all the fundamental notions of Jainism. Discussing the species of human beings it provided a list of 26 countries of the Aryans, which is important for the study of ancient Geography.

The fifth, sixth and seventh *Upangas* are scientific works dealing with Astronomy and Geography.

The remaining 5 *Upangas* from one chapter each of the *Nirayavali Sutta,* having legendary contents.

Ten Painnas

Painnas are minor works corresponding to the *Parisistas* in Vedic literature. They are said to be the compositions of Prtyeka Buddhas, *i.e.,* the souls attaining realization in their independent way. The subject-matter of *Painnas* is miscellaneous. Most of them deal with how a *Bhikkhu* renounces his body in the last days. There are two types of death. The death of a true aspirant is *Panditamarana*. He renounces all attachment in his last days and dies peacefully. On the other hand the death of a disbeliever is *Bala marana.* Even in his last days he keeps himself attached to his wealth, relatives and body. He dies a painful death. The *Painnas* describe both types of death in detail. *Tandula Veyaliya Painna* deals with human physiology.

The *Sthanakavasi* sect of Jains does not recognize this class of works as canonical.

Six Chheda Sutras

The term *Chheda* means a cut. A punishment of cut into the period of ascetic life is proposed when a monk is found guilty. On this basis, the entire class of works dealing with the punishments and prohibitions is known as *Chheda*. It is important for a comparative study of the ascetic life.

Four Mula Sutras

The term *Mula* is interpreted in many ways. The most probable explanation is that a text of these *Sutras* was learnt by heart. The tradition continues even now. This class consists of the following four works :

1. Uttarajjhayanani.
2. Avassaya.
3. Dasaveyaḷiya.
4. Pinda nijutti.

Uttaradhyayana is one of the most valuable works in the canon. It is a religious poem consisting of 36 chapters. The *Santi Parvan* of the *Mahabharata, Dhammapanda* and *Sutta Nipata* of the Buddhist and *Uttaradhyayana* stand on a par; and we can learn that the same current of ascetic poetry runs through all the three traditions. The series of gnomic aphorisms, parables and similes, dialogues and ballads found in all the three systems represent a common heritage.

Uttara is a fine piece of Prakrta poetry as well. It presents many narratives in a fascinating style.

The first chapter deals with the rules of discipline to be observed by a disciple. "One should always be meek, and not to be talkative in the presence of the wise; one should acquire valuable knowledge, and avoid what is worthless." He should not speak unsaked, and asked he should not speak a lie. He should not give way to his anger, and bear with indifference the pleasant and unpleasant occurrences.

The second lecture deals with the troubles in the path of ascetic life which a monk should bear and face boldly. If a layman abuses a monk the latter should not grow angry. If a monk hears bad words, cruel and rambling ones, he should silently overlook them, and not take them to heart. A monk should not be angry if beaten, nor should he entertain sinful thoughts. Knowing patience to be the highest good a monk should meditate on the Law (*Dharma*).

The third lecture, the "four Requisites", stresses the value of human life and its utility for spiritual development. It says, "Four things of paramount value are difficult to obtain here by a living being, human births, instruction in law, belief in it and energy in self-control."

The fourth lecture deals with the impurity and ephemeral character of worldly pleasures. The following stanza reminds us of the famous line by Naciketas in the *Kathopnisad* :

"Wealth will not protect a careless man in this world and the next. Though he had seen the right way, he does not see it, even as one in the dark whose lamp has suddenly been put out."

"Though others sleep, be thou awake! Like a wise man, trust nobody, but be always on the alert.

The fifty lecture gives a beautiful description of the two types of death, that of a fool and the wise.

The ninth lecture gives an account of a royal sage Nami, who lived an unattached life like Janaka of the *Upanisads*. Nami also ruled Mithila and showed his unconcern when the name of Janaka in the *Mahabharata* also.

In the tenth lecture life is compared with the leaf of a tree which can fall any moment.

The eleventh gives a true definition of the learned person (*pandita*). The twelfth is an account of Hari Kesi, a monk coming from Candala family. He goes to a sacrificial performance, the Brahmins assembled there hate him and a discussion follow. It is a vivacious dialogue between a proud Brahmin and a despised ascetic. The contrast is set forth between the formalism and ceremonialism of the priestly class on the one hand the self-control and the virtuous life of the pious monks on the other. In the splendid dialogue too, between the *Purohits* and his sons, the ascetic ideal is set forth against the Brahmanic ideal as the better and higher one. This conversation is found also in the *Mahabharata*, the *Puranas*, and in the *Jatakas*, in part even literally. This proves that it belonged to the general Indian ascetic poetry.

If I were asked to suggest a single work from the Jain canon to be included into the great scriptures of the world I would suggest *Uttaradhyayana*.

The second *Mula Sutra* is *Avassaya*. It is an essential part of the daily *rites* of a monk who has to recite it every morning and evening for self-purification.

The third is *Dasaveyaliya*. It is also meant for a monk. It begins with the three-fold way of *Dharma, i.e.*, non-violence, self-control and penance. As a matter of fact the letter too are incumbent on the follower of non-violence. A monk's search for food is beautifully compared with that of a bee. A bee collects his food from many flowers. He satisfies his hunger without disturbing the latter. Similarly, a monk should go to many houses taking a morsel everywhere. He should satisfy his hunger without becoming a burden on others. The questions are asked as how to walk, how to stay, how to sit, how to sleep, how to eat, and how to drink, so that one may not acquire sin. They are answered in the same strain, *viz.* that one should walk carefully, sit carefully, and so on. Here the author gives a gist of the religion in one word. While the *Bhagavadgita* teaches a man to become *yogin*, this *sutra* teaches him to become *yati* (self-controlled). But ultimately, both come to the same thing.

The fourth *Mula Sutra* is *Pinda Nijjutti*. It is peculiar to the monks only and does not posses any general interest.

The two *Chulikas* of the *Nandi Sutra* and the *Anuyoga dvara* are works on Jain epistemology and logic and reflect the influence of the period of logic in Indian Philosophy.

Commentaries

There are four types of commentaries on the canonical texts. They are not mere explanations but show a later development of the subject. They are also helpful in keeping the old tradition alive.

(*a*) *Nijjuttis* are the oldest type of commentaries. They are ten in number and written in Prakrit verses. All of them are ascribed to Bhadrabahu who died 170 years after the death of Mahavira. But some of them are decidedly the works of the second Bhadrabahu who lived in the 5th century A.D.

(*b*) After *Nijjuttis* we have *Bhasas* (*Bhasyas*). They also are in Prakrit meters and so mingled with the *Nijjuttis* that it is difficult to make a distinction. The *Bhasa* on the *Avassaya* known in Sanskrit as *Viseavasyaka* Bhasya is an *encyclopaedic* work. It has a Sanskrit commentary as well.

(*c*) *Chunnis* are small commentaries by Sanghadasa Ganin. They are very important for knowing the old tradition.

(*d*) *Tikas* are Sanskrit explanations by Abhayadeva, Malayagiri and Silanka.

Thus the canon of Svetambaras consists of the texts with four types of commentaries.

The *Salkhandagama* and *Kasaya Bahuda*, the canon of Digambaras also contains many commentaries. Out of them *Dhavala* and *Jayadhavala* are most famous and regarded very highly. They are very big in size and full with information.

Non-Canonical Scriptures

The contribution of Jains towards the literature of India

is large in extent as well as variety. This is not the occasion to survey the entire literature. I shall refer to a few works only which have exercised a great influence on the Jain tradition.

1. *Tattvartha Sutra* comes first in this category. It is held in high esteem by Digambaras as well as Svetambaras. The former worship it like the canon. It is an aphorism in ten chapters. The last five chapters of it are devoted to the way of spiritual development.

Tattuartha is commented both by Svetamabara as well as Digambaras Acaryas of high reputation. Of course, Digambaras commentaries are more scholarly. Pujyapada, Akalanka and Vidyananda, the three stalwarts of Jain literature, have written excellent commentaries on it. They are important contributions to philosophy and logic. Among Sevetambaras a commentary by the author himself and another by Siddha Sena Ganin are more prominent. Thus, the *Tattvartha* with its commentaries, serves as independent literature on all aspects of Jain religion and philosophy.

2. Next, we come to the works of Kundakunda, a mystic philosopher. He was a prolific writer particularly on Jain mysticism. Dr. A.N. Upadhye has surveyed his works in his scholarly introduction to *Pravacanasara*. Kundakunda's Trinity of *Samayasara, Panacastikaya-sara* and *Pravacanasara* has exercised great influence on the entire Jain literature. A scholarly edition of *Samayasara* by Prof. Chakravarti has appeared from Bharatiya Jnanapitha, Kashi.

3. Next we should specify the literature on the theory of *Karman* which is a speciality of Jainism. It is said that this literature forms a part of the extinct *Purva* literature. We have six *Karma granthas, Kammpayadi* and *Pancasangraha* in this class. The *Karmakanda* of *Garmmalasara*, though a later work, is important from the subject point of view. *Labdhisara* and *Ksapanasura* also treat of the same subject.

4. The fifth century is marked by a new development in the history of Jainism. The religion which developed so far in

an independent and scheduled manner came into clash with rival systems. Mystic appeal gave way and the support of logic became inevitable. The era is marked by the pioneer work of Siddhasena and Samantabhadra. They gave a logical interpretation to the Jain theory of non-absolutism.

Sidhasena is credited with three works :

(*a*) Sanmati-tarka—It is a remarkable contribution showing depth, originality and logical approach. In reality Non-absolutism is a logical interpretation of the Jain principle of Non-violence, and *Sanmati-tarka* represents it fully. It has a voluminous commentary by Abhaya-deva, beautifully edited by the great Pandits Sukh Lal and Becharadasa. A critical English edition of the text, with elaborate introduction has appeared from the Jain Svetambra Education Board Bombay.

(*b*) Sicasena's second work is *Nyayavatara*. It is small treatise on Jain logic. It has been edited with English translation by Dr. P.L. Vaidya.

(*c*) His third contribution is thirty-two *Dvatrimsikas* (works having thirty-two verses each). Out of them only twenty-two are available which deal with various topics. Siddhasena is regarded as a great logician in Jain tradition.

Samanta Bhadra was known as a *stutikara, i.e.,* the writer of prayers. Most of his works are in the form of devotional prayers. But they are pithy with philosophical depth. His *Devagama-stotra* with its commentaries by Akalanka and Vidyananda stands highest in the Jain literature on philosophy. He examines in it the criterion of a preceptor, with a reliable authority and scrutinizes all the systems one by one. His *Yuktyanusasana* and *Svayambhustotra* also are a valuable contribution. *Ratnakarana Shravakchara* a work on the ethics for a layman also is ascribed to him. But scholars have raised a doubt about his authorship.

5. We have already referred to the *Visesavasyaka Bhasya* by Jinabhadra. It is a monumental work of the Agamic tradition. With it the Agamic period closes and the period of logic begins.

6. Aklanka, Vidyananda, Haribhadra, Manikyanandin, Devasuri, Prabhacandra, Abhayadeva, Hemchandra, Mallisena and Yasovijaya are some of the names which stand high in this field. Haribhadra Hemchandra and Yasovijaya have contributed towards *Yoga* or the system of spiritual development also. Their works stand a good comparison with the Yoga systems of Patanjali and Buddhism. *Samadhi Tantra* by *Pujyapada, Dhyanasataka* by Jinabhadra and *Janarnava* by Subhacandra also are valuable contribution to *Yoga.*

Works in Indian Dialects

The contribution of Jains towards the languages of South is remarkable. The author of the *Kural,* the great epic of Tamil, was a Jain poet. In Kannada also the contribution begins the *Kavirajamarga* by Nrpatunga, the first emperor of Karnataka. It has its golden age in the tenth century with the contribution of Punna, etc., and continued for a pretty long period. Prof. Chakravati has surveyed the contribution of Jains towards southern languages in Jain Antiquary.

Among the Northern dialects Gujarati and Rajasthani literature show a dominating influence of Jain scholars while in Hindi also their contribution is creditable. The autobiography of Banarsi Das is the first work of its kind in Hindi literature. For the study of Apabhramsa, the Jain contribution forms the very backbone.

Jain Mystics of the Modern Period

Among the mystics of India in the Muslim period and afterwards Ananda Ghana, Vinaya Vijaya and Raya Chand occupy eminent position. The last was regarded by Mahatma Gandhi as his *Guru.* His letters and *Atmasiddhi Sastra* are a valuable contribution.

Conclusion

The above is a brief survey of the great scriptures of Jains. The value of a scripture can be judged by its capacity for moulding a *Sattvika* life, and I can say, Jain scriptures have played a creditable role in this respect. It is unfortunate that they are now the property of a sect, followed mostly by businessmen, whose method of worship lies in storing and not in reading or practising. It is time that we look towards the entire literature as the human contribution for peace and happiness. All the great scriptures should be translated into the great languages of the world to make a healthy world culture.

5 FUNDAMENTAL PRINCIPLES

Lord Mahavira, the last Tirthankara of the Jainas, is described as a supreme personality and acknowledged as 'a great Brahmana', 'a great guardian', 'a great guide', 'a great preacher', 'a great pilot', and 'a great recluse'. Around his personality there gathered a large number of men and women belonging to different castes and classes. His disciples and followers sincerely believed that their master was, whether walking or sitting, gifted with a supreme knowledge and vision of the *summum bonum*. It is this earnest belief in the greatness of the Teacher that induced them to repose their trust in him and in his words. To them, he stood as a living example of highest human virtue and perfection. His life was to them a perennial source of light and inspiration. His sufferings and forbearance kept them steady in all their trials and tribulations. And his teachings and instructions were for them not ordinary words but utterances of one who saw the light of truth and was able to lead others along the path to enlightenment.

His Clan

'Mahavira' or the Great Hero was not the personal name of the religious teacher. He was better known to his contemporaries as Nigantha, Nataputta-Nigantha of the Nata or Naya Clan. This name is composed of two separate epithets. Nigantha and Nataputta, the first of which is religious and the second secular. He was Nigantha (Nirgrantha) in a literal as well as in a figurative sense—unclothed without and free from all worldly bonds and ties within. He was called Nataputta because he was a scion of the Naya, Nata or Jnatri clan of the Kshatriyas. Just as the Buddha was called Sakyaputta because he was a scion of his clan, so was Mahavira called Nataputta because he was a scion of the Nata Clan.

His Birth and Parentage

The Jaina tradition places the birth of Mahavira in the year 599 B.C. He belonged to Kasyapa gotra. He was a son of Kshatriya Siddhartha, also known as Sreyamsa and Yasamsa, and of Kshatriyani Trisala, also known as Videhadatta and Priyakarini of the Vasishtha Gotra. His mother was a sister of Chetaka, one of the kings of Vaisali. His parents, both lay followers of Parsva, were pious and chaste, virtuous and strict. They rigorously observed the principles of Jainism.

One incident regarding the birth of Mahavira, which has been mentioned by some Svetambara works, cannot be ignored. It is said that Mahavira was first conceived in the womb of a Brahmin lady called Devananda but was later transferred to the womb of Tisala Khattiyani as Tirthankaras are not born in the Brahmin families. The Bhagavati Sutra puts this episode into the mouth of Mahavira himself. The incident as described there related to Devananda and Usabhadatta, the original parents, coming to see Mahavira when the latter had become famous as a preacher. On seeing Mahavira milk began to flow from the breast of Devananda due to the strong motherly love she bore towards him. Gotama asked his Master the reason for this upon which the latter admitted that he was the son of Devananda. The text goes on to say that these original parents of Mahavira accepted the order of their Jaina son. This may be one of the causes of his having Brahmin disciples.

Curiously enough, the tradition about the transfer of the womb goes back to the beginning of the Christian era or even earlier, as it is found depicted in one of the Mathura Sculptures. This story seems to have been borrowed from the Puranic story of the transfer of the embryo of Krishna from the womb of Devaki to that of Rohini. This incident regarding the transfer of the womb had been discredited by the Digambaras.

H. Jacob thinks that Siddhartha had two wives, the Brahmani Devananda, the real mother of Mahavira, and the Kshatriyani Trisala. The name Risabhadatta has been invented by the Jainas in order to provide Devananda with another husband. Siddhartha was connected with persons of high rank and great influence through his marriage with Trisala. It was, therefore, profitable, if not probable, to give out that Mahavira was the son, and not merely the step-son, of Trisala, for the reason that he should be entitled to the patronage of her relations. The Jainas, preference for Kshatriyas rather than for Brahman is also proved by this curious legend. In the *Bhagavati Sutra*, there is no mention of the change of Mahavira's embryo, and Devananda has been stated to be the mother of Mahavira. It is reasonable to assume that Risabhadatta and Devananda were original parents of Mahavira, but they might have given Mahavira to Siddhartha and Trisala to be adopted by them.

Before birth, Mahavira's mother is said to have seen a number of dreams. According to the Svetambaras, they numbered fourteen. These fourteen dreams, according to the *Kalpa Sutra*, were (1) an elephant; (2) a bull; (3) a lion; (4) the anointing of the goddess Sri; (5) a garland; (6) the moon; (7) the sun; (8) a flag; (9) a vase; (10) a lotus lake; (11) an ocean; (12) a celestial abode; (13) a heap of jewels; and (14) a flame. The Digambaras, who describe sixteen dreams, insert the visions of a throne of diamonds and rubies, and also of a great king of the gods dwelling below the earth. They also assert that she saw the sun before she dreamt about the moon. In place of a flag, they affirm that she saw two fishes. They also assert that she witnessed two vases instead of one, filled with pure water. The interpreters foretold that the child would become either a universal monarch or a prophet possessing all possible knowledge. Since it is a legendary account, it is not necessary to believe that the mother of the *Tirthankara* actually saw all the dreams. The birth of great men has often afterwards been made a theme for some of the most fanciful and superhuman legends the world has known.

Birth Place

The early scriptures of both the Svetambaras and the Digambaras agree that Kundapura or Kundagrama was the birth place of Mahavira. After examining the evidence contained in the *Acharanga Sutr*a, the *Kalpa Sutra,* the *Uttaradhyayana Sutra* and the *Bhagvati-Sutra-Tika,* it becomes clear that Jainism had a great stronghold in the area of *Vaisali-Kundapura* of the Videha country during this period and that Mahavira was closely associated with this area. The name *Visalie i.e., Vaisalika* was given to Mahavira in the *Sutra-Kritanga. Vaisalika* apparently means a native of Vaisali, the capital of Videha country. Thus it is clear that Mahavira was born at Kundapura near Vaisali in the Videha country.

From the seventh century onwards, the gradual decline of Vaisali began and the Jainas came to forget the birth place of the last Tirthankara. Some Digambara Jaina works place Vaisali under Chetaka in Sindhu-Vishaya or Sindhu-desa. To them Tirabhukti became Sindhu-Vishaya. Evidently, however, Vaisali was not situated in Sindhu-Sauvira. K.P. Jain suggests two reasons for this confusion. Firstly, it may be that the authors have equated Sindhu-desa with Vrijidesa, and, secondly, there might have been a confusion especially because Ujjayini in Avanti, too, was called Visala, and there was the Sindhu river in the adjoining territory for which reason it was called Sindhu-desa in the middle ages (8th to 15th centuries A.D.) Since the Digambara writers, K.P. Jain adds, lived more in the Ujjayini region, they appear to have confused Ujjayini (which was also called Visala) with the Visala, little knowing that another Visala different from their own existed in Eastern India.

Efforts have recently been made to find out the birth place of Lord Mahavira, the son of the Jnatrika leader of Kshatriya-Kundapura or Kumalapura and the maternal son of Lichchhavia chief. While the Digambara Jainas found a village called Kundalapura near Nalanda, the Svetambara Jaina found a site called Kshatriyakunda near the village Lachhwad of Lachhuar in South Monghyr. These came to be regarded as the birth places of Lord Mahavira by the respective sects. Temples and *Dharmasalas* were constructed and the Jaina pilgrims began to pour into these places. Thus while the real birth place was forgotten, other places came to be recognized as such.

The present site, Kshatriyakunda, near Lachhwad, cannot be the birth place of Lord Mahavira because if formed part of Anga, and not of Videha. Modern Kshatriyakunda is situated on the mountain while there are no references to mountains in connection with ancient Kshatriyakunda of Kundapura in the Jaina scriptures. Near the present Kshatriyakunda, no traces of such ancient places as Vaisali, Vanijyagrama, Kollaga Sannivesa and Karmaragrama are found. The nullaha near it is not the Gandaki river.

In the *Mahavagga* of the Buddhists, it has been said that Buddha, while sojourning at Kotiggama, was visited by the courtesan Ambapali and the Lichchhavis of the neighbouring capital, Vaisali. From Kotiggama, he went to where the Natikas lived. There he lodged in the Natika Brick Hall. From there he went to Vaisali where he converted the general-in-chief (of the Lichchhavis), a lay disciple of the Nirgranthas. H. Jacob has identified Kotiggama of the Buddhists with Kundagama of the Jainas. Apart from the similarity of the names, the reference to the Natikas, apparently identical with the Jnatrika Kshatriyas to whose clan Mahavira belonged, and to Siha, the Jaina, points to the same direction. Kundagrama, therefore, was probably one of the suburbs of Vaisali, the capital of Videha. This conjecture is borne out by the name *Vesalie, i.e., Vaisalika* given to Mahavira in the *Sutrakrigangu. Vaisalika* apparently means a native of Vaisali; and Mahavira could rightly be called as such when kundagrama was a suburb of Vaisali. H. Jacob regards Kundapura as only an insignificant place and believes that the sovereign of it could at best have been only a petty chief. The identification of Kotiggama with Kundapura seems to be doubtful, and both seem to be independent villages.

A.F.R. Hoernle has clearly shown that Vaisali is the birth

place of Mahavira. Vaniyagama was another name of the well-known city of Vaisali, the capital of the Lichchhavi country. This city, commonly called Vaisali, occupied a very extended area, which included within its circuit, besides Vesali proper, several other places such as Vaniyagama and Kundagama. They still exist as villages called Baniya and Basukunda.

The identification of Vaisali with the group of remains associated with the village of Basarh in Muzaffarpur District, some forty km. To the north of Patna, is conclusively proved by the survival of the ancient name with only slight modifications; by the geographical bearings taken from Patna and other places; by the topographical details compared with description recorded by Yan Chwang, the Chinese pilgrim in the seventh century and by the finding on the spot of sealings of letters inscribed with the name *Vaisali*.

The identification of ancient Vaisali and Kundagrama or Kundapura with Basarh and Basukunda respectively has been supported by several other scholars such as T. Bloch, S. Stevenson, *N.L.* Dey and *B.C.* Law. Some of these scholars consider Kunapura, Vaniyagama, Kollaga Sannivesa and Karmaragrama to be the suburbs of Vaisali. This view does not seem to be correct. These were independent villages which may be identified with the modern villages of Basukunda, Baniya, Kolua and Kumana Chhapargachhi respectively. Brahmanakunda and Kshatriyakunda were the two wards of Kundapura, and between them was situated Bahusala Chaitya. Vaisali and Kundapura were situated on the eastern bank of the Gandaki river, while Karmaragrama, Kollage Sannivesa, Vanijyagrama and *Dvipalasa Chaitya* on the west.

Childhood

There are scriptural anecdotes, myths and miracles connected with the childhood of Mahavira. It is stated in them that his birth was celebrated alike by gods and men, and it was received by his parents with the loftiest expectations. On the day of his birth, the prisoners in Kundapura were released. Festivals kept the whole town bound in mirth and joy for ten days after which many offerings were made to the gods. His parents named him 'Vardhamana' or the 'Properous one', because with his birth, the wealth, fame and merit of the family increased.

The two ascetics, Sanjaya and Vijaya, became somehow suspicious about the nature of some object. As their suspicion immediately disappeared at the sight of Lord Mahavira soon after his birth, they therefore gave him the name *Sanmati* in devotion.

The scriptures of both the Svetambaras and the Digambaras relate the legends of Mahavira's supreme valour and how easily he excelled all his companions in strength and physical endurance during boyhood. One day, playing with his friends in the garden of his father, Mahavira saw an elephant, mad with fury and with juice flowing from his temples, rushing towards him. His companions, all boys, shocked and frightened at the sight of this imminent danger, deserted their comrade and ran away. Without losing a moment, Mahavira made up his mind to face the danger squarely, went towards the elephant, caught hold of his trunk with strong hands and mounted his back at once.

Another legend tells how, when Mahavira was playing with the same children at *Ambali Pipali* (a short of 'tick or 'tig') among the trees, a god disguised as a dreadful snake appeared on a tree. All his companions were alarmed and fled away. Mahavira, mustering courage, remained calm. He caught hold of the snake and threw it away. The god again decided to frighten the child by carrying him high up into the sky on his shoulders. Mahavira, however, was not in the least alarmed, and seizing this opportunity of showing his superiority over the immortals, whacked the god and pulled his hair so hard that he was only too ready to descend and get rid of his obstreperous burden. As he stood fast in the midst of dangers and fears, patiently enduring all hardships and calamities, adhering to the chosen rules of penance, and as he was wise, indifferent to pleasure and pain alike, rich in self-control and gifted with fortitude, the name *Mahavira* was given to him. As he devoid of love and hate; he was called

Sramana.

In person, Mahavira seems to have been handsome and impressive. He was clever and was possessed of a very keen intellect. The *Kalpa Sutra* mentions that from his very birth, he possessed 'supreme, unlimited and unimpeded knowledge and intuition.' We may assume that he received the usual education and training of a Kshatriya aristocrat in literature and philosophy, in military and administrative sciences, and in music and fine arts.

Life of a Householder

On the question of Mahavira's marriage, there is a fundamental difference of detail between the Digambara and the Svetambara accounts. The Digambara works deny the fact of Mahavira's marriage. On the other hand, in the Svetambara accounts, there is an allusion to his marriage. In his youth, Mahavira was however, given to contemplation and had begun to entertain plans of renunciation. His parents tried to solve the problem by marrying him off to a beautiful young woman, Yasoda, a Kshatriya lady of Kaundinya *Gotra*, who soon presented him with a daughter named Anojja. Anojja was married to Jamali, a Kshatriya, who after becoming Mahavira's follower created a schism. Mahavira's grand daughter, who belonged to the Kausika *Gotra*, had two names : Seshavatt and Yasovatt.

Mahavira's paternal uncle was Suparsva. His elder brother was Nandivardhana and his elder sister Sudarsana. His parents died when he was thirty years old. Afterwards, his elder brother, Nandivardhana, succeeded his father. With the permission of his brother and other authorities, he carried out his long cherished resolve and became a monk with the usual *rites*. The Digambara works do not mention the names of his elder brother and elder sister. According to them, Mahavira embarked upon his spiritual vocation during the lifetime of their parents. At first his parents were opposed to the idea of their delicately natured child undergoing all the hardships that fall to the lot of a houseless mendicant, but at last they acquiesced.

His Ascetic Life : His Twelve Years of Preparation

The *Acharanga Sutra* has preserved a sort of religious ballad giving an account of the years during which Mahavira led a life of the hardest asceticism, thus preparing himself for the attainment of the highest spiritual knowledge. The account given in the *Kalpa Sutra* substantially agrees with that of the *Acharanga Sutra*. Both the *Acharanga* and the *Kalpa Sutra* narrate the story of his *Sadhana* in such a manner as to suggest that he had to make superhuman efforts before he could aspire to obtain the coveted position of a *Kevalin*. It is remarkable that this account of *Mahavira Sadhana* given in the *Acharanga* and the *Kalpa Sutra* does not bring in Gosala to form an episode. It is only from the *Bhagavati Sutra* and the *Uvasagadasao* the we know that the Ajivika Teacher Gosala lived in the company of Mahavira for a period of about six years during this ascetic period of Mahavira's life.

Mahavira renounced the world at the age of thirty, It seems that he joined the order of Parsva of which his parents were lay followers. Whereas the Digambaras believe that Mahavira abandoned clothes at the time of his initiation, the Svetambaras hold that he abandoned them after thirteen months. The *Acharanga Sutra* gives the following account of his ascetic life.

For a year and a month since he renounced the world Mahavira did not discard his clothes. Thereafter, he gave up his garments and became naked. Even when he used his robe, he used it only in winter. For more than four months many living beings gathered on his body, crawled about it, and caused him pain. Then he meditated, walking with his eye fixed on a square space before him of the length of a man. Many people assembled, shocked at the sight; they stuck him and cried. He renounced the company of the female sex and of all householders. When asked, he gave no answer; when saluted he gave no reply. He was beaten with sticks, and struck by sinful people.

For more than a couple of years, he led a religious life without using cold water; he lived in solitude, guarded his body, had intuition, and was calm. He carefully avoided injuring the meanest form of life. He did not use what was expressly prepared for him. He consumed clean food. He did not use another's robe, nor did he eat out of another's vessel. Disregarding contempt, he went with indifference to places where food was prepared he was not desirous of eating delicious food, nor had he any longing for it. He neither rubbed his eyes nor scratched his body.

Mahavira sometimes lodged in workshop, assembling places, wells or shops; sometimes in manufactories or under a shed of straw. He sometimes took shelter in travellers' halls, garden-houses, or towns; sometimes in a cemetery, in relinquished houses, or at the foot of a tree. At these places, he spent thirteen long years meditating day and night exerting himself, undisturbed strenuously. He did not seek sleep for the sake of pleasure; he would wake up himself and sleep only a little, free from cares and desires. Waking up again, he would lie down exerting himself; going outside for once in a night, he would walk about for an hour. In these resting places, he had to face manifold calamities. Crawling or flying animals attacked him. Bad people, the guard of the village, or lance-bearers assaulted him. Always a master of himself, he endured these hardships as he wandered about, speaking but little. Ill treated by the wanderers, he engaged himself in his meditations, free from resentment. Always calm and cool-headed, he patiently bore the pains caused by grass, cold, fire, flies and gnats.

Mahavira traveled in the pathless country of Radha, in Vajrabhumi and Svabharbhumi, where he used most comfortless beds and seats. The rude natives of the place attacked him and unleashed their dogs to bite him, but he never used his sticks to keep them off. Being perfectly enlightened he endured the abusive language of the rustics. Sometimes when he did not reach the village, the inhabitant met him on the outskirts and attacked him, saying ' Get away from here.' He was struck with a stick, fist, or lance; he was hit with a fruit, a clod, and a potsherd. When once he sat without moving his body, they cut his flesh, tore his hair or covered him with dust. They disturbed him in his religious meditation. Abandoning the care of his body, he endured all pains free from desire.

Mahavira was able to abstain from the indulgence of the flesh, though he was never attacked by any illness. Whether wounded or not, he never had any desire for any medical treatment. Purgatives and emetics, anointing of the body and bating, shampooing and learning of teeth did not behove him, after he learned that the body is something unclean. In the cold season, he meditated in the shade, and in summer, he exposed himself to the heat. He lived on rough food : rice, pounded jujube, and beans. Using these three kinds of food, he sustained himself eight months. Sometimes he ate only the sixth meal, or the eighth, the tenth and the twelfth. Sometimes he ate stale food. He committed no sin himself, nor did he induce others. He meditated persevering in come posture, without any motion whatsoever; he meditated in mental concentration on the things above, below, beside, free from desires. He meditated free from sin and desire, not attached to sound or colours; though still an erring moral, he never acted carelessly.

Thus, like a hero at the head of a battle, he bore all hardships, and, remaining undisturbed, proceeded on the road to deliverance. Understanding what truth is and restraining his impulses for the purification of his soul, he finally liberated himself.

The account of Mahavira's ascetic life given in the *Kalpa Sutra* is as follows. When the moon was in conjunction with the asterism *Uttaraphalguni*, he, after fasting two and a half days without drinking water, put on divine robe, and, quite alone, nobody else being present, tore out his hair and, abandoning his house, entered the state of houselessness. For more than a year he wore clothes. Afterwards, he walked about naked, and accepted the alms in the hollow of his hand. Fore more than twelve years, he neglected his body and took no care of it. With exemplary equanimity he bore, experienced and suffered all pleasant or unpleasant occurrences arising from divine powers, men or animals.

Henceforth, the ascetic Mahavira remained circumspect in speech, movement begging, accepting anything, and carrying his outfit and drinking vessel. He guarded his thoughts, words, acts, senses and chastity. He moved without wrath, pride, deceit and greed. He remained calm, tranquil, composed, liberated, free from temptations, without egoism, and without property. In short, he had cut off all earthly ties, and was not stained by any worldliness. As water does not adhere to a copper vessel, so sins found no place in him. His course was unobstructed like that of Life. Like the firmament, he wanted no support, and like the wind he knew no obstacles. His heart was pure like the water in autumn. He remained unsoiled like leaf of a lotus. His senses were well protected like those of a tortoise. He lived single and alone like the horn of a rhinoceros. He was free like a bird. He was always walking like the fabulous bird, Bharunda. He was valorous like an elephant, strong like a bull, unassailable like a lion, steady and firm like Mount Mandara, deep like the ocean, mild like the Moon, refulgent like the Sun and pure like excellent gold. Like the earth, he patiently bore everything and like a well kindled fire, he shone in his splendour.

Out of all the eight months of summer and winter taken together, Mahavira spent only a single night in villages and only five nights in towns. He was indifferent alike to the smell of ordure and of sandal, to straw and jewel, dirt and gold and pleasure and pain. He was attached neither to this world nor to the world beyond. He desired neither life nor death. He arrived at the other shore of the *Samsara*, and exerted himself for the suppression of the defilement of *Karma*.

With supreme knowledge, intuition conduct, valour, uprightness, mildness, dexterity patience, freedom from passions, control, contentment, and understanding Mahavira meditated on himself for twelve years on the supreme path to final liberation which is the fruit of veracity, control, penance and good conduct.

The *Kalpa Sutra* gives a list of forty-two rainy seasons spent by Mahavira since he renounced the life of a householder. He stayed the first rainy season in Asthikagrama, three rainy seasons in Champa and Prishtichampa, twelve in Vaisali and Vanijyagrama, fourteen in Rajagriha and Nalanda, six in Mithila, two in Bhadrika, one in Alabhika, one in Panitabhumi, one in Sravasti and the last one in the town of Papa in king Hastipala's office.

B.C. Law thinks that the *Kalpa sutra* list of places is worded according to the idea of succession and chronology. The idea of succession is suggested by two expressions : 'the first rainy season in Asthikagrama' and 'the last rainy season in Papa or Pava'. Accordingly he suggests the names of places where Mahavira spent the twelve rainy seasons of his ascetic life. He stayed the first rainy season in Asthigrams, three rainy seasons in Champa and Prishtichampa and eight in Vaisali and Vanijyagrama. This view does not appear to be correct. Except the first and the last, the other places have not been mentioned in chronological order but in groups.

According to a commentary on the *Kalpa Sutra*, Asthigrama was formerly called Vardhamana. It would perhaps be more correct to say that Asthigrama was the earlier name of Vardhamana (modern Burdwan). But none need be surprised if Asthigrama was the same place as Hatthigama (Hastigrama) which lay on the high road from Vaisali to Pava (probably modern Kasia). Champa was the capital of Anga which was conquered in Mahavira's time by Srenika Bimbisara and permanently annexed to Magadha. Its actual site is probably marked by two villages of Champanagara and Champapura near Bhagalpur. Prishtichampa must have been a place near Champa. Valisali is identified with modern Basara in Vaisali, a district of Bihar. It was the chief seat of government of the Vriji-Lichchavis in Mahavira's time. Vaniyagama is the same as modern Bania, a village near Basarah. Rajagriha (modern Rajgir) was the capital of Magadha in Mahavira's time. Nalanda is identified with modern Bargaon, 10 km. to the northwest of Rajgir in the district of

Nalanda near Bihar (Biharsharif). Mithila was the capital of prosperous kingdom of Videha. It is identified with Janakapur, a small town within the Nepal border, north of which the district of Muzaffarpur and Darbhanga meet. Badrika, which is the same name as the Pail Bhaddiya, was an important place in the kingdom of Anga. It was visited by Buddha and is identified with modern Monghyr.

Alabhika, which is the same as the Pali Alavi, is identified by A. Cunningham and A.F.R. Hoernle with Newal with Aviwa, 40 km. north-east of Eatwah. It lay between Savatthi and Rajagriha. Panitabhumi, which is the same as Paniyabhumi, was a place in Vajrabhumi, a division of the pathless country of Radha. Sravasti was the flourishing capital of the kingdom of Kosala in Mahavira's time. It is identified with sahet-Mahet on the bank of the Rapti. Papa, which is the same name as the Pali Pava, was one of the chief seats of government of the Mallas. It was in Mahavira's time one of the halting stations on the highway from Vaisali to Kusinara and Kapilavastu. A. Cunningham took it for the modern village, Padaraona, 18 km. to the N.N.E. of Kasia. It is identified with a place located at a distance of ten km. from Biharsharif in Patna District.

One important event of this period of Mahavira's life was his meeting with Gosala Maukhaliputta, the head of the Ajivika sect. From the account given in the *Bhagvati Sutra*, it is known that during the second year of his ascetic life, Mahavira stayed at Nalanda during the rainy season. At this time, Gosala, who was then wandering about in the country showing pictures to the people at large, happened to arrive and put up there. Owing to Mahavira's extraordinary self-restraint, his impressive habits of meditation, his capacity to prohesy things correctly and to the fact a rich householder Vijaya, of Rajagriha had shown respect and hospitality to him, Gosala was attracted, and wanted to be his disciple, but Mahavira declined his request. His prayer was not granted on two successive occasions even though the Master was entreated by the rich householder, Ananda and Sudarsana.

In the meantime, Mahavira went to the settlement of

Kollaga, at some distance from Nalanda, where he was hospitably greeted by the Brahmin Bahula. (Kollaga is identified with the modern village Kolhuda.) Gosala proceeded towards Rajagriha and its suburbs to find out Mahavira but in vain. He came back to the weaver's shed of Nanda where he gave away his cloths, vessels, shoes, and pictures to a Brahmin of the place, shaved off his hair and beard, and in despair departed in search of the Master. On his way, he came across Kollaga where he saw people praising Bahula's liberality towards Mahavira.

Gosala continued his search of Mahavira and at last succeeded in finding him out at Paniyabhumi. He again requested him with greater earnestness to make him his disciple. This time his request was granted, and both Mahavira and his disciple Gosala lived together for six years in Paniyabhumi, practising asceticism. Afterwards, they started from Paniyabhumi to Kurmagrama, and on from Kurmagrama to Siddharthagrama. Siddharthagrama is probably the same as Siddhangram in the Birbhum District. While at Kurmagrama, they met an ascetic named Vesayana who remained seated with upraised arms and upturned face in the glare of the Sun, while his body was swarming with lice. Gosala enquired whether he was a sage or a bed of lice. Vesayana became very angry and attempted to strike Gosala with his supernormal powers. Mahavira explained to him the severs ascetic discipline by which such powers could be obtained.

While at Siddharthagrama, Gosala uprooted sesame shrub and threw it away. Owing to a lucky fall of rain, the shrub came to life again. From this, he jumped to the conclusion that all plants were capable of reanimation. He drew even further conclusion that not only plants, but in fact all living beings were capable of reanimation. His theory of reanimation and other doctrines did not find favour with Mahavira who believed in the freedom of the will. Henceforth Gosala severed his connection with Mahavira and established a separate sect known as Ajivika.

B.M. Barua is of the opinion that the Jaina account of Gosala is biased and that it cannot therefore be relied upon. It is equally possible that Mahavira in the beginning of his ascetic carrier might have become a disciple of Gosala. Gosala was recognized as a teacher at least two years before Mahavira. He predeceased Mahavira by some sixteen years. There is a discrepancy between the accounts of the *Bhagavati* and the *Kalpa Sutra*. According to the former, Mahavira spent six years in Paniyabhumi in the company of Gosala, while the latter gives him only one year in that place, but six years in Mithila. The inference from these two somewhat contradictory accounts seems to be this—that in the second year of his monkhood, Mahavira left the religious order of Parsvanatha, and joined the school of Gosala. And when six years afterwards the difference of opinion led Mahavira to leave that school, he founded a new school of his own and organized a religious order mainly after the model of Parsvanatha. This view of B.M. Barua's appears to be only imaginary and is not supported by any solid dependable evidence. There are clear proofs that from the beginning of his ascetic life, Mahavira became a Jaina monk and that he did not join any religious order afterwards.

The incidental enumeration of the places visited by Mahavira in the *Bhagavati Sutra* during his ascetic life does not tally with those given in the *Kalpa Sutra*. The *Bhagavati* associates Nalanda, Rajagriha, Paniyabhumi, Siddharthagrama and Kurmagrama with his early wanderings. The *Uvasagadasao* mentions Vanijyagrama, Champa, Baranasi, Alabhji (Pali Alavi), Kampilyapura, Polasapura, Rajagriha, and sravasti as the places that were visited by Mahavira. Both the *Bhagavati Sutra* and the *Uvasagadasao* would have us believe that he received extraordinary respect from certain rich householders even long before his jinahood. Baranasi is no other than modern Benaras. Kampillapura is identified with; Kampil in the Farrukabad District. Polasapura has not been identified, but at the time of Mahavira, it was within the kingdom of king Jiyasattu, the ruler of Kosala.

The *Avasyaka Niryukti*, the *Avasyka Churni*, the *Avasyaka*

Bhashya, the *Avasyaka Tika*, the *Kalpa Sutra Tika*, and the *Mahavira Charitras* written by Nemi Chandra, Guna Chandra and Hema Chandra somehow give us a detailed account, with chronological succession of Mahavira's itinerary. Though based on tradition these are still very late works and cannot be wholly relied upon. Their motive was sometimes to glorify Lord Mahavira and present him as a superhuman being, rather than as an ordinary mortal. One important conclusion may be drawn that Jainism had penetrated to far-flung areas so that at the time of composition of these works, their authors expressly mention the visit of Lord Mahavira to these places in order to impress the masses, but actually the spread of Jainism during the time of Mahavira there seems to be quite impossible.

When Mahavira was thirty years old, he renounced the world with the permission of his elder brother, Nandivardhana, and his relatives. With people pursuing him, he set out from Kundagrama in the dark of Margasirsha on the tenth day in winter by; simply putting on a divine garment (*Devadussa*). He came to the garden of Nayasandavana situated in the northeast direction on the outskirts of Kundaggama. At this place, the renuciation ceremony of Mahavira was celebrated with great rejoicings. He is said to have given the first half of his garment to a Brahmana.

First Year

In the evening of the same day, Mahavira left Nayasanda for Kumaragama. There were two routes by which this journey was performed, one by water and the other by land. Mahavira preferred the latter and reached Kumaragama. Now this village is famous by the name of Kammana-Chhapara. Here, Mahavira stood in meditation but was harassed by a cowherd who took him for a thief and wanted to hit him. Next day, Mahavira proceeded to Kollage Sannivesa where he broke his fast. From there, he started for Moraga Sannivesa and reaching there, stayed in a hermitage. Next day, he left Moraga Sannivesa but again came back to this place after eight months. Then he proceeded to Atthiyagama, where he put up in the shrine of

Sulapani. Here Salapani Jakkha is said to have caused Mahavira many troubles but the latter bore them with his wonted equanimity and patience. Thus Mahavira spent his first rainy season at Atthiyagama.

Second Year

From Atthiyagama, Mahavira again came to Moraga Sannivesa where lived an ascetic named Achchhandaka. Then he started for Vachala, which was divided into Uttaravachala and Dakkhinavachala, and between them flowed the rivers Suvannakula and Ruppakula. When Mahavira was going from Dakkhinavachala to Uttaravachala, the remaining half of his garment got entangled in the thorns on the bank of Suvannakula. From this time onwards, Mahavira became a naked monk. There were two routes to Uttaravachala, one through the hermitage named Kanakakhala and another from outside it. Mahavira chose the former one which was more difficult. At Uttaravachala, he had to face a poisonous snaked named Drishtivisha. From Kanakakhala, he travelled to Seyaviya where he was received by King Paesi. T. W. Rhys Davids identifies this place with Satiabia and Vost with Basedita, Twenty-five km. from Sahet-Mahet and ten km. from Balarampur. Mahavira attived at Surabhipura from Seyaviya after crossing the Ganges, and afterwards proceeded to Thunaka Sannivesa where he stood in meditation. The place was situated in the country of Mallas to the north-west of Patna on the right bank of the Gandaki. From here, Mahavira proceeded to Rayagiha and sojourned in a weaver's shed in Nalanda where he passed the second rainy season. Here Gosala met him and the two left for Kollaga together.

Third Year

From Kollaga, Mahavira and Gosala came to Sunnakhalaya and then to Bambhanagama. This Bambhanagama lay in a route from Rajagriha to Chama. From this place, they reached Champa where Mahavira spent the third rainy season.

Fourth Year

From Champa, Mahavira and Gosala arrived at Kalaya

Sannivesa and thence to Pattakalaya. At both these places, Gosala was insulted for his misbehaviour. Then, both came to Kumaraya Sannivesa where Mahavira practised meditation in the garden, Champaramanijja. Then they proceeded to Choraga Sannivesa where they were taken to be spies and were taken prisoners. Choraga Sannivesa may be identified with Choreya in Lohardugga District in Bengal. From this place, they travelled to Pitthichampa where Mahavira passed the fourth; rainy season.

Fifth Year

From Pitthichampa, Mahavira and Gosala proceeded to Kayangala, now identified with Kankajol in Santhal *Pargana* in Bihar. At this place, some ascetics were staying with their families. Gosala is known to have misbehaved with them and was therefore punished. Then both came to Savatthi and, later, to Haledduga. Here under a big turmeric tree Mahavira stood in meditation. His feet are said to have been burnt by fire. Meditation over, both proceeded to Nangala where Mahavira stood in meditation again in the Vasudeva temple. Gosala was punished once again for his misdemeanour. Then, they arrived at Avattagama where Mahavira spent his time in meditation in the Baladeva temple and Gosala was taken to task for his misbehaviour. Continuing their travels in this region, they reached choraya Sannivesa from where they journeyed to Kalambuka Sannivesa. Here both were tied by Kalahasti and were beaten; later on, they were set at liberty by Kalahasti's brother, Megha, who recognized Mahavira. Then they journeyed to the country of Ladha where Mahavira had to endure various kinds of painful sufferings. Ladha or Radha comprises the modern districts of Hooghly, Howrah, Bankura, Burdwan, and the eastern part of Midnapore. From this place, they moved on towards Punnahalasa where some robbers made a dastardly attempt on Mahavira's life. Undaunted, they travelled to the city of Bhaddiya where Mahavira passed the fifth rainy season.

Sixth Year

From Bhaddiya, both Mahavira and Gosala travelled to

Kayalisamagama, and then onward to Jambusanda and Tambaya Sannivesa. Jambusanda was located between Anbagama and Bhoganagara on a route from vaisali to Kusinara. Then they arrived at Kuiya Sannivesa where, suspected of beings spies, they were kept as prisoners, but were later released at the intercession of two sisters, Vijaya and Pragalbha. Kuiya or Kupiya is identified with a place located at a distance of ten km. from the Khalilabada Mehadavala road in Khalilabad Tehsil of Bhuhabasti District.

Now Gosala and Mahavira parted with each other. Mahavira left for Vaisali where he stood in a blacksmith's shed. The blacksmith, seeing Mahavira naked, ran to hit him. Afterwards, Mahavira proceeded to Gamaya Sannivesa where he was honoured by Vibhelaka Jakkha. From this place, he travelled to salistsayagama where the demoness Kataputana caused him much trouble. After six months, Gosala again joined Mahavira at this place. Finally, Mahavira visited Bhaddiya in order to spend the sixth rainy season there.

Seventh Year

Then Mahavira and Gosala travelled together in the country of Magadha. In the course of the Journey, Mahavira decided to spend the seventh rainy season at Alabhiya.

Eighth Year

From Alabhiya, Mahavira and Gosala set out for Kundaga Sannivesa. At this place, Mahavira stood in meditation in the temple of Vasudeva. Gosala was again beaten for his bad manners. Then they visited Maddangama and stayed in the Baladeva temple. Afterwards they came to Bahusalagagama where Mahavira was harassed by Salejja Vanamantari. From this place, they proceeded to the capital Lohaggala where the royal servants suspected them to be spies and caught them. Later on they were set free at the intercession of Uppala who is said to have arrived there from Atthiyagama. Lohaggala may be identified with Lohardaga situated in the region which forms the central and north-western portion of the Chhota Nagpur Division. From Lohaggala, they went to Purimatala where Mahavira stood in meditation in the garden of Sagadamuha. Primatala may be identified with Purulia in Bihar. From there, they travelled to Unnaga and on to Gobhumi. At last they reached Rayagiha in order to pass the eighth rainy season.

Ninth Year

From Rayagiha, Mahavira and Gosala again set out for a Ladha country which is non-Aryan. In the course of this journey, they passed through Vajjabhumi and Subbhabhumi, where Mahavira had to endure all sorts of tortures. Sometimes people surrounded him and set their dogs upon him. Mahavira got no shelter in this region. He passed the ninth rainy season in this country.

Tenth Year

Mahavira and Gosala then travelled to Siddhattapura and Mummagama. Soon they returned to Siddhatthapura. It may be the same as Siddhangrama in Birbhum district. Severing his relations with Mahavira again, Gosala now went to Savatthi while Mahavira visited Vaisali where the republican chief Sankah saved him from the trouble caused by the local children. From here, Mahavira crossed the river Gandai by boat and reached Vaniyagama. He then proceeded to Savatthi where he passed the tenth rainy season.

Eleventh Year

From Savatthi, Mahavira set out for Sanulatthiyagama, which may be identified with Dalabhum in Singhbhum District in Bengal. He then went to Pedhalagama and stood in meditation in the garden of Pedhala in the shrine of Polasa. In this region of the Mlechchhas, Mahavira had to suffer much. He travelled later to Valuyagama, Subhoma, Suchchhetta, Malaya and finally on to the Hatthisisa. At all these places, apparently located in the north-west part of Orissa, Mahavira had to undergo extreme physical torture. Afterwards he reached Tosali where he was suspected to be a robber and hit hard. The place is now identified with Dhauli and some neighbouring places in Orissa. Then he travelled to Mosali where he was caught under the suspicion of a dacoit and brought before the king, but he was soon released. Mahavira again returned to Tosali and found himself in great troubles. He was actually to be hanged here but was luckily rescued by Tosali Kshatriya. Then he arrived at Siddhatthapura from where he preceeded to Vayaggama. For a period of six months, he had to bear great hardship at all these places. From Vayaggama, he proceeded to Alabhiya and then to Seyaviya and Savatthi. At last, passing through Kosambi, Vanarasi, Rayagiha and Mithila he spent the eleventh rainy season at Vaisali.

Twelfth Year

From Vaisali, Mahavira came to Sumsgumarapura which is identified with a hilly place near Chunar is Mirzapur District. He proceeded thence to Bhogapura, which lay between Pava and Vaisali, and to Nandiggama, from where he travelled to Mendhiyagama. Afterwards he proceeded to Kosambi, where he received his alms after a period of four months. From Kosambi, he set out for Sumangalgama and then for Palayagama. Finally, he reached Champa for spending the twelfth rainy season.

Thirteenth Year

From Champa Mahavira came to Jambhiyagama. Kalyana Vijaya identifies it with Jambhigaon near the river Damodar in the Hazaribagh District, but it must be located somewhere near modern Pavapuri in Bihar. From this place, he reached Mendhiyagama. Then he visited Chhamanigama where a cowherd is said to have thrust iron nails into his ears. In this conditon, Mahavira is said to have reached Majjhima Pavi where the nails were removed from his ears.

Mahavira's Penance in a Cemetery at Ujjain

According to the Svetambaras, Mahavira was born with three kinds of knowledge : *Matijnana, Srutajanana* and *Avadhijnana*. He also gained the fourth kind of knowledge, *Manahjparyayajnana*, by which he knew the thoughts of all sentient beings possessing the five senses in the two and a half continents till some time after his initiation to asceticism.

According to the Digambaras, Mahavira failed to gain it, though he performed meditation for six months, sitting absolutely motionless. At the end of the six months, he went to Kulapura where its ruler, Kuladhipa, came and did him honour, washed his feet with his own hands, and having walked round him three times, offered him rice and milk. There Mahavira took as his first meal (*Paranum*) after fasting for six months. He returned to the forest and wandered about in it performing twelve kinds of penances, but still the knowledge was withheld from him. At last he visited Ujjayini and did penance in a cemetery there when Rudra and his wife tried in vain to interrupt him. It was only after overcoming this temptation and again embarking upon his forest life of meditation that, according to the Digambara belief, he obtained *Manahparyayajnana*.

Kevalajnana

The period of twelve years spent in penance and meditation was not fruitless, for in the thirteenth year, Mahavira at last attained supreme knowledge and final deliverance from the bonds of pleasure and pain. The Jainas themselves have described this most important moment of the prophet's life.

> "During the thirteenth year, in the second month of summer, in the fourth fortnight, the light (fortnight) of *Vaiskha*, on its tenth day, called *Suvrala*, while the moon was in conjunction with the asterism Uttara-Phalguni, when the shadow had turned towards the east, and the first wake was over, outside of the town Jrimbhikagrama on the northern bank of the river Rijupalika, in the field of the householder Samaga, in a north-eastern direction from an old temple, not far from a *Sal* tree, in a squatting position with joined heels exposing himself to the heat of the Sun, with the knees high and the head low, in deep meditation, in the midst of abstract meditation, he reached *Nirvana*, the complete and full, the unobstructed, unimpeded, infinite and supreme, best knowledge and intuition, called *Kevala*."

When the venerable Mahavira had become an *Arhat* and a *Jina*, he was a *Kevalin*, omniscient and comprehending all objects; he knew all the conditions of the world, of gods, men and demons; whence they come, where they go, whether they are born as men or animals, or become gods of hell-beings; their food, drink, doings, desires, open and secret deeds, their conversation and gossip and the thoughts of their minds; he saw and knew all the conditions in the whole world of all living beings.

At this time, Mahavira (the great hero) or Jina (the conqueror) was forty-two years old; and from this age, he entered upon a new stage of life that of a religious teacher and the head of a sect called the Nirgranthas, 'free from fetters'. He went from place to place for the propagation of his doctrine, and for making converts. His first declaration about himself aroused confidence among his followers and urged them to follow his example in their own life. The Buddhist texts give us an idea of his first declaration which is as follows :

I am all-knowing and all-seeing, and possessed of an infinite knowledge. Whether I am walking or standing still, whether I sleep or remain awake, the supreme knowledge and intuition are present with me—constantly and continuously. There are, O Nirgranthas, some sinful acts you have done in the past, which you must now wear out by this acute form of austerity. Now that here you will be living restrained in regard to your acts, speech and thought, it will work as the non-doing of *Karma* for future. Thus, by the exhaustion of the force of past deeds through penance and the non-accumulation of new acts, (you are assured) of the stoppage of the future course, of rebirth from such stoppage, of the destruction of the effect of *Karma*, from that, of the destruction of pain, from that, of the destruction of mental feelings, and from that, of the complete wearing out of all kinds of pain."

First Sermon

When Mahavira attained kevalahood, a *Samavasarana* (religious conference) was held on the bank of the river Ujjuvaliya, but it is said that the first discourse of Mahavira remained unsuccessful. Then after traversing twelve *yojanas*, he is said to have returned to Majjhima Pava where the second *Samavasarana* was convened in the garden of Mahasena. Here after a long discussion on various and philosophic points, Mahavira converted to Jainism the eleven learned Brahmanas who had gone there to attend the great sacrifice performed by a rich Brahmana named Somila.

According to the Digamabara scriptures, even after obtaining *Kevalanjnana* (Enlightenment) at Jrimbhikagrama, Mahavira did not break his vow of silence taken from the time of *Pravrajya*, and wandering continuously for sixty-six days in silence, reached Rajagriha, the capital of Magadha. Outside the city of Rajagriha, at Vipulachala where he settled, a *Samavasarana* was held for his first sermon. First of all he converted eleven learned Brahmanas, including Indrabhuti Gautama, who were known as his disciples (*Ganadharas*). King Srenika with the members of the royal family, including his queen Chetana, and the whole army came to the *Samavasarana* to pay homage to Mahavira as well as to listen to his first sermon. It is said that the kind asked him several questions concerning the faith and all of them were satisfactorily answered.

Eleven Disciples (Ganadharas)

First of all, Mahavira by his preaching converted to Jainism the eleven learned Brahmanas who became his disciples, his eleven *Ganadharas*. They listened to Mahavira's discourses and heard the gentle, thoughtful answers he gave to all questions. Finally, being convinced of the truth of his views, they became his disciples or *Ganadharas*. The eldest was Indrabhuti, then followed Agnibhuti, Vayubhuti, Vyakta, Sudharma, Mandikata, Mauryaputra, Akampita, Achalabhrata, Metarya and Prabhasa. The first three Ganadharas were brothers and belonged to the Gautama *Gotra*, and were residents of Gobbaragama. The fourth belonged to the Bharadvaja *Gotra* and was the resident of Kollaga Sannivesa; the fifth belonged to the Agni Vesyayana

Gotra and was the resident of Kollaga Sannivesa; the sixth belonged to the Vasishtha *Gotra* and was the resident of Moriya Sannivesa; the seventh belonged to the Kasyapa *Gotra* and was the resident of Moriya Sannivesa; the eighth belonged to the Gautama *Gotra* and was the resident of Mithila; the ninth belonged to the Harita *Gotra* and was the resident of Kosala; the tenth belonged to the Kaudinya *Gotra* and was the resident of Tungika Sannivesa; and the eleventh belonged to the same *Gotra* and was the resident of Rajagriha. These Ganadharas were all Brahmana teachers, and all except Indrabhuti and Sudharma, died during the life-time of Mahavira. They are said to have been versed in the twelve *Angas*, the fourteen *Purvas* and the whole *Ganipidaga* (the basket of the Ganis).

The Digambaras have some different names for these *Ganadharas* and give a different account of Gautama's conversion. According to Gunabhadra the eleven names are as follows: Indrabhuti, Vayubhuti, Agnibhuti, Sudharma, Maurya, Maundra, Putra, Maitreya, Akampana, Andhavela or Anvachela and Prabhasa. Indrabhuti became a very learned *pandita* and grew extremely vain of his learning. One day, however, an old man appeared and asked him to explain a certain verse to him. Mahavira had, the old man said, repeated the *Sloka* to him, but had immediately afterwards become so lost in meditation that he could get no explanation of it from the saint, and yet he felt that he could not live unless he knew the meaning. The verse contained references to *Kala* and *Dravya, Pancha Astikaya, Tattva* and *Lesya*, not one of which could Gautama understand, but being too true a scholar to pretend to a knowledge which he did not possess, he sought out Mahavira to ask for an explanation. The moment he was in the presence of the great ascetic, all his pride in his fancied learning fell from him, and he besought Mahavira to teach him. He not only became a convert himself, but took over with him his five hundred pupils and his three brothers. In the Digambara Jain *Pattavalis*, Sudharma comes after Indrabhuti, and Sudharma was also known by the name of Lohirya.

One significant fact about these *Ganadharas* is that all of them were Brahmins, which proves that among the Brahmins also an ideological revolution was taking place and compelling them to give up their traditional grooves of thoughts advocating ritualism. Further, it was this intelligentsia that predominantly included the Brahmins who helped him spread his faith.

Four Orders of the Jaina Community (Samgha)

Mahavira possessed a unique power of organization. By his wonderful personality and organizational skill, he attracted a large number of people, both men and women, to be his disciples. From them therefore grew the four orders of his community: monks, nuns, laymen, and laywomen.

The chief among his followers were the fourteen thousand monks placed under the charge of Indrabhuti Gautama. Mahavira resolved to combat by regulations and organization those special temptations and dangers which beset ascetics in their wandering life. For this purpose, he divided fourteen thousand monks into nine regular schools called *Ganas*, placing each school under the headship of one of his chief disciples or *Ganadharas*. The leading *Ganadhara* had five hundred monks under him, but some of the others had only three hundred or two hundred and fifty. These *Ganadharas* were to guide and instruct separate groups of Nirgranthas.

Besides the fourteen thousand monks, a great multitude of women followed Mahavira, and of these some thirty-six thousand actually renounced the world and became nuns. At their head was Chandana, a first cousin of Mahavira's, or, as other accounts have it, his aunt.

Mahavira's third Order consisted of laymen numbering about one hundred and fifty-nine thousand with Sankha Sataka at their head. These laymen were householders who could not actually renounce the world but they at least could observe the five small vows called *anuvrata*. The similarity of their religious duties, differing not in kind but in degree, brought about the close union of laymen and monks. Most of these regulations meant to govern the conduct of laymen were intended apparently to make them participate, in a measure and for some time, in the merits and benefits of monastic life without obliging them to renounce the world altogether. "The genius for organization which Mahavira possessed." S. Stevenson rightly observes, "is shown in nothing more clearly than in the formation of this and the order of laymen. These two organizations gave the Jaina a root in India that the Buddhists nerves obtained, and that root firmly planted amongst the laity enabled Jainism as we have seen, to withstand the storm that drove Buddhism out of India."

Their fourth and last Order consisted of devout laywomen or *Sravikas* numbering about three hundred and fifty-eight thousand with Sulasa and Revatt as their heads. Their household duties prevented their becoming nuns but still they served the ascetics in many ways. The number of members in the four Orders of the Jaina Community is exaggerated, but There is little doubt that Mahavira converted a large number of people to Jainism.

The Digambaras believe that Mahavira did not travel alone but that wherever he went he was accompanied by all monks and nuns who had entered his Order. He preached in a language which they call *An-akshari*, which was unintelligible to the common people; so Gautama acted as his interpreter and translated all he said into Ardha-Magadhi.

Places of Rainy Seasons (Chaturmasa)

The *Jaina Kalpa Sutra* gives the names of the places where Mahavira spent one or more rainy seasons since he became an ascetic after renouncing the world. He stayed the first rainy season in Asthikagrama, three rainy seasons in Champa and Prishtichampa, twelve in Vaisali and Vanijagrama, fourteen in Rajagriha and Nalanda, six in Mithila, two in Bhadrika, one in Alabhika, one in Panitabhumi, one in Sravasti and the last one in the town of Papa in King Hastipala's office. This list is neither exhaustive nor chronological though it covers broadly the forty-two years of his itinerary. It is rather difficult to distinguish the places he visited during and after the period of his ascetic life merely on the basis of the list supplied by the *Kalpa Sutra*. There is no doubt that the *Kalpa Sutra's* authority on the itinerary of Mahavira is ancient and fairly reliable. It gives us a fair idea of the area over which he wandered propagating his faith. When the places are correctly identified, we come to know that this area roughly covered the modern State of Bihar and some parts of Bengal and U.P.

The Jain tradition which mentions Mahavira's visit to Vitibhaya, the capital of Sindhu Sovira, to preach to king Uddayana, is of very doubtful veracity. The earliest reference to this visit is found in the *Bhagavati* and later on in certain *Churnis* which perpetuate the tradition. It is quite possible that in later times, when Jainism spread to Western India, the Jainas, in order to impress the masses of this region, wanted to point out that their association with them was not new. In order to trace the beginning of this association from the earliest times they concocted the story of Mahavira's visit to King Uddayana.

The late Jaina works describe Mahavira's itinerary exhaustively and chronologically, but the description does not seem to be fully reliable. After attaining *Kevalajnana*, Mahavira spent no less than thirty rainy seasons at the following, places yearwise—(1) Rajagriha, (2) Vaisali, (3) Vanijyagrama, (4) Rajagriha, (5) Vaijyagrama, (6) Rajagriha, (7) Rajagriha, (8) Vaisali, (9) Vaisali, (10) Rajagriha, (11) Vaijyagrama, (12) Rajagriha, (13) Rajagriha, (14) Champa, (15) Mithila, (16) Vanijyagrama, (17) Rajagriha, (18) Vanijyagrama, (19) Vaisali, (20) Vaisali, (21) Rajagriha, (22) Nalanda, (23) Vaisali, (24) Vaisali, (25) Rajagriha, (26) Nalanda, (27) Mithila, (28) Mithila, (29) Rajagriha, and (30) Apapapurt.

Influence on Lay followers (Sravakas)

First of all, Mahavira seems to have tried to attract those householders who formed a large body of lay disciples by laying down certain rules of conduct. Gautama Indrabhuti was taken to task by the Master when he sought to claim a difference in degree in this respect between a recluse and a lay disciple. The gift of supernormal vision was no monopoly of any Order or caste or sex. In this matter, Mahavira made no distinction between men and men, or between men and women. He did not enjoin one set of rules for male recluses and another for those of the fair sex, one set of rules for male lay disciples and another for female lay disciples. When he wandered about in the country, he was accompanied by male as well as female recluses.

Mahavira not only taught his followers to observe penances and live a life of restraint in all possible ways but also watched how they had been progressing. He also encouraged them in the study of the *Purvas* and in developing their power of reasoning and arguing. The Buddhist records themselves attest that there were some able and powerful disputants among the Nirgrantha recluses and disciples.

The lay disciples of Mahavira and the lay supporters of his Order, both male and female, are all mentioned as persons of opulence and influence. At the same time, they were noted for their piety and devotion. Their contemporaries, including kings and princes, consulted them on many affairs and matters. Among them, Ananda and his wife Sivananda from Vanijagrama, Kamadeva and his wife Bhadra from Champa, Chulanipriya and his wife Syama, Suradeva and his Dhanya from Baranasi, Chullasataka and his wife Pushya from Kampilyapura, Kundakolita and his wife from Kampilyapura, Sardalputra and his wife Agnimitra from Polasapura and Mahasataka from Rajagriha and Nandinipriya and his wife Asvini, and Salatipriya and his wife Phalguni were the most well known lay disciples of Mahavira.

The Pali *upali sutra* introduces us to the rich householder upali of balakagrama, near Nalanda, who was lay disciple of Mahavira and a liberal supporter of the recluses of his Order both male and female. We are indeed told that a very large, number of the inhabitants of Balakagrama, headed by Upali became lay disciples of Mahavira. The bankar Mrigara or mrigadhare of sravasti, father-in-law of the Buddhist lady visakha, is mentioned as a lay disciple of Mahavira and lay supporter of the Nirgrantha recluses.

The Jaina *Bhagvati Sutra* speaks of two other rich householder Vijaya and Sudarsana, among the lay disciple of Mahavira. Of these the former was a citizen of Rajagriha.

Royal Patronage

Not only the rich bankers and merchants, but even kings, queens, princes, and ministers became lay disciples of the Jaina Tirthankara Mahavira. His personal connections with the various rulers were through his mother, Trisala, the Lichchhavi princess, and his maternal uncle, Chetaka, the king of Vaisali. According to Jaina traditions, kings like Srenika, Kunika, chetaka, Pradyota, Satanika, Dadhivahanna, Udayana, Viangaya, Virajasa, Sanjasa, Sankha Kasivaddhana and others are said to be his followers. Queens like Prabhavati of Udayana, Mrigavati and Jayant of Kosambi, queen of king Srenika and Pradyota, and princesses like Chandana, the daughter of the king Champa, followed Jainism. Princes called Atimukta, Padma, grandson of Srenika, Megha, Abhaya and others are said to have joined the Order of Jainism. The royal patronage must have facilitated the spread of Jainism.

Both Jainism and Buddhism claim most of the contemporary rulers of this period as followers fo their respective religions. It seems that it was the general policy of the rulers of this and even of later times to show reverence to the teachers of different sects. As Srenika's father is said to be a follower of the Parsvanatha sect which had also its stronghold at Rajagriha, it is natural the Bimbisara was inclined towards Jainism. The *Uttarddhyayana Sutra* relates how Bimibisara, 'the lion of the kings' with the greatest devotion visited the other 'Lion of homeless ascetics' (*Anagara-Siham*) at a *chaitya* with his wives, servants and relations, and became a staunch believer in the Law. R.K. Mokkerji and other historians have identified this ascetic with Mahavira because of the expression *Anagara Siham*, while others consider him to be a different ascetic, Anathi of the Nirgrantha Sect. His Jaina learning may have been due to his wife Chellana, who was a daughter of Chetaka of Vaisali. Hemachandra tells the story that "when the country was under a blight of cold, the king accompanied by Devi

Chellana went to worship Mahavira". The fact that Mahavira passed fourteen rainy seasons at Rajagriha is sufficient to prove that he exercised some influence over both Srenika and Kunika, the rulers of Magadha. According to the Jaina texts, Mahavira was always treated by them and other members of the royal family with the utmost respect. On one occasion, Srenika is said to have issued a proclamation promising financial support to the relatives of those who enter the Jaina holy order.

Srenika's son Kunika is represented in the Jaina texts as a Jaina. These texts are partial in freeing him from the charge the Buddhist texts level against him. The *Aupapatika Sutra* throws special light ‹ n the cordial relations between Kunika and Mahavira. Kunika is known to have appointed a special officer known as *Pravritti Vaduka Purusha* to inform him about the wandering and daily routine of Mahavira. It contains an account of Mahavira's *Samosarana* in Champa and Kunika's pilgrimage to this place. He was frequent visitor to Mahavira with his queens and royal retinue. He had an intimate connection with him both at Vaisali and Champa, and openly declared before Mahavira and his disciples his faith in him as the true teacher who had made clear the true path of religion based on renunciation and non-violence. Kunika was succeeded by his son Udayabhadra, who in the lifetime of his father served him as the Victory at Champa. He was a devout Jaina, fasting on the 8th and 14th *tithis.* He is also known to have built a Jaina shrine (*chaityagriha*) at the center of the town, Pataliputra.

In the Buddhist texts, Srenika and Kunika are known by the names of Bimbisara and Ajatasatru and both were devoted to the Buddha. Bimbisara accepted Buddhism, and his coversion was celebrated by inviting the Buddha and his disciples to meals which he himself served at the place, and then by announcing his donation of the park, Veluvana, to the Buddha and the *Samgha.* At another time, when the Buddha had no money with which to pay the ferry-man who carried him across the Ganga, the emperor granted remission of these ferry charges to all ascetics out of his regard for the master. After the murder of his father, Ajatasatru paid a visit to the Buddha in his Mango-grove. He also erected a *Stupa* over the relics of the Lord Buddha. He gave full facilities for the holding of the General Council of the Buddhists in the Saptaparni cave at Rajagriha shortly after the Buddha's death.

At the time of Mahavira, Udayana was a very powerful monarch of Sindu Sauvtra. He is said to have been related to Mahavira through his wife Prabhavati, a daughter of king Chetaka. It is said that once Udayana thought of paying a visit to Mahavira, who was in Champa at that time, and that the latter knew his thoughts and came down to his capital Vitabhaya in order to ordain him. Udayana anointed Kesikumara, his sister's son, on the throne and joined the order under Mahavira. He is known to have attained perfection. The Buddhist scriptures describe Udrayana or Rjdrayana of Sindhu Sauvtra, with Roruka as his capital, as a Buddhist. It is said that an image of the Buddha was sent by king Bimbisara to king Udayana to acquaint him with the Buddhist religion. In course of time, he gave his throne to his son Sikhandi and joined the Buddhist order under the influence of his queen Chandraprabha.

According to Jaina traditions, Pradyota, a follower of Mahavira, tried all he could for the propagation of Jainism. Mahavira was related to Pradyota, because Siva, the daughter of his maternal uncle Chetaka was married to him. Pradyota is said to have installed the *Jivanta* (life-time) *Svami* images of Mahavira at Ujjain, Dasapura and Vidisa. According to the Buddhist, Pradyot was converted to Buddhism by Mahakachchayana.

Chetaka, the ruler of Vaisali, was a follower of Mahavira. It was only due to his influence that Vaisali became a stronghold of Jainsim and that Mahavira visited this place from time to time. Chetaka had seven daughters, the eldest of whom was married to king Udayana of Vatsa and the youngest to King Srenika Bimbisara of Magadha. One joined the religious Order of Mahavira and the other four were married to the members of the royal family. There may be some truth in the suggestion made by C.J. Shah that these princesses were instrumental in the propagation of Jainism in Northern India.

It is significant that Buddhist books do not mention Chetaka at all, though they tell us about the constitutional governement of Vaisali. Buddhist took no notice of him as his influence was used in the interest of their rivals. Simha, A Lichchhavi general, was among the lay disciples of the Jaina Tirthankara.

Looking at the great importance of Champa in the Jaina annals, there in nothing strange if one assumes that its ruler, Dadhivahana, followed Jainism and held Mahavira in high esteem. His daughter Chandana of Chandanabala was the first woman who embraced Jainism shortly after Mahavira had attained the *Kevala*. As Champa became a great centre of Jainism, Mahavira spent three of the rainy seasons at this place.

The ruler of Kausambi was king Satanika to whom was married Mrigavati, the third daughter of Chetaka. Both the king and the queen were devotees of Mahavira and followers of the Jaina Order. The Jaina tradition also affirms that the king's Minister (*Amatya*) and his wife were Jainas by faith. Saranika's son and successor was Udayana. The Jaina literature claims him to be a follower of the Jaina Order. On the other hand, the Buddhist scriptures tell us that Udayana was at first not favourably inclined towards Buddhism, but later, however, he became a devotee of the Buddha.

Savatthi, Baranasi, Kampillapura, Mithila, Polasapura and Alabhia were all important towns visited by Mahavira within the kingdom of king Jiyasattu. Jiyasatu (*Jita-satru*, conqueror of enemies) seems to be a title of the king like the epithet *Devanampiya* of Asoka. Jiyasattu seems to be no other than Pasenadi or Prasenajit of Kosala. The *Rayapaseniya Sutta* records a dialogue between Kesi and Paesi, when the latter, being influenced by the teachings of the former, became a *Samanovasaga*. Kesi, a follower of Parsva, was a Jaina recluse who is represented in the *Uttaradhyayana Sutra* as the contemporary of Mahavira and Gautama Indrabhuti. Paesi or Pradesi may be identified with Pasenadi or Prasenjit of Kosala. From the Buddhist texts, it is known that Prasenajit was a great admirer of the Buddha though he was not converted to Buddhism.

After giving up his flourishing kingdom of Dasarna, Dasamabhadra, who was the contemporary of Mahavira, became a monk. Dasamabhadra is not known from any other source. Dasarna is identified with Vidisa or Bhilsa region in Madhya Pradesh. The early association of Jainsim with this area is clear even from the Jaina traditions which aver that Vajrasvami and other Jain pontiffs obtained liberation in the hills, Kunjaravarta and Rathavarta, in the neighbourhood of Vidisa.

Karakandu, king of Kalinga, is known to have adopted the faith of the Jinas, and, after placing his son on the throne, exerted himself as 'Sramana'. This proves the existence of Jainism in this Province from very early times, but it is very difficult to say when Karakandu lived in Kalinga. It was a Jaina stronghold, at least from the time of Lord Mahavira. The Jaina *Harivamsa Purana* informs us that Lord Mahavira had preached his faith in Kalinga. The *Haribhadrtya Vritti* on *Avasyaka* confirms Mahavira's visit to the country of Kalinga and adds that the king of that country was a friend (or relation) of his father's. The reference to Nandaraja as having taken away the image of Jina from Kalinga in the inscription of Kharavela is very interesting as it proves the existence of image-worship among the Jainas even in the fifth century B.C.

There are traditions even of Mahavira's visit to South India. From the *Jivundhara Charita* of Bhaskara, it is known that Jivandhara, who was the ruling chief of this region at this time, was a Jaina. He cordially received Mahavira and became an ascetic after obtaining *diksha* from him. Jivandhara seems to be an imaginary name. Actually speaking, there was no such ruler whose kingdom extended to and comprised Southern India during this period.

Mahavira is known to have converted to Jainism a prince

named Ardraka who became a monk. He was so much influenced by the teachings of Mahavira that he always supported Jainism in his disputations with the teachers of different religions. This Ardraka is identified with the prince of the Persian emperor Kurusha (558-530 B.C.). Both the emperor and the prince are believed to have sent presents to the king Srenika and his son Abhayakumara of Magadha who also in return dispatched their presents to them. It is said that first of all Abhayakumara enlightened Ardraka with the teachings of Mahavira. In course of time, Ardraka joined the Order of Mahavira.

On the basis of an evidence furnished by a very late period, Mahavira is known to have propagated his message even in the region now known as Rajasthan. There is an inscription of 1276 A.D. which begins with a verse which tells us that Mahavira in person came to Srimala. This is supported by the *Srimala-mahatmya,* a work of *c.* the thirteenth century A.D., which gives an account of the dissemination of Jainism in Srimala, Disgusted with the behaviour of the Brahmanas of Srimala. Gautama Ganadhara went to Kashmir where he was converted to Jainism by Mahavira. After his return Srimala, he converted the Vasiyas to Jainism and composed the *Kalpa Sutra,* the *Bhagavati Sutra Janmasutra* and other works. An inscription of 1396 A.D., found on the door of the chief shrine in Jivantasvami Sri Mahavira Jaina temple at Mungusthala Mahatirtha, 7 km. west of Abu Road, shows that Lord Mahavira visited Arbudabhumi, and an image was consecrated by Sri Kesi Ganadhara during the 37th year of the life of Mahavira. These statements are of a very late date and, therefore, cannot be easily relied on. But from them it can be legitimately deduced that in the 13th century A.D., Jainism was considered to be a very old religion in Rajasthan.

Not only the rulers but also several contemporary clans were the followers of the religion of Mahavira. There are many stray references in the Jaina *Sutras* which prove that the Lichchhavis followed the Jaina faith. Their capital , Vaisali, formed one of the headquarters of the Jaina community during the days of the Mahavira. Out of the forty-two rainy seasons of his ascetic life, Mahavira spent twelve at Vaisali. Like the Lichchhavis, the Vajjis, who in fact cannot be strictly differentiated from the Lichchhavis, came under the influence of Lord Mahavira, for Vaisali seems to have been regarded also as the metropolis of the entire Vajji Confederacy. The Jnatrikas of Kundagrama, who formed one of the most important clans included in the Vajjian confederacy, were also his followers. The other clans of the Vajjian confederacy must have been naturally affected by the doctrines of Nataputta. It is among these confederate Kshatriyas that Mahavira was born and found strong supporters of his religion. The Mallas also seem to have cherished a feeling of respect and sympathy for the great prophet and his doctrines. The Ugras and the Bhogs are repeatedly mentioned in several of the oldest sacred books as being among the most prominent of the earliest converts.

It is clear from the above discussion that though only a few of these kings can definitely be identified, the late tradition without much historical support brings nearly all the kings of North India in those days under the spiritual sway of Mahavira in one way or the other. While some of the names of these rulers seem to be imaginary, others might have flourished long after Mahavira. From this evidence only one significant conclusion can be drawn, namely, that in course of time, Jainism spread in different parts of India and received royal patronage. During the period of Mahavira, its influence seems to have been confined only to the modern states of Bihar and some parts of Bengal and U.P. and it is probably that most of the ruling chiefs of this area patronized Jainism.

Mahavira and the Buddha

The evidence of Buddhist literature is adequate enough to prove that Mahavira was a contemporary of the Buddha. Although they had not personally met each other, there were occasions when they felt interested in knowing and discussing each other's view through some intermediaries. Dirghatapasvi and Satyaka (Pali Sachchaka) among the Nirgrantha recluses, and Abhaya, the prince, Upali the banker, and Simha, the

Lichchhavi General among the Jaina laity, loom large among sea of the world, were straying or perishing by sinking or drowning or floating.

Mahavira, who was the wisest sage the world has known possessed infinite knowledge and faith. This wise man had explored all beings, mobile or immobile, high or low, eternal or transient. Like a lamp, he saw the Law in a true light. He knew this world and the world beyond. His knowledge was inexhaustible like the water or the sea. As he had mastered all philosophical systems, he understood the doctrines of the Kriyavadins, of the Akriya vadins, of the Vainayikas, and of the Ajnanavadins. His perception was infinite.

He endured severe tortures and penance in his life in order to annihilate his *karmans.* He bore everything like the earth. Having conquered the passions which defile the soul : wrath, pride, deceit, greed, the great sage did not commit any wrong, nor did he cause any wrong to be committed by others. He observed the chastity, the highest type of austerity, by abstaining from women. He practiced the highest contemplation, which is the purest of the pure—pure without a flaw. He granted protection to all and was the most vigorous. He wandered about without a home and crossed the flood of the *Samsara.* He renounced everything because he had broken away from all ties.

Mahavira was a great reformer. Since many abuses had crept into Jainism, he did his utmost to remove them. For this, he had to bring about some changes even in the traditional religion coming from Parsva. He added the vow of chastity and emphasized the importance of nudity. Though his teachings were based on the old religion, he made a more systematic arrangement of its philosophical tenets. All these point to his great reforming zeal.

Mahavira possessed a great organizing capacity, and he made the laity participate in the *Samgha* along with the monks. He encouraged a close union between laymen and monks by advocating similar religious duties for both, duties that differed not in kind but in degree.

6 THE WAY OF INNER DEVELOPMENT

I

The modern man has begun to realize that humanity is suffering so much not from scarcity or ravages of nature but from its own inner conflicts, its pride and prejudices, its favours and disfavours and its convictions based on mere caprice. It is not the material necessities but the unbridled lust for power and domination nursed by the individual or a group that causes wars, which leave behind the seeds of mutual hatred and perpetual enmity. Time-honoured friendship and mutual confidence come to an end and neighbours begin to look at one another with suspicion. Fear takes the place of love and the entire strcture of mental attitude is changed. Foremost preference is given to the preparations of deadly weapons. The man power and all resources of the nation are harnessed to the interest of war. Nazis thought that they were born to rule the world. This false notion threw the entire world in the clutches of war with its long lasting after effects. It is time that we think of not only famines and scarcities but also of the complex that are still dividing the humanity, even when natural barriers and boundaries have lost their significance. The atomic research has made the problem still graver. On one side, there is comfortable proposed by the principle of live and let live. On the other hand, there are atom and hydrogen bombs ready for total annihilation of the human species. We have to make our choice. In the first case, we must learn to rise above the complex narrowing the vision of man. We shall have to see that conceit, zealousy, mutual hatred, greed for power and domination and such other passions are no more our guides.

We shall have to remove the narrow walls of 'I' and 'mine' and learn thinking welfare of not only ourselves or a particular group but that of the entire humanity living in every corner of the world, or rather, of every being possessing life. We shall have to share the piece of bread in our possession with our starving neighbours even at the expense of our own hunger. It is in this perspective that I have chosen spiritual realization as my subject. The way to spiritual realization means the way to conquer these complexes and passions.

It is useless to discuss hare what happens after realization or the condition of soul in that state. The propounders of different system of philosophy have given, in their own way, different explanations, which is just like an attempt to know the peak of a mountain sitting in a closed room. If you want to have a clear vision of the peak you will have to open the doors, move towards the mountain and climb it step by step. It is almost essential. Otherwise, your knowledge would remain merely a guess work. Similarly, to try understand the nature of salvation with an opposite move is a useless attempt. A wishful thinking. Logicians have discussed the subject and formed different ideas according to their fancy. But, they are and will remain for ever, far from the reality. A thing of realization cannot be expressed in words. It is beyond even mental approach. The Acharya says—Logic cannot reach it, intellect cannot grasp it.

Really speaking, the discussion whether the ideal of salvation is attainable or not attainable does not serve any purpose. What is important is the way prescribed for it. It is certain that the traveller of this path does contribute to the happiness of his own self as well as of the world. The quantity of mental satisfaction increase as he moves further and further. No doubt, he does not add to our material gain; yet, he provides a sure remedy to the sufferings where material gains have failed. Further, it can be asserted, without an inch of hesitation, that the traveller of this path never suffers and none suffers through him. He is danger to none and none is danger to him. He is a blessing to himself, blessing to the Society and blessing to even his enemies. Lord Krishna says in the Gita— "O Arjuna ! rest assured that a devotee of mine never perished."

The school of Indian Philosophy hold different views regarding the nature of realization. But they are one not only in prescribing a way to it but also in the salients features of that way. The scope of his paper is not sufficient for a co-operative study. Here, I shall try to show the way as prescribed by Jainism.

The soul, according to Jainism, consists of four Infinites, i.e., Infinite Knowledge (*Ananta Jnana*), Infinite Intuition (*Ananta Darsana*), Infinite Happiness (*Ananta Sukha*) and Infinite Potency (*Ananta Virya*). They are natural characteristics of the soul and get full manifestation in the state of salvation. These powers of the soul are neutralized by the karmic influence in the state of spiritual bondage, the state of beings engrossed in worldly affairs. The way to salvation means the effort of the soul to remove karmic obstruction and regain its natural state of four Infinites lying dormant since the time immemorial. Thus, the nature of obscurance, its gradual removal and the means for that remove are the main factors to be considered to have a clear glimpse of the Jaina way to spiritual realization.

The cause of obscurance is known as *karman*. It is composed of material substance known as *Karma vargana*. The soul disturbed by the activity of mind, speech or body attracts the dirt of that substance and is thereby petrified. The passions of anger, conceit, crookedness and greed give duration and intensity to that dirt. Stronger the passions the dirt of *karman* will last for a longer duration and affect the soul more severely. The accumulated *karman* expires after giving its fruit when the term of its duration is over. At the same time new disturbance causes new accumulation. This process is confined from the time immemorial and will continue as long as the new accumulation is not stopped and the old one is experienced away or cast off through other measures. The way to salvation means a deliberate attempt on the part of the soul, for purification from the dirt by stopping the new accumulation and destroying the old one.

The function of *karmic* dirt is divided into two main groups. the *karmans* that impress the potencies of soul are known as *Ghati karmans* and those related with new projection are *Aghati karmans.* Both of these groups are further divided into four each.

(A) *Ghati Karmans*

1. *Jnanavarana*—Obscurance of knowledge.
2. *Darsanavarna*—Obscurance of Intuition.
3. *Mohaniya*—Perversion.
4. *Antaraya*—Obstruction in attainments.

(B) *Aghati Karmans*

1. *Vedaniya*—Sensation of pleasure or pain.
2. *Ayusya*—Birth and life in a particular kingdom.
3. *Nama*—Physique or constitution of the body.
4. *Gotra*—High or low birth.

The problem of spiritual development is concerned mainly with the first group.

Umasvati prescribes three virtues paving the way to salvation. They are—Right Knowledge, Right Attitude and Right conduct. Knowledge in itself is neither right nor wrong. It is right when possessed by a person with Right Attitude and wrong in reverse case. Thus, Right Attitude and Right Conduct play the main part. Both of them are connected with Mohaniya karman. The ladder of salvation means, therefore, gradual freedom from the effect of *Mohaniya*.

Mohaniya is further divided into *Darsana Mohaniya* (the cause of perverted attitude) and *Charitra Mohaniya* (the cause of perversion in conduct). Darsana Mohaniya has three types:

1. *Mithyatva Mohaniya* : The cause of wrong attitude, which makes the man extravagant seeking happiness

in external objects and taking body and other material things as his own self.

2. *Misra Mohaniya* : The cause of mixed attitude fluctuating between right and wrong.
3. *Samyaktava Mohaniya* : Mohaniya without the potency of perversion.

Charitra Mohaniya is further divided into 25 types :

1-16 — Four degrees of the effect of anger (*Krodha*), Conceit (*Mana*), Crookedness (*Maya*) and greed (*Lobha*) each. These degrees are known as *Anantanubandhi*, *Apratyakhyani*, *Pratyakhyanavarana* and *Sanjvalana* respectively.

17-25 — Nine semi-passions (no-*Kasayas*) of laughter (*hasya*), liking (*rati*), disliking (*arati*), fear (*bhaya*), grief (*soka*), hatred (*jugupsa*), sexual desire of a female (*striveda*), sexual desire of a male (*purushveda*) and sexual desire of the third gender (*Napunsakaveda*).

The aspirant climbs higher and higher by gradually subduing the above-mentioned degrees of passions. This is beautifully shown in the Jaina theory of fourteen *Gunasthanas*. The first four *Gunasthanas* are mainly related with different aspects of *Darsana Mohaniya* and five to twelve with those of *Cartira Mohaniya*. The last two are the stages of complete realization, one with activity and the other without activity.

Pujyapada in his '*Samadhia Tantra*' sums up these stages in three categories of *Bahiratman*, *Antaratman* and *Paramatman*. The soul in the first category is extravagant and seeks happiness in external objects, takes external objects as his own self and thus goes astray from its own nature. In the second category it is introvert and tries to realize its own nature. The third category represents the stages of perfect realization. An aspirant is advised to abandon the first and try to attain the third through means of the second. The first *Gunasthana* shows the state of *Bahiratman*, two to twelve that of *Antaratman* and the last two that of *Paramatman*.

The states of soul are judged through *lesyas*-thought points also. They are six in number and symbolise the thoughts according to the intensity of violence. The first *lesya* is Krishna (black) symbolizing the thoughts of most cruel nature. Then, there are *nila* (blue), *kapot* (light blue like the colour of a peageon), *Tejas* (firy), *Padma* (lotus colour) and *Sukla* (white). The thoughts of a person with *Sukla lesya* are of the purest nature. The *lesyas* numbering two to five symbolize the intermediate stages.

The yoga system divides the flow of mental activity into *Sansara pragbhara* and *Kaivalya pragbhara,* showing the bent of mind towards the pleasure of world and the spiritual realization respectively. They are just life the states of *Bahiratman* and *Antaratman* as shown above.

The Buddhist holds five states of *prthagjana, srotapanna sakadagamin, anagamin* and *arhat.* The first state contains the idea of *bahiratman,* the next three of *antaratman* and the last one of *paramatman.*

The Jaina literature on *karman* and *gunasthana* describes the above path minutely with every detail. Haribhadra, Subha Candra and Yasovijaya have explained it on the lines of yoga system. But, the theory of *gunasthana* serves as back bone for all the methods.

The first *gunasthana* is known as *Mithya drsti.* It represents the state of wrong attitude. The soul is rotting in it from the time immemorial without finding the real path. As a matter of fact it is not a step towards realization, as may be assumed from its inclusion into fourteen steps, but the lowest state where the spiritual journey is not even begun. Nevertheless, there are some stages even before the beginning of that journey and they are included into the first *gunasthana.*

We have already stated that *karmic* effect is the main cause of soul's wanderings in this world. This effect is sometimes thick and sometimes thin. When it is thick the soul is lead astray. When it is thin the soul takes a turn towards the real path, but without a definite start. We can compare these occasional inclinations with wanderings of a traveller who has lost his path in a jungle. He is sometimes, far from the real path and sometimes very near. But, in no case finds it. His coming near the path is merely an accident. It is useful only if he proceeds further in the same direction and happens to perceive the path. On the contrary, if in his bewilderment he turns his face again to the wrong direction, his coming near the path is futile.

Three Karmans and Grantha Bheda

The state when accidentally the burden of *karmans* is somewhat lightened and the soul feels an urge for inner realization, is known as *yathapravrti karana*. It is not reached through a deliberate and systematic pursuit but comes as an accident. The Jaina scriptures compare it with a stone rolling into a hilly foundation. The stone rolling unconsciously in the stream gets a round shape as the image of *Saligram* a *Hindu God*. The stone did not desire or strive for obtaining that shape, but the turn of events changed it into that form. Similarly, the soul with perverted attitude is unable to make a discrimination between right and wrong, nor does it make any deliberate attempt for realizing the truth. Still, accidently it reaches a stage when the major part of accumulated *karmans* is removed through experience of its fruit and the new accumulation is not so heavy that the duration of entire stock comes within a limit. As its result the feels an urge for inner purification. But, this urge is not so strong as to force the aspirant to a definite start. It rises innumerable times without having a permanent effect. Death of a beloved person, destruction of a thing extremely desired for or such other phenomena generally produce this type of attitude temporarily.

In the latter case the soul advance further and reaches the stage of *Apurva karana*. The karmic stock is further reduced in this stage and the soul takes a decisive step. This step is the most important in career of an aspirant. It is known as *apurva* as it was never achieved before. The aspirant, in this stage, reaches the point of breaking the tie of perversion.

The third step is *Anivrttikarana*, reached on breaking the tie of perversion. The aspirant attains it after subduing the five types of *Mohanlya i.e., Mithyatva Mohanlya* and *Anantanubandhi* degree of four passions and thus reaches the fourth *gunasthana*. It is known *anivrtti*, because, the aspirant, having once attained it, is never lost. By taking this step the soul limits its wanderings in the Universe. It comes to the path of light from that of darkness.

The second *gunasthana* is known as *Sasvadana*. It is not attained in the ascending order but in retrogression when the soul has fallen down from a higher stage and has not yet touched the ground.

The third *gunasthana* is known as *Misra* and represents the stage of mixed attitude. It is caused by the rise of Misra *Mohaniya*. The aspirant in this stage is not firm in his convictions and wavers between right and wrong. This state lasts for a short while only. After that the aspirant either goes down by resorting to wrong attitude (*mityyadrsti*) or moves further by taking a right attitude.

The fourth *gunasthana* is *Samyagdrsti* attained by the aspirant with right attitude and a firm faith in truth. His passions (*kasayas*) become mild and last for a short period only. They are week in intensity as well. Roughly speaking, the person whose enmity or other passionate feelings last for a duration of more than one year is considered to be under the effect *Anantanubandhi* and, therefore, not a *Samyagdrsti*. It is necessary for a Jain to purify his heart of all passions at least once a year. This is why the Jains are so particular in observing the festival of Paryushar which is an annual festival of self-purification and introspection.

A *Samyagdrsti* is expected to possess the following five virtues :

1. *Sama* : Natural tranquility of soul caused by subsidence of passions.
2. *Samvaga* : The sense of discrimination between right and wrong.
3. *Nirveda* : A dislike towards the pleasure provided by the satisfaction of senses.

4. *Anukampa* : Kind heartedness and generosity. A natural desire to see every body happy.
5. *Astikya* : The firm faith in truth.

His heart is generous and full of love for others. He desires for the happiness of all and tries to help miserable persons. Amitagati has beautifully depicted his behaviour in the following lines :

Sattvesu maitrim gunisu pramodam,

Klistesu jivesu krpaparatva,

Madhyastyyabhavam Viparltavratan,

Sada mamatma vidadhatu deva.

O Lord! may my soul cultivate the habit of friendship with all beings, pleasure to see the virtuous, kindness towards the afflicted and indifference for opposition.

The fifth *gunasthana* is *Desavirati*. The aspirant in the fourth was expected to have a right attitude. He did nothing on the practical side. He was not expected to observe any vows or practice restraints necessary for self-purification. This start is made in the fifth *gunasthana*. It is attained after subduing *Apratyakhyanavarana i.e.* the second degree of passions. Here, the aspirant is expected to purify his heart every four months. He takes the vows of a householder and leaves the acts of gross violence, falsehood, theft and sexual blasphemy. In short he is expected to refrain from all acts amountable to a crime. He must obey the laws of state breaking of which amounts to theft. In addition he should fix limit for his possessions. He should prepare a list of everything he wants to own for his personal use and should not go beyond the limit fixed therein. It is also expected that he should go on curtailing that list and have daily scrutinization. He should also fix limits in all the directions for his economic or political exploitations. Further, a *Shravaka*, as the householder is called in this stage, observes some vows or penances for self-purification as his daily or periodical duties. He is generous to a guest of good conduct and serves him with food and other necessities with a heart full of devotion.

The Jain *sravakas* held an honourable position in society as well as state in the past. They were trusted by the state in all confidential matters and approached by other persons for proper advice and other help. The *Uvasogadasao* describes the conduct of ten householder devotees of Mahavira. They were city fathers in real sense.

The sixth *gunasthana* is *Pramatta sanyata.* The aspirant upto the fifth stage is a member of society and carries his duties and obligations towards himself as well as the society. He enjoys the family life and external pleasures in a moderately controlled form, not forgetting the supreme object and other duties. His character is well balanced without resorting to either extreme of looseness or complete renunciation. In the sixth *gunasthana* he leaves family life and joins the order of medicants. He devotes his entire life to the attainment of spiritual realization. He refrains from not only the gross sins but from the sins of minor nature also. He is not to kill any animal whether movable or immovable harmful or not harmful. Similarly, he is not to speak a lie in any way, not to take even a trivial thing without asking permission of the owner and hold any property. The vows of a monk are called *Mahavratas* (complete vows) in contrast with *Anuvratas* (partial vows) of a householder.

This stage is reached after subduing *Pratyahyanavarana i.e.* the third degree of passions. A monk is expected to purify his heart every fortnight. He has to observe *pratikramana* (repentance for the sins committed knowingly or unknowingly) and other purifications daily.

This stage is known as *Pramatta-sanyata,* because the aspirant, though observing complete restraint is open to negligence or slips.

The seventh *gunasthana* is known as *Aparamattasamyata.* It should be remembered here that the third degree of passions was subdued in the sixth stage. After that there remains the fourth degree of *samywalana* only. This is the mildest form of passions. It is compared with a line drawn in water, which vanishes no sooner it is drawn. Similarly, the passions of *samjvalana* degree do not last for any duration. Nevertheless, their rise is not stopped completely. The aspirant in seventh stage tries to control that also. This stage is called *Apramatta,* because, the aspirant is always alert not to allow any slipping. Here, the aspirant wins three types of stronger sleep also.

Note : According to Jainism there are five types of sleep which are the effect of *Darsanavarana* :

1. *Nidra* : Ordinary sleep.
2. *Nidra nidra* : Deep sleep where one is not able to open his eyes even when awake.
3. *Pracala* : Drowsiness.
4. *Pracala pracala* : Heavy drowsiness causing the flow of saliva and movement of limbs.
5. *Styanagrdhi* : Somnabulism; speaking, walking and doing other actions under sleep.

An aspirant in seventh stage is free from the second, fourth and fifth types.

This alertness is not permanent. It comes and goes according to the fluctuations of mind. Consequently, the aspirant struggles between the sixth and seventh stages. His position is compared with a log of wood moving up and down with the turn of waves.

The eighth *gunasthana* is known as *Apurva karana.* The aspirant, in the seventh stage, was described as starting his struggle against slipping. He reaches the eighth stage in case he wins the struggle and finds himself fully equipped to subdue the remaining portion of passions. It is known as *Apurva* because the soul gets such purification as was never achieved before. Here, he aims at the complete victory over passions for the first time.

Two Srenis—This complete victory is effected in two ways. Some aspirants have their passions and complexes subsided and feel perfect tranquility on the surface. The subsided complexes lie in subconscious mind waiting for provocation to come to surface. There are others who destroy the very root of those complexes leaving no more a chance for their rise. The first type is known as Upasama *sreni* and the second as *Ksapaka sreni. Upasama* means subsidence and Ksapaka means destruction. They are compared with two methods of water purification. The dirt in water can either be removed for ever through filtering process or can be subsided in the bottom through chemical process. In latter case the slightest disturbance is sufficient to make the dirt reappear while in the first case the purification is permanent. Similarly, passions and complexes can either be removed for ever or subsided in the bottom. In first case the aspirant is without any danger of falling down. In second case the complexes lie dormant in the subconscious mind waiting for provocation, when they rise again and the aspirant falls down. The stories of great yogins falling down from the peak of high spiritual attainments confirm the above fact.

Upto the seventh stage the aspirant adopted mainly the path of *ksayopasam i.e.,* partial subsidence or destruction and partial rise without the fruit giving intensity (*pradesodaya*). The subduing of *anantanubandhi* etc. in previous stages did not meant their destructing or subsidence but rise without the fruit giving potency. The aspirant from the eighth stage begins his purification by subsidence or destruction in reality. The soul is empowered here with to reduce the effect of *karmans* in respect of duration as well as intensity. This potential reduction is carried in the following five ways :

1. *Sthitighata* : Reduction of the enduring period allotted to the karmans in store.
2. *Rasaghata* : Reduction in fruit giving intensity.
3. *Gunasreni* : To convert the karmans of longer endurance into those with endurance of not more than a *muhurta* (48 minutes).
4. *Guna sankrama* : To convert the *karmans* with intensive

degree into those with milder degress.

5. *Anya-sthiti-bandha* : To accumulate new *karmans* of very short duration and low intensity to which those of longer duration and higher intensity are converted.

There are three feats (*karanas*) which the aspirant undertakes gradually for this reduction.

1. *Yathipravrtti karana* : Inclination of the soul towards subsidence or destruction without actual step.
2. *Apurva karana* : First step towards complete subduing through subsidence of destruction.
3. *Anivrtti karana* : To bring soul in such a state of purification when further progress becomes automatic. This progress is uniform and depends no more on individual effort. The eighth stage is known as *Apurva karna* on account of the second feat in form of five reductions. The aspirants in this *gunasthana* do not necessarily have uniformity in the level of their self-purification at the moment of first entrance on further advance. There are innumerable degrees according to the status of individuals. For this very reason the eighth *gunasthana* is known as *Nivrtti* also showing the absence of uniformity in spiritual progress.

The ninth *gunasthana* is known as *Anivrtti*. The aspirant after reducing the stock of *karman* through the means of *sthitighata* etc. comes to a point when his progress becomes automatic. Consequently, all the aspirants make a uniform advancement. All of them are on the same status in the first and succesive moments of their progress. This uniformity is known as *Anivrtti*.

These two *gunasthana* last not more than a *muhurta* (48 minutes). They are also known as *Badara Samparaya* (with big passions) in contrast to *Suksma Samparaya* (with small passions), the tenth *gunasthana*. Anger, conceit and crookedness are regarded as big passions in relation to greed which is recognized as the small passion. The first three continue upto the ninth stage only and greed continues upto the tenth. At the end if the eighth stage the aspirant subdues six types of semi-passions also, namely, (1) laughter, (2) liking, (3) disliking, (4) fear, (5) grief, and (6) hatred. By the end of ninth he subdues three types of sexual desire in addition to the *sanjvalana* degree of anger, conceit and crookedness. Then, there remains the *sanjvalana* degree of greed only, which is subdued by the end of the tenth.

The tenth *gunasthana* is known as *Suksma-samparaya* on account of its subduing all the passions except *sanjvalana* type of greed.

The eleventh *gunasthana* is *Upasanta-Mohaniya*, meaning a complete subsidence of *Mohaniya*. This stage lasts for a short period only after which the subsided passions rise again and the aspirant falls down. In his backward movement he may stop at the sixth, fifth or fourth stage or come down to the bottom. But, this position does not last for unlimited period. Within a specified period, known as *Ardha pudgala paravartan* as the maximum he makes fresh attempts with a renewed strength and ultimately succeeds by adopting the course of *Ksapaka sreni*.

The twelfth *gunasthana* is *Ksina-Mohaniya* showing the complete destruction of Mohaniya. The aspirant with *Ksapaka sreni* does not undergo the eleventh stage and reaches the twelfth direct.

The thirteenth *gunasthana* is *Sayogikavalin*. At the end of the twelfth the aspirant destroys other *ghati karmans* also and attains all the four infinites. He attains Infinite knowledge (*Kavalajnana*) due to the destruction of jnanavaranly, Infinite Intuition (*Kevaladarsana*) due to the destruction of *Darsana-varaniya*, Infinite Happiness due to the destruction of *Mohaniya* and Infinite Power due to the destruction of *Antaraya*. The four *aghati karmans* still continue upto the end of life. The aspirant in this stage is called *Arhat* or *Kavalin*, corresponding to the *jivanmukta* of other systems. This stage is known as *sayogin*, because the activity of three yogas *i.e.* mind, speech and body continues.

The fourteenth *gunasthana* is known as *Ayogikevalin,* where the activity of yogas is stopped completely. This state corresponds to the *Asamprajnata samsdhi* of yoga system. It is also known as Sailesi showing immovability like the king of mountain. The aspirant stays in this position for a short while only, namely the period required in pronunciation of five short vowels. At the end of it the soul shoots up like an arrow till it reaches the top of the universe. It rests there forever in the abode liberated souls. This is how the career of search after soul is completed.

One can see from the above description that spiritual development means gradual freedom of the soul from karmic bondage. It is, therefore, necessary here to mention in brief, the nature of bondage, its causes and means of freedom.

Bondage means the accumulation of *karmic* matter by the soul. The latter when disturbed by certain activity, attracts the atoms of matter known as *karmavarjana*. These atoms are blended with soul like water with milk and affect soul by their chemical action. The question how a material thing can have its chemical action on an immaterial thing is replied by the Jainas on the basis that the soul under bondage is not quite immaterial. It is a blend of mind and matter. The pure, soul, as it is in the state of salvation, is never so affected. The question about the first relation between soul and *karman* is ruled out by holding the relation as without beginning and not admitting a first movement. This is a common problem of all systems and is replied in the same way.

This bondage is classified in the following four types related with the nature, quantity, enduring period and intensity in fruit :

(*a*) *Parkrabandha* : Regulating the varieties of *karman* accumulated on a certain activity.

(*b*) *Pradeshabandha* : Regulating the quantity of particles of each variety.

(*c*) *Sthitibabdha* : Fixing the enduring period of a particular particle.

(*d*) *Anubhaga bandha* : Regulating the intensity of fruit of a particular particle.

Yoga (the activity of mind, speech and body) and *kasaya* (passions) are the means affecting this bondage. The first two *bandhas* are regulated by *yoga* and the latter two by *kasaya*. The number and nature of the particles to be accumulated are fixed according to the disturbance caused by the *yoga*, and the enduring period as well as the intensity in fruit is fixed according to the degree of passions. In the thirteenth stage passions are destroyed completely. Still the *karmic* influx continues owing to the activities of *yogas*. But the particles accumulated in that stage are without the capacity of giving fruit or enduring for a period on account of their being not accompanied by passions.

An activity is either beneficial or harmful. Beneficial activity is not induced by passions. The *karmic* accumulation resulting from it does not give bitter fruit. On the other hand harmful activity causes such accumulation as puts the soul to suffering and miseries. Both types of activity are known as *Asrava* meaning the influx of *karman*. It has five types of *Mithyatva* (wrong attitude), *Avirati* (indiscipline), *Pramadh* (negligence), *Kasaya* (passions) and *Yoga* (three types of activity).

One has to refrain from all the five types of Asrava to check the *karmic influx*. The aspirant aiming at the complete freedom from *karmic* bondage has to stop the new flux, as well as consume up the accumulated stock. The process of this consummation is called *nirjara*. The Jain literature prescribes various penances and other practices for it, namely, twelve types of penances (*tapas*), twelve contemplations (*bhavanas*), four meditations (*dhyanas*), the vows of a monk and a householder and such others. Kundakunda, Jindabhadra, Pujyapada, Haribhadra, Subha Candra, Hema Candra, Yosovijaya and other scholars have written systematic treatises on the subject. The reader is adviced to consult them for a detailed study.

The above is a short account of the process of self-realization as prescribed by Jainism. It is useful not for salvation only but also for a man who wished to live happy life by rising above the inner conflicts and complexes. It is regrettable that the supreme science of leading a happy life has been wrongly confined to transcendental purposes only with the assumption that its benefits are not connected with the present life. But it is a wrong notion. The man, however materially rich may he become, shall have to learn, sooner or later, this science if he seeks real happiness and wants to save himself from destruction. The fear of atomic weapon can be cast off only if the man learns to live amicable and peacefully. We hope, U.N.O. and the individuals wielding the destiny of mankind, will pay attention to the above fact and make the teaching of self-discipline an essential part of the study for builders of the new world.

II

Right attitude (*Samyak Darshan*) is the first and foremost qualification of an aspirant. Whether the aim is mundane or supermundane, the goal material or spiritual, it is important as a requisite of success. Every system of religion has prescribed it as the starting point of the spiritual journey. It consists in the right selection of , first the ideal, secondly that of the preceptor who can show the way theoretically as well as practically and thirdly the way itself. In the solutions of political, social and other problems also it hold an important function.

The Vedanta prescribes the following four requisites of an aspirant :

1. Perception of the distinction between what is permanent and what is temporary. In the field of valuation it is a distinction of permanent values from the temporary ones.

2. Detachment from all the objects of the temporary values, attainable in this world or in the next.

3. A calm temperament, undisturbed by external effects, which consists of : (i) mental equilibriums, (ii) control of the sensual desires, (iii) abstinence from external inducements,

(iv) tolerance and fortitude against hardships, (v) concentration, and (vi) faith or devotion.

4. A desire for release (mukti).

Of actions, Vedic tradition mentions three types :

1. The actions to be performed as daily or occasional duties, such as daily prayers or purificatory baths to be taken on certain occasions. These acts do not yield any positive result but neglect or non-performance of them is a sin. They protect the person from the accumulation of new 'dirt' obscuring the spiritual qualities.

2. Acts performed with a particular motive, such as the sacrifices performed of obtaining kingdom, wealth, progeny, etc.

3. Acts prohibited by the scriptures, which bring sin to the doer.

The aspirant is required to give up the last two types and continue the first for long. Gradually his heart will be purified and he will have an inclination towards higher values. His aim will shift from the temporary to the permanent.

Patanjali compares the mind to a river having a shifting Current. Sometimes the Current is directed towards lower values and sometimes towards the higher values. There are five states of mind, of which the first three express the lower tendency and the remaining two the higher. The first three are : (1) the state of engrossment in external objects; (2) The state of ignorance or obscurity; and (3) the state of fluctuation when the mind is unsteady, inclining sometimes inward and sometimes outward.

The two higher states are : (1) the state of concentration; and (2) the state of control when the mind is absolutely free from thought.

Buddhism describes the two groups of states as respectively that of a layman (*puhujana*) and that of one who has entered the current of higher values (*sotapanna*).

In Jainism the right attitude has been described

elaborately. Its constituents, causes, perversions and other things have been discussed in detail. This is useful to an ordinary aspirant also. According to Jainism, the right attitude has two aspects—the internal and the external. The internal aspect is related to the requisite purification of soul.

The soul is compared to a traveller wandering in the forest who has lost his way. Sometimes he is far from the path and sometimes comes near and enters its borders without realizing it. In spite of a physical contact with the path he is not conscious of it; consequently the next moment he loses it and goes astray. Perchance it happens that when he enters the border through the instruction of a preceptor or the direction of his inner voice he comes to recognize the path. This is quite a new incident in his career. Jainism analyses this process into three 'feats.' The first is 'the accidental feat' (*Yathapravratikaran*), *i.e.*, touching the path accidentally without consciousness of it. The second is "the novel feat" (*apurvakaran*), one which was never experienced before. The third is "the feat of non-return" (anivratikaran), when the aspirant is fixed on the path and cannot be misled.

This is possible only when the *karmas* or the matter polluting the soul are reduced to within a reasonable limit. This pollution is known as *moha*, illusion, or perversion, which is again divided into two, *viz.*, perversion in attitude and perversion in conduct. The latter is elaborated in four types of passions : anger, concert, crookedness and greed. Only when the effect of the two types of *moha* is reduced to below a certain maximum, and the inner light of the soul therefore beings to pierce it with its rays, does the right attitude dawn.

The external form of right attitude consists in three 'adoptions' : of a right ideal; of a right preceptor and of the right path. In Jainism the ideal is presented by the perfect soul free from the obscuring, debasing or weakening pollutions. This ideal is personified by the *Arihanta, i.e.*, the perfected soul in physical existence, and the *Siddha, i.e.*, the same out of physical existence. The right preceptor is not only cognizant of the way but is a traveller on it who has renounced all other ambitions and activities and made this journey the sole aim of his life. He voluntarily impose on himself all the disciplines, restrictions and rigorous required for progress in that journey. The path is that taught by the perfected souls, those perfect in knowledge and perfectly free from attachment and hatred or other passions.

Though Jainism also deteriorated later into a sect and the above three constituents of right attitude were identified with particular personal beings, in the beginning they were stated in a form absolutely free from that bias. Pure Jainism is the worship of pure principles, unalloyed and unbiased. The Jain hymn of solution recited at the beginning of every auspicious undertaking is free from any personal name. Out of the five solutions mentioned in it the first two go to perfected souls and the remaining three to the followers in that journey in their different functions.

The effect or creative power of the right attitude varies according to the strength of faith and detachment from lower values. Three types of faith are distinguished according to their comparative creativity.

1. Creative (*karak*). The faith or attitude which impels a person to action. Action is the standard by which to judge the strength of belief. If we sincerely believe in an idea, we must act accordingly; otherwise we lack in belief.

2. Appreciative (*rochak*). The inclination towards a noble object to the extent of mere commendation. The person with this type of faith tries to induce others to act and puts the proposal forward in an attractive manner, but he himself is not impelled to act. We might compare him with an artist who can move the audience with music, dance, dramatic acting or some other performance full of pathos but who is unmoved himself. Much modern leadership can be thus classed.

3. Illuminative (*dipak*). A lamp shows the path to others but itself does not get any profit. Similarly, a person who can explain the subtleties of the spiritual path to others, who helps others in the journey by illuminating the path, without moving

himself, belongs to this type. It is mere scholarship without life.

There are five perversions of attitude obstructing the way to righteousness. As a matter of fact, they are mental weaknesses.

1. The perversion of attaching secondary importance to righteousness (*abhigrahic*). Many persons adopt the path of righteousness for some other ulterior motive. To adopt a principle to please an influential person, for wealth, for fame or for any other motive except the principle in itself is a perversion of this category. Religious system have adopted the method of inducement in their propagation. They pointed out the future pleasure of heaven and this world as the result of their renunciation in this life. The person was promised hundreds of beautiful damsels as the result of celibacy in this life. A drunkard was promised a heaven where fountain of wine are flowing. These inducements divert the attention of the aspirant from the supreme values to lower desires. Similarly to adopt political life not as a career of service to the nation but with a view to occupying chairs, gathering influence or with some other ulterior motive is a perversion of this type.

2. The perversion (*abhiniveshic*). To follow a path merely to satisfy an egoistic temperament. A person knows that the path adopted by him is wrong. Yet he sticks to it because any change hurts his sense of pride. This perversion is common among religious preachers in high positions who continue the same preaching even after ceasing to believe its truth. It requires great courage to correct oneself, particularly in an esteemed position after the accumulation of fame and popularity. It is really a tragedy that the person, though aware of his mistake, is not allowed to correct himself. This is why the seeker of truth is enjoyed to run away from fame or other egoistic fascinations.

3. The perversion of doubt (*samshayic*). To be continually doubtful in mind, without resolution or determination leading to action. The progress of a person with this perversion is hampered by fluctuations. He does not gather enough force

to rise to his feet and move.

4. The perversion of undeveloped consciousness (*anabhog*). This is found among the animals, who are devoid of any consciousness of lower or higher values, creatures of instinct.

Jainism holds further that knowledge and without a right attitude is a perverted knowledge and conduct without it is a perverted conduct. Knowledge is no doubt a power which can be used for a good as well as a bad purpose. When the object is bad, the power or instrument leading to its attainment also comes in the same class. Similarly if a power is used for a good purpose, it becomes good. Power in the hands of a devil is known as *asuri shakti* (devilish power) and the same in the hands of a god becomes divine (*daivi shakti*). Thus the perversion or purity of knowledge is not intrinsic but pragmatically determined, according to the attitude of knower. The same rule applies in the case of conduct also. Thus attitude is the main standard of valuation. A person with the right attitude but devoid of knowledge and conduct shall get them in due course, but the person far advanced in knowledge and conduct but with perverted attitude may or may not reach the right attitude. In other word, sincerity of purpose, purity of aim and a sense of correct valuation are the foundation of individual as well as national character. Any nation without this sincerity may express its religiosity in high-sounding terms but cannot make any real progress. A rêligious preacher may possess a beautiful art of expression but cannot purify himself without this sincerity. And scholarship without it is merely a tormenting of words.

7 VOWS FOR A HOUSEHOLDER

Jainism prescribes two codes of conduct for morality and spiritual development. The higher code is meant for the monks who have renounced the worldly life and are free from social obligations. The lower code is meant for the laity striving for salvation without renouncing the social responsibilities. This latter code provides valuable material for the organization of a healthy and prosperous society.

It is divided into twelve vows further classified into three groups. The first group consisting for five vows presents a code for ethical conduct. The second group consisting of three presents a discipline subsidiary to the main ethical code. The remaining group consisting of four vows is meant for refinement or the unfoldment of the dormant spiritual qualities.

A vow is graded on the basis of three types of commitments. The three commitments are : *(i)* to do oneself; *(ii)* to order; and *(iii)* to comment upon a sin committed by someone else. Of each grade there are three instruments *i.e.* mind, speech and body. Thus there are nine ways of committing a sin and to refrain from all of them by observing vows is possible for a monk only. A householder is advised to refrain from as many of the nine as possible, according to his capacity and inner strength.

Non-violence

According to Jainism life is divided into two broad divisions of stationary beings and moving beings. The former group includes the four elements *viz.* earth, water, fire and air along with vegetable life, while in the latter are included all the moving animals beginning with Amoeba upto human and divine beings.

The first vow of a householder is related with non-violence. Abstinence from 15 types of acts causing violence is included in it. A householder decided to refrain from deliberately killing all innocent living beings. Here the adverb deliberately and the adjective innocent are significant. In case an animal is killed without intention to do so or is killed by way of punishment the vow is not broken. Thus a king is permitted to punish the offender or his enemy. In the war he can attack the fighting men only. To kill innocent women and children is against the code. (In the present atomic warfare uninvolved population in the cities is the main target.)

There are five transgressions related with the vow of non-violence concerned with household animals and slaves. These are :

(*i*) to tie the animal or a slave tightly,

(*ii*) to beat him severely,

(*iii*) to cut his lines or tail,

(*iv*) to load him with heavy burden, and

(*v*) to keep him hungry or thirsty.

Truth

The second vow is pertaining to truth. The observer makes a decision not to speak gross untruth which may harm the listeners or the concerned. The untruth is mainly elaborated as follows :

(*i*) The untruth about a girl at the time of betrothal *i.e.*, exaggeration of her merits and concealments of her demerits.

(*ii*) The untruth about cattle at the time of their selling.

(*iii*) The untruth about land.

(*iv*) To embezzle or speak untruth about the trust.

(*v*) False evidence.

The five transgressions of the vows are as follows :

(*i*) Allegations without proper thought and investigation.

(*ii*) Allegations on personal talking secretly.

(*iii*) To disclose private talk held with wife or some other lady.

(*iv*) False instructions or preaching.

(*v*) To forge documents.

Non-stealing

The third vow is related with honestly or abstinence from theft. The gross form of theft is elaborated as follows :

(*i*) by digging it out from the truth,

(*ii*) by breaking open the lock or by opening it with a key *i.e.* burglary,

(*iii*) Robbery, and

(*iv*) to take up anything without the permission of the owner when the latter is within the knowledge.

The five transgressions of this vow are as follows :

(*i*) to accept anything brought by a thief,

(*ii*) to appoint thieves or decoits for material gains,

(*iii*) to do anything illegal or prohibited by the law of the Government.

(*iv*) dishonesty in weighing or measuring the commercial commodities,

(*v*) deceiving through imitation.

The above two vows *i.e.* truth and non-stealing are significant in the field of social behaviour and business.

Sexual Discipline

The fourth vow is related with sexual discipline. The householder is enjoined to be satisfied with his own wife and at the same time prohibited to have sexual relations with any married woman other than his own wife.

In ancient society women were divided into three categories :

(*i*) One's own wife

(*ii*) The wife of some one else

(*iii*) *i.e.* unassociated women—prostitutes etc.

The higher morality demanded that a person should confine himself to the first category *i.e.* to his own wife only, but the lower morality did allow a relation with the common women. Though denounced in the field of religion it was not thought to be anti-social. Any sexual connection with the second category *i.e.* married woman other than one's own wife was considered immoral as well as anti-social. A Jain householder is not permitted to have any relation with such a woman. As far as the third category is concerned he is given a choice but he is advised preferably abstain from it.

The five transgressions of this vows are as follows :

(*i*) to have sexual relation with the woman engaged for a short period.

(*ii*) unmarried,

(*iii*) to satisfy the sexual desire unnaturally,

(*iv*) to have an intense sex-desire,

(*v*) to indulge in the conjugal relation of human beings or animals other than his own family or possessions.

Non-possession

The fifth vow is concerned with material possession. The householder is advised to limit his possessions. The five transgressions are as follows :

To transgress the limit of :

(*i*) gold, silver, etc. or the wealth in coins, valuable metals and jewels,

(*ii*) immovable property *i.e.* the land, house etc.

(*iii*) live wealth of cattle and slaves,

(iv) food grains and other commodities,

(v) ordinary metals other than silver and gold as well as utencils and other articles made of them.

Selflessness

The sixth vow puts a limit on the area of exploitation. A householder is instructed to limit the area of commerce, harvest, industry and other commercial enterprises. This vow serves two-fold purpose. Firstly puts a check on unrestrained material ambitions which keep the man constantly in a state of unrest. Secondly it avoids mutual conflict in the uncontrolled desire for commercial exploitation and political subjugation which has led the world to the verge of total annihilation.

This vow has the following transgressions :

To cross the self-imposed limits

(*i*) in the space above,

(*ii*) in the space below,

(*iii*) in other directions,

(*iv*)to extend the limits of land possessions, and

(*v*) to forget the limit while engaged in exploitation.

Cutting the Daily Requirements

The seventh vow puts a limit on the commodities of daily use. The householder fixes the number of commodities used in food, drink, bath, journey, furniture etc. In this vow the limitation is not on the possessions actually but on their real use for necessity or enjoyment. These commodities are divided into twenty-six categories covering the whole sphere of daily life.

Behaviour and Orderliness

The eighth vow puts a check on the useless efforts amounting to violence. The householder is warned against doing anything to violent or causing any inconvenience to others without a passive interest. This purposeless violence is divided into four categories.

(*i*) committed through depressive or violent thought (*i.e.* anger),

(*ii*) committed through negligence under intoxication or passions,

(*iii*) to supply weapons, or

(*iv*) to give instructions for violence.

The five transgressions are :

(*i*) to indulge in useless movements and facial expressions under sex desire,

(*ii*) to move foolishly hand, feet, eyes or other parts of the body without any purpose,

(*iii*) futile and obstinate talks,

(*iv*) disordering furniture or other commodities,

(*v*) to increase unnecessarily the articles of daily use.

Thus we see that this vow demands orderliness in household effects and the behaviour expected from a civilized person.

Shikshavratas

The 'Shikshavratas' are the last four vow meant for the discipline for character. They are religious practices for spiritual refinement.

The ninth vow is *'Samayika' i.e.* the practice of *Samata* (equlity) in life through the equilibrium of mind, speech and body. The observer decides to refrain from all acts of sin for a limited period. It has five transgressions :

Wrong application of

(*i*) mind,

(*ii*) speech,

(*iii*) body,

(*iv*) to become unaware of the vow undertaken, and

(*v*) fickleness in the observation of the vow.

The tenth and eleventh vows also prescribe a life of seclusion from worldly activities for a period of twenty-four hours. In one of the above two vows fast is prescribed during this period and in the other not. The observer is expected to devote his time in self-analysis and meditation.

The twelfth and the last vow is related with charity. A householder is expected to be hospitable and charitable whenever a guest of good character comes to his door in need.

There is one more vow which is observed at the approach of death. A Jain is advised to relinquish attachment with all the wordly objects *viz.* house, wealth, family and even the body itself, when he finds that the latter is unable to do the function for which it is meant. According to Jainism life in itself is not the aim but a means to achieve the same *i.e.* unfoldment of the spirit. Hence when an aspirant observes that instead of becoming an instrument his body is an impediment, he gives up food and drink and calmly waits for his last moment. This vow also has five transgressions :

To have a desire for

(*i*) this world,

(*ii*) next world,

(*iii*) prolongation of life,

(*iv*) early death, and

(*v*) wordly enjoyments.

He is forbidden to desire anything. He must not cover either life or death. Thus he passes away peacefully with a perfect equilibrium of mind.

There is a religious *rite* for every Jain known as '*Pratikramana*' which is to be observed twice a day. The word *Pratikramana* means retracting or going back. During it the observer dwells upon his past conduct and expresses his regret for any transgression of the vow or vows taken by him. As said before, one *Pratikramana* is observed at the sunset when the conduct of the day is celebrated upon and the other early in the morning when the conduct of the night is taken into account.

II

Pancha Shila, pronounced as Pansil in Pali, is a Buddhist term, but its implications are universal. It constitutes the foundation of ancient morality. Every religion, has accepted it as basic code for social as well as the individual conduct. It is the primary requirement of a good citizen. The person neglecting it is regarded a danger to society. He is a sinner as well as a criminal.

In the Theravada Buddhism five principles are recited along with hymn of refugee on every auspicious occasion. After salutation to the Buddha a monk recites three times the hymn of refugee, repeating "I go to the Buddha for refuge, I go to the doctrine (*Dharma*) for refuge, I go to the order for refuge." Then he takes a pledge for the five moral precepts. By the first pledge he declares to abstain from *Pranatipata, i.e.,* injury to life, by the second from taking anything without permission of the owner, by the third from sexual immorality, by the fourth from falsehood and by the fifth from taking intoxicants. A Buddhist promises to observe these five precepts immediately after declaring his faith. They are also known as five Shiksa Padas. In the Mahayana school the same are included into Shiksa Paramita, *i.e.,* Perfection in conduct. This is the second perfection out of the ten, which a Bodhisattva attains in his spiritual journey. The first perfection is Dana *i.e.* charity; which is a beginning on the way to great compassion, Mahakaruna, a special contribution of the Mahayana Buddhism.

In the *Yoga Sutra* of Patanjali the first four of these precepts have been recognized as the first four of five 'yamas', which constitute the primary equipment of the traveller on the path of yoga. Patanjali further says that the five vows are eternal and universal. Their application is not limited to a particular caste, country, time or occasion. They are universal. Similarly, they do not admit of any exception.

Manu, the first law-giver of the Hindu Society, enjoins them as '*Samasika Dharma*' *i.e.* the duty of a man in brief. They resemble five of the ten commandments of Moses, which were reuttered and confirmed by the Christ too. They are found in the *Quran* also, though not in one place. The Jain scriptures recognize them as '*Vratas*'. In the case of a monk they are complete and , therefore, termed as *Mahavratas* (great vows). While in the case of a householder they limited and termed as *Anuvratas* (smaller vows).

Any number of quotations can be cited here from the great scriptures of the world. The followers of different religious systems may disagree in the conception of God, Soul and Universe. They descend to bitterness in actual practice, but in the basic code of morality, mainly they are in agreement.

Historical Aspects

We have seen that the number five is common to most of the systems. But, there is a difference in detail, which is important for a study of the ethical history of India. In the non-Buddhist systems generally, we have non-possession (*aparigraha*) in place of abstinence from intoxicants. It appears that the fifth vow did not exist in the ancient code and was added later according to necessity. This proposition is supported by the Bodhayana *Dharmasutra* as well as by the tradition of Jainism. In the Bodhayana we have the first four vows only. In the Jain tradition also we find that the order of Parshwanatha, the 23rd Thirthankara, admitted four vows only which were called *Yamas*. The discipline of Parshwanatha was known as Chaturyana.

Bodhayana is clear in not providing any place to non-possession. But, there is some anomaly in the Jain tradition. The *Thananga Sutta* states the fourth vow as Bahiddha-danao viramana. Abhayadeva, the well known commentator on Jain canon, interprets bahiddha as parigarha or property. But, his interpretation does not confirm with the Suyagada, where Bahiddha means sexual intercourse. If we examine the above controversy in the light of Bodhayana, which provides a striking resemblance to the Jain ascetic practices, the contention of the Suyagada seems more reasonable.

Further, the Uttradhyayana states that the order of Parshwanatha allowed garments for monks. They used to put on even costly garments with various colours. It had a result of degrading effect. The monks showed attachment to fine clothes. Mahavira did not like it and, therefore, stressed upon nakedness. It shows that Mahavira, being very keen on one attachment, could introduce non-possession and not celibacy as the fifth vow.

Buddhism, accepts abstinence from all intoxicants in place of non-possession. But, there is no doubt about its later introduction. Because, the first four Shilas are always found together while the fifth is many times omitted.

Moreover, celibacy is the fundamental code of ascetic tradition. It is, inconceivable, particularly for a sect following the severest form of asceticism, to leave it altogether.

It means that the earliest form of ethical code consists of the first four precepts only and non-possession is a later addition. But, the ethical code of the ancient Vedic Aryans was somewhat different. It was national and aimed at material prosperity. The ideal of spiritual development in it, is later development. A national ethics prescribes one code of behaviour with the members of its own class and a different one for others. The above-mentioned four precepts were good as long as the mutual behaviour of Vedic Aryans was concerned. But, they were not recommended in dealing with the *ab origines.* Moreover, the fifth vow of aparigraha went against the very spirit of Vedic ritualism. A society striving for material prosperity cannot favour an ideal like non-possession. Roughly, the Vedic religion enjoins three-fold duty *i.e.* sacrifice, study and gifts to Brahmanas. Of course, truth, penance, patience, forbearance and such other virtues are recommended as divine other virtues are not essentials of morality. They were easily over looked when they conflicted with material interest.

The ascetic tradition framed its code of morality mainly

for the recluse who is free from social obligations. In this tradition the life of a householder is an excuse, allowed to the weak lacking in strength to follow the path of an ascetic. Thus possession and property, (a virtue for the householder), were thought as sin for the ascetic. On the other hand Brahmanical ethics lays emphasis on the life of a householder. While framing a code, it kept in view the family life. The life of an ascetic, there was the life of retirement, of a pensioner. The Vedic tradition believed in the social unit, where the individual was only a part; forfeiting all its interests and privileges in the welfare of society. On the other hand, the ascetic tradition held the individual in itself, as a unit. The society, it contended, was formed for the comfort and development of the individual. In the Vedic tradition the individual is meant for society, while in the ascetic tradition society is meant for the individual. Later, when the two traditions got mixed and the synthesis of the two framed a new culture, all the social as well as individual virtues got their proper place. The ascetic tradition, so far emphasising a negative aspect only took the positive side too into consideration and the Vedic tradition, on the other hand accepted spiritual development and the ultimate aim of life.

This compromise between prosperity and renunciation was not possible in external behaviour. Consequently, the qualities of heart came into forefront. The mechanical form of religion gave way and the subjective aspect came into prominence. Both, the Vedic as well as the ascetic tradition established a real contact with life. Non-violence, which in ascetic tradition meant merely non-killing developed into the positive quality of Universal love, where social as well as the individual virtues are infused together. The vow of abstinence from telling a lie came to be recognized as speaking what is beneficial, brief and sweet. Non-stealing in recognizing the social as well legal rights of others. Abstinence from sexual inter-course into mental chastity and non-possession into non-attachment. This healthy synthesis was really a remarkable step in the history of civilization.

Let us now discuss the development of the individual precept in the main systems of India, *i.e.*, Hinduism, Buddhism and Jainism. Hinduism, for this purpose, should be further divided into Brahmanic Hinduism and ascetic Hinduism.

In Brahmanic Hinduism, as I have already stated, sacrifice, study and gifts to Brahmans are the main duties of a householder. Every person according to the Vedic society, is born with three debts or obligations. The debt of Gods is repaid through sacrifice, that of the ancient sages through study and that of the ancestors through the birth of a male child.

We can see here that all the three duties are very important for a society. The sacrifices apart from their transcendental value, which I think was a later development, were nothing but social gatherings. The Aryans used to assemble together, sing and dance, eat and drink, worship fire and thus develop their social life. Then, we have the study of ancient lore which infused pride for noble heritage, the feeling which is essential for preservation and growth of a society. The birth of male child was necessary for continuance as well as the strength of society. Social development was the basic standard for valuation in Vedic society. Killing of animals was a necessary part of the social gatherings of non-vegetarian society. Consequently, the principle of non-violence automatically came into disregard. On the contrary a person of means not performing bloody sacrifices came to be regarded as a sinner. Similarly, celibacy was a sin as long as one did not see the face of a son. At the time of marriage the bride was enjoined to give birth to ten sons. In this society violence and sexual intercourse are not sins by themselves, but only when they interfered with social set up. The check aimed at only the social stability. Within the limits they were not only allowed but encouraged and were prescribed as social obligations.

Later, when spiritualism got dominance over secularism and universal ethics got more appreciation. Brahmanical tradition also accepted non-violence etc. as the basis of morality. But, it was careful not to injure the interest of the institute of sacrifices. It held that violence committed for the sake of sacrifice is not a sin. In due course dispassionate thinkers, like Vachaspati Mishra, came forward and held that violence in sacrifice also is a sin. But, at the same time they said, it is amply repaid by the virtue accumulated through the sacrifice. In Jainism also, when building of temples, pilgrimages with great pomp and show and such other works with the name of Prabhavana got more importance there arose a school which held that violence for religious acts was not a sin.

Anyhow the influence of the creed of non-violence was so strong that it changed fundamentally the Brahamanic notion of morality. The institution of animal sacrifice is now a thing of the past. Public opinion is deadly against it. Even the orthodox Brahmans do not follow it in practice.

The ascetic Hinduism, represented by the systems of Sankhya, Yoga, Pancharatra, Bhagavata etc., is totally against violence. The *Yogasastra* gives it a subjective consideration. Vyasa in his commentary on the aphorisms of Patanjali defines non-violence as freedom from malice.

While describing the influence of non-violence Patanjali says that even born enemies leave their enmity in the presence of a person who has inculcated the ideal or non-violence into his life. The followers of Yoga had a firm belief in the maxim that contempt breeds contempt and love breeds love.

The followers of Bhagavata cult emphasize love and devotion. They are strictly vegetarians and regard killing of animals as the greatest sin. The cult of Vaishnavism, spread along with Jainism in Gujarat and Rajasthan in the north and into the whole of south has exerted a great influence in creating a temperament of non-violence among the people. Even the Muslims of these parts dislike killing or impeaching animals. They are less quarrelsome and believe in compromise more than in fight.

The growth of Vaishanavism and Jainism side by side in the same region and period suggests that they were against mutual hatred. They followed a common way of life, possessed a generous mentality and bore a charitable attitude towards the neighbour and his belief. In Gujarat still there are many families where different traditions are followed by the individual members according to their choice without any restriction. If the wife is a Jain the husband is a Vaishnava and their relations are very sweet. Both the traditions have infused in their life a sense of mutual love and tolerance. Sometimes, one can further observe that it is not only a tolerance but positive respect for all that is divine, for the sanctity of all faiths and creeds.

In the Mahayana Buddhism the ideal of non-violence has developed into a special form. Here, it is merely a negative virtue, but positive to the extreme. The Bodhisattva sacrificing his life to feed birds and insects is nothing but the extreme form compassion which would appear non-sense to the humanist. The Vedic systems allow these extreme forms in a certain stage only. When the aspirant has risen above all passions and crossed the narrow boundaries of wordly relations, he is free to act as he likes. When the causes of distraction are removed control from outside becomes unnecessary. Passions are the cause of violence and when they are removed the person becomes non-violent naturally and reaches the state of perfect character. According to the non-Buddhist systems the journey of the spirit ends with this. But in Buddhism the new ideal of *Mahakaruna i.e.* Great compassion; emerges after that stage and the Bodhisattva tries for salvation of other suffering people. He does not enter into *Nirvana* as long as there is a single soul suffering from the miseries of this world.

Another speciality of Buddhism is its emphasis on the subjective side. It prescribes many formulae for the cultivation and purification of mind.

In Jainism the cult of non-violence has taken quite a new turn. It has become the very foundation of Jain religion as well as philosophy.

The basic principle on which the Mahavira's massage of non-violence stands is the feeling of equality (*Samata*). In

Ayara he says "You yourself are the being which you intend to ill-use, you yourself are the being which you intend to insult, you yourself are the being which you intend to torment. You yourself are the being which you intend to prosecute."

Every monk and householder recites in his daily prayers. I have friendship with all and enmity with none.

This fellow-feeling has developed into the following four respects, which cover the region of Jain philosophy and region :

1. Respect for Life;
2. Respect for Mind;
3. Respect for Man; and
4. Respect for Personal Effort.

The first thing is respect for life. Mahavira was against the supremacy of a few over others. He did not like that the existence of one class should be confined to the 'comfort of others'. All animals, whether human beings or lower ones possess equal right to live. It is against morality that man should consume the life of other animals for his personal enjoyment. The basic principle of morality, according to Mahavira, is the feeling of equality. Ones being virtuous or otherwise depends upon the amount of the sense of equality practiced by him in the actual life. "Samayae samano hoi". A Sramana becomes through Samata this was the basic announcement of Mahavira. Fear, hatred, malica, envy and all other sorts of passions weakening the self, come from the feeling of inequality. If a man respects his own life he must respect the life of his fellow beings as well; and we can say this is the first step towards democratic Universe.

Analysis and classification is a speciality of the ancient religions : particularly, that of Buddhism and Jainism. In Jain Scriptures non-violence is classified into one hundred and eight types, which is interesting to note how the ancient sages were careful about their conduct.

The first three types are related with the three steps

towards commitment of an action. They are Samramha *i.e.* *(1)* intention to commit a sin; *(2)* Samarambha preparation; and *(3)* Arambha—actual doing. Each of them is further divided into three types of responsibility, *i.e.* *(1)* to do himself, *(2)* to order, and *(3)* to approve.

Each of the nine types is further divided into three instruments of the mind, speech and body. They are further divided into four motive passions; anger, conceit, crookedness and greed which induce a person to commit violence. This analytic approach helps an aspirant in self-scrutiny. He can know clearly in what respect he is responsible for a particular misdeed and how he should be careful to keep himself away.

In the early canonical literature respect for life is the dominating theme and this is the essence of Jain religion. On its negative side it stresses non-injury and on the positive side friendship with a feeling of equality.

The Tattvartha defines violence as injury to ones vitalities (*prana*) out of negligence (*pramada*). There are ten vitalities, *i.e.* the five senses, mind, body, speech, breathing and life. The enumeration of these vitalities is very significant. It shows that violence means not only a injury to life but to put any obstacle in the free movement of a living being. To put censor on one's speech, to deprive one from the acquirement of knowledge which he can do through the senses, to put improper pressure on ones mind, to put restriction on ones physical movement and all other acts of this type are violence. The term negligence (*pramada*) in the definition, explains the motive. It means all types of negligence leading the aspirant astray from the goal of spiritual purification, all acts that pollute the soul and make it extrovert. They are divided into five classes of : *(1)* Intoxication, *(2)* Objects of sense-enjoyments, *(3)* Passions, *(4)* Slumber, and *(5)* Futile gossip. If all of the above considerations are kept in view, one can clearly observe that the principle of non-violence, as developed in Jainism, safeguards all social and individual rights of a person. It provides equal right to every being not only to live but to fully develop and exercise all his potencies.

Respect for Mind

The respect for life gradually developed into respect for mind and it is the basis of Jain logic. We generally abuse our opponent as a liar without understanding his viewpoint. If we show same respect for the mind of our opponents as we have for our own, much of the unnecessary controversy would cease. This respect for mind has developed into the theory of Non-absolution or Anekanta Vada. Prof. A.B. Dhruva has designed it as 'Intellectual non-violence.'

It should be stated here that Jainism is a staunch realist. It does not admit anything as purely subjective and proposes that all viewpoints with apparent contradiction, emerge from experience. They are based on a corresponding objective quality. The difference lies in the individual choice only, and, we should have the same respect for choice of the so-called opponent as we have for our own.

In a cultured society we do show proper regard for different tastes and choices. But that regard is confined to physical comfort only. In the intellectual field we do not show the same sense of culture. The contribution of Jainism in this respect is unique. In the present age, when democracy is regarded as a sign of culture, the principle of respect for mind is not only highly useful but imperative.

Respect for Man

The third thing is respect for man. This eliminates all types of discrimination based on sex or caste. Jainism admits that every human being, whether a Brahman or the so-called lowbred possesses soul with similar qualities and, therefore, is equally entitled to all religious duties which are the way to spiritual development.

In the order of Mahavira there were many monks who came from *chundala* or other low caste and enjoyed same status as the monks from noble families. The monk who was junior even by one day used to salute his senior without any consideration of high or low birth.

Respect for Personal Effort

The fourth but one of the most important point is, respect for personal effort. Jainism believes that a person himself is responsible for his happiness and miseries. Curses and boons, which were a dominating factor in the Puranic age, have no place here. The respect for personal effort has developed into the Jaina theory of *Karman;* which is foundation of Jain ethics in its spiritual aspect. There are fourteen steps, known as 'Gunasthanas' constituting the ladder to salvation. The aspirant climbs its steps by step removing the obstruction of *Karman.* At the end, when the soul is fully purified of the Karmic pollution, it is liberated and becomes *'Mukta.'*

Jainism does not believe in an Almighty Creator. It holds that every soul can become 'paramatman' when fully purified. Boons and curses or dependance on the pleasure of some Almighty being is against the principle of equality; which Jainism is prepared to leave in no circumstances.

Truth

While accepting truth as one of the great vows, main emphasis is laid on the motive. Truth does not mean merely the statement of a fact, but at the same time the language of the student should be inoffensive and the motive beneficial. In case a statement leads to harm others, though logically true, it is not allowed. Similarly, a harsh or pinching word also is disallowed. Thus, we can see that in the ascetic tradition, including all the three systems of Jainism, Buddhism and Hinduism, truth is motivated with non-violence.

As a matter of fact, truth occupies a prominent position in the path of knowledge, while in the path of action it is subordinate to non-violence.

The path of knowledge is the path of Philosophers. For them truth is supreme. But for man of action truth is only a supplement to non-violence. In certain cases when he has to forego either of the two, he will prefer non-violence.

It is clearly stated in the Jnanarnava that the vows of truth etc. in their real sense, form a part of the great vow of non-violence.

Non-stealing

The vow of non-stealing roughly means not to take anything without permission of the owner. But, ultimately, it aims at taking nothing which is not ones due. To usurp others right through robbery, diplomacy or any other device is stealing and it is a sin. The term 'one's due' has two implications. Firstly, one must earn before possession. Secondly, one should not go beyond the limit that is necessary to his life. He should not be a burden to society by putting his obligations on others. At the same time he should not hoard, which means starvation for other members. He should apply his surplus strength for the benefit of society or his own spiritual development but in no way in robbing others, through any means barbarian or the so called civilized.

Celibacy

In the Vedic Hinduism to marry and have progeny was a social obligation. But, in the ascetic tradition it was totally denounced. Ultimately they came to a compromise in the state of a householder. Both traditions prohibited the sexual inter-course beyond one's wife duly married. I have already stated the different attitudes in the case of a householder. For Vedic Hinduism it is an obligation which can be fulfilled only through the birth of a male child. But in the ascetic tradition it is an excuse. The former looks it as a necessity while the latter as a distraction, an obstacle in the spiritual progress.

In Sanskrit celibacy is generally termed as Brahmacharya which means treading into the soul. Any act, therefore, which disturbs the concentration on soul or which leads towards extraversion is 'Abrahmacharya.'

Non-Possession

Non-possession or *'aparigraha'* is the last vow. In Buddhist Panchasila it has been substituted by abstinence from intoxication. In Jainism, as I have already stated, it did not exist before Mahavira. In the *Yogasutra*, as in the case of other yamas it has got a subjective definition in the form of non-attachment. Vedic Hinduism does not recognize it at all, as it goes against the social organization which aims at prosperity.

In the beginning *parigraha* meant any type of possession. An ascetic was enjoined not to keep anything except what was necessary for observance of religious *rites,* and a householder also was instructed to narrow, as far as possible, the limits of his possession. But later on *aparigraha* came to be interpreted as non-attachment with its widest implications, and in this sense both, the ascetic as well as the Vedic traditions united. In course of time non-attachment became the principal aim of spiritual practices. Jainism and Buddhism preached it through non-violence while the *Bhagavadgita* taught it through dispassionate action. Both, the actionists and non-actionists you may call them as escapists of have equally accepted it as the fundamental principle of spiritual development.

According to Jainism *moha* is the main obstacle in the path of salvation. It has two sides—*(1) Raga* (attachment), and *(2) Dvesha* (hatred). The first is the subjective sides of *parigraha* and the second that to violence. Thus on subjective consideration *aparigraha* is as important as non-violence.

In the Vedanta this principle has developed into the absence of egoism. An aspirant is instructed to abandon the complex of 'I' and 'mine'. Thus, in the Vedanta one can see, it is the only target of spiritual journey, and I think the Vedanta supersedes all other systems in this respect.

If we carry it further we have to learn non-attachment towards not only external objects but the internal notions and feelings as well. If we learn non-attachment with our pre-conceived thoughts, prides and prejudices we can easily arrive at the truth. The Jain theory of non-absolutism is nothing but a method for dispassionate thinking. Further we have to learn non-attachment towards our caste, creed, country, tradition and all other things, attachment to which is highly commended by the so-called cultured society, in high sounding works like patriotism etc. and which is the poor case of all international crises.

Conclusion

The above is a short introduction to the five precepts that are regarded as foundation of ethics. All religious system have accepted them as far as theory is concerned while in practice they have evolved a national ethics of their own, which is the root cause of all conflicts and consequent evils.

Human mind is so framed that it gets more inspiration from national ethics. Hundreds of examples can be cited where people have sacrificed their wealth, position and even life for the sake of their country, sect or other unit. But there are very few who have dome the same for Universal welfare. Whenever a passionate appeal is made on the name of a particular sect, or nation we have good response. Thousands and thousands sacrificed their lives for the war known as crusade, which is reality, went against the spirit of Christianity. Muslims and Hindus are not behind in this type of blood-stained history. But, appeal for universal welfare does not prove so inspiring.

If we try to find out the reason behind it, we shall realize that the national ethics provides enough scope for the satisfaction of one's baser instincts. Sometimes, an unbridled expression of these very instincts, is eulogized as the virtue of high order. Anger and thirst for blood are praised as bravery, conceit and vanity as national pride. Crookedness and fraud as diplomacy and greed for domination as ambition. They are regarded as essential parts of service to the nation or the religion. Plunders and cruelties perpetuated on the enemy are thought as a part of the crusade. On the other hand the Universal ethics cannot provide cheap rewards of this type. Here, one has to subdue his baser instincts and it requires a long period of restraint, continence and arduous practices. The aspirant has to check external longings and conquer the forceful urge of habits and predispositions.

Moreover, national ethics is a type of intoxication. It appeals to the sentiment induces one for prompt action. The Universal ethics on the other hand appeals to reasoning which is extremely useful to find out a theory, but lacks in force for practical purposes. And this places a real problem before us. Hinduism has found out a solution in neglecting neither of the two. It holds, that both are not only necessary but compliment to each other, if applied properly. National ethics is unavoidable upto a certain stage of society. But the leaders must aim at the Universal ethics and be clear in their mind that national aspiration does not mean dominance or prosperity at the expense of others. At the same time it should be realized that the service to one's nation is only a step towards service to the entire universe.

The same is the criterion for cultural development. An individual or a nation is cultured to the extent it has inculcated Universal ethics in its life.

8 FIVE TYPES OF KNOWLEDGE

I

The problem of knowledge, in general is divided into three branches of Psychology, Epistemology and Logic. But the present treatment if confined to the contribution of Jainism towards the first two branches only.

Psychology of Knowledge

Jaina psychology can be analysed under the following three heads :

1. Organs of knowledge.
2. Their function for producing cognition.
3. The stages of knowledge, from sensation to judgment.

The organs—In discussing the causation of knowledge generally the following four factors come into consideration :

1. The soul.
2. The mind.
3. The senses.
4. The object.

The Soul

According to Jainism the soul is permanent substance. It possesses consciousness as its natural attributes. There is no soul without consciousness and no consciousness without soul. This consciousness expresses itself in all the psychological functions of knowing, feeling and willing. The first, *i.e.*

knowing is its natural and pure manifestation while the remaining two are mixed. In feeling consciousness is mixed with the effect of *Vedaniya karman* (see theory of *karman*) and in willing with that of *Mohaniyakarman*. But knowing is natural. Here, the soul does depend upon any external assistance. As there is heat in the fire and coolness in the water, similarly, we have knowledge in the soul.

A question arises if knowledge is a natural and permanent attribute why it is phenomenal. It appears after some positive effort and vanishes automatically. Similarly, when all the souls possess this attribute equally, why there is inequality in knowledge. Jainism replies these objections through the theory of obscurance. Out of the eight *Karmans* accepted by Jainism the first, second, fourth and eighth are known as *ghatins*. They put obstructions in the natural expression of soul. The first two are related with the obstruction of conscious manifestation. They are compared with a cloud obscuring the light of the sun. The removal of that obscurance is necessary for knowledge. The liberated soul, which is free from this obscurance, gets the full manifestation. Infinite knowledge dawns there in full bloom without any external dependence. There, it is constant as well as similar in all states and persons.

Mind and the Senses

The mind and each of the senses are divided into two aspects, *i.e.* the physical aspect and spiritual. In the physical aspects the senses are parts of the physique of a living being. They are material as the body itself. They are further divided into the internal part and the external part, which is interesting for the study of ancient physiology. In the spiritual aspect they are nothing but the soul itself. They only represent the various expressions of the powers and the soul and their applications. This spiritual aspect is again divided into Power (*labdhi*) and Application (*upayoga*). In the process of knowledge the physical mind and the physical senses play the part of window only. A man sitting in the closed room cannot see anything outside even with perfect vision. The window enables his to peep outside. The sphere of objectivity depends upon the size of the window. Similarly, the man is confined into the closed room of *karmic* obscurance. A hole into that obscurance enables the person to look at the external object. As the window is nothing but a natural outlet for the sense of vision, similarly the senses are nothing but partial removal of *karmic* obscurance. Thus, the senses in their positive aspect are nothing but soul.

The Object etc.

Now we come to the fourth category of the object, light etc. Jainism does not give them any importance in the causation of knowledge. They are admitted as occasional helper but not as essentials. In illusion the object which exists does not appear. On the other hand that which does not exist appears.

It means that the presence of object is not a necessary condition. The *Nyaya* system includes big dimension, manifestation of colour, and light also in the causation of visual perception. But Jainism does not feel this necessity. The questions, why there is no reception in darkness, why we do not see atoms or air etc. are replied by the theory of capacity. It is the capacity provided by the removal of obscurance which regulates all the gradations or limitations in knowledge. Though contact between senses and the objects is not regarded as essential condition, yet it has been accepted in the case of four senses. The mind and the sense of vision do not require any physical contact with the object, about which the system of *Nyaya* is very particular.

Thus, we can see that soul is the only efficient as well as material cause of knowledge. The same is agent. The help of other accessories is negative *i.e.*, their contribution is confined to the removal of the obscurance. The Ayaranga says, "The soul is knower, the instrument of knowledge also is soul."

It should be clarified here that the systems of Sankhya Vedanta and Buddhism make a distinction between the discursive knowledge and the transcendental knowledge. In the former type matter, (*prakrit*) or nescience (*avidya*) plays the prominent part.

According to the Sankhya knowledge means a simultaneous reflection of the object as well as consciousness (*purusa*) into *buddhi*, a product of the matter. Of course, consciousness also has its share by way of reflection. But, the material cause of a reflection is not the reflectee but the reflector. Thus knowledge according to Sankhya is a mode of matter. Jainism does not accept any contribution on the part of matter. All modes belong to the soul. Secondly, Jainism does not believe in the theory of reflection or representation. It holds that the objects are presented to the soul direct.

According to the Vedanta, discursive knowledge is a complex phenomenon. It analyses the appearance into two parts. One part is consciousness and the other the object. As far as consciousness is concerned it is nothing but soul. There is no difference between Jain and the Vedanta in this respect. But, in case of the object the Vedanta holds that it is supplied by nescience. The mind, which is a product of *avidya*, goes out through the channel of cognizing senses and establishes a contact with the object. There, it performs two-fold function. Firstly, it removes the obscurance for manifestation of consciousness. Secondly, it projects an object which gives the knowledge a form. Jainism does not admit this illusory projection.

According to Yogachara Buddhism, all concepts are subjective. They are products of past impressions.

Thus, in discursive knowledge all the three systems recognize the contribution of matter or nescience in their own style. But according to Jainism subjective contribution is confined to the act of feeling and willing only. As far as knowing is concerned, it is purely objective. The transcendental knowledge according to them is devoid of all concepts. The discursive knowledge is both, a cause as well as the effect of something different from soul. The transcendental knowledge in pure consciousness, unpolluted by the association of object. Jainism does not support the above view. It does not make any qualitative difference between the two. Ordinary cognition of a layman, is as true as the cognition of an omniscient. The difference lies in quantity only. The cognition of ordinary person is confined to the consideration of one aspect only, while that of omniscient covers all the aspects. The former is partial while the latter is complete. Jainism contents that 'incomplete' does not mean wrong. It is wrong only if the cognizer is impertinent as to reject other aspects. Thus, wrongness is not connected with the appearance, but, with the attitude behind it. This is why in early Jainism the basis of truth and falsehood is not objective validity, but, attitude of the subject. If the cognizer possesses a right attitude his knowledge is right. If, on the other hand, his attribute is perverted the knowledge is wrong.

Of course, Yasovijaya Upadhyaya (1820 A.D.) has interpreted the Jaina theory also under the Vedantic influence. He admits that the complete knowledge is pure manifestation of the soul, while incomplete one is produced by the soul assisted by the *karman* obscuring complete knowledge. But his theory is not supported by the old tradition.

The *Nyaya* also holds knowledge as, the attribute of soul, but, according to him it is not a permanent factor. It is not natural but, Adventitious. Through the collocation of certain factors it appears in the first moment, exact in the second and disappears in the third automatically. In the states of sleep and salvation it is totally absent. According to Jainism it is the very essence of soul and never totally absent. One cannot conceive the fire without warmth. Similarly, the soul without knowledge is inconceivable.

Umaswati has given knowledge as the definition of soul. Vidyananda, while explaining the above, differentiates it from ordinary types of definitions and says that it is the very essence of the soul. It is definition as well as the definee, while ordinary definitions are mere definitions.

The Nature of Obscurance

The soul is, by nature, cognizer and the object knowable. There is a permanent relation between the two as knower and the knowable. There is no limit to this relation, as far as capacity is concerned. The soul possesses the power to know all the objects and even more if they happen to be. It is like the scorching sun which can illumine all objects. But that power is restricted by the *karmic* obscurance. Yasovijaya (the reader is advised to refer the chapter on *karman* for this purpose) compares this obscurance with a cloud obscuring the sun. It is a material substance attached to the soul. It pollutes the purity of the latter and does not allow it to shine in full brightness.

The Theory of Upayoga

The question may arise : if obscurance is the only regulating factor, where is the use of sense organs. We cannot see an object with close eyes with any amount of *ksayopasama*, as the partial removal of obscurance is recognized.

The Jaina reply to this question is a bit complicated. There are ten completions (*paryapti*) they say, which a being completes gradually after entering into the womb of the mother. The five senses and the mind constitute one completion each. The animal after completion of visual sense is supposed to possess the power of listening, and so on. The gradation in these powers depends upon the capacity of the completions. There are two factors which lead to the completion of the senses of knowledge. The responsibility for creating physical senses, goes to *Namakarman*. The spiritual senses being the faculties of soul itself, are restored by the *ksayopasama*. Thus *ksayopasama* is responsible in providing a faculty with the birth. It is also responsible to later developments for good or bad. But, it has no control over the day-to-day appearances. It limits the knowing capacity in every sense. It is there even when the sense are no more in action. Similarly, there is no difference in *ksayopasama*. When we apprehend a lion or a cloth, requiring the same amount of knowing capacity. Thus, *ksayopasama* is responsible for providing a capacity only, which is known as *labdhi* in Jain terminology. The day-to-day phenomena of cognition are regulated by the theory of *Upayoga* or application. The physical senses are useful in the function of application, without which the faculties do no work.

The Jain term for all types of cognitive activity is *Upayoga*.

It means application of the cognitive power possessed by the soul naturally or through restoration as the result of the removal of obscurance.

Division of Knowledge

The term knowledge denotes a judgment. It is the stage of conclusion in the process of thinking. But in discussing the psychology of thinking one has to consider the preceding stages also, beginning with the first sensation or inclination of the soul to know the object. We have stated above that the comprehensive Jaina term, for this purpose, is *Upayoga.* It is divided as follows :

1. Nirakara Upayoga or Darsana.
2. Sakara Upayoga or Jnana.

Nirakara Upayoga or Darsana

There is much controversy about the actual position of *darsana.* Commonly it is held as the first general appearance, apprehending mere existence. But this view does not hold good with the conception of *Vyanjanavagraha* which is defined as the first contact between senses and the object, and which is accepted as the first stage of *jnana.* No appearance, whether general or particular, is possible before that contact; and thus, the possibility of *darsana* before that a stage is out of question. On the other hand it is accepted unanimously that *darsana* must precede the first stage of *jnana.* In order to remove this anomaly some *Acharyas* have accepted *Avagraha* and *Iha,* the first two stages of knowledge preceding the judgment (*avaya*) as *Darsana.* But it a rough estimate. The point has been discussed elaborately by Brahmananda, the commentator on *Brhaddravya Sangraha* and in *Dhavla* by Vireswara. Both of them hold that *Darsana* in actual sense, is the first inclination of soul for knowing the object, the action of senses begins after this inclination. It is activity of pure consciousness before the entrance of the object into the sphere.

Darsana is generally compared with the indeterminate perception of the *Nyaya* or Buddhist perception. But, this comparison holds good only if the common view is held.

Division of Darsana

Darsana is divided into four types :

1. Caksurdarsana : The inclination preceding visual cognition.
2. Acaksuradarsana : The inclination preceding the cognition arising from other senses and mind.
3. Avadhidarsana : The inclination preceding the extra-ordinary perception with limited sphere.
4. Kevaladarsana : The inclination preceding perfect knowledge.

Sakara Upayoga or Jnana

Jnana means judgment. As stated above it is last stage of thinking process. Jaina psychology divides the process into four stages. These stages are related with the ordinary perception only arising through the senses and the mind, which constitutes the first type of its five-fold division. It is better, therefore, to have an idea of the division of *jnana*. It is divided into the following five types :

1. Matijnana : Knowledge through the senses and the mind.
2. Srutajnana : Verbal knowledge.
3. Avadhijnana : Extraordinary perception with limited sphere or clairvoyance.
4. Manohparyayajnana : Knowledge of the states of mind.
5. Kevalajnana : Perfect knowledge.

Matijnana

Mati includes all types of sense-experience. It is also known as *Abhinibodhika*. It is divided into the following four stages :

Avagraha—Sensation
Iha —Proposition
Avaya—Judgment
Dharana—Confirmation.

Avagraha is again divided into Vyanjanavagraha and

Arthavagraha. Vyanjanavagraha means a contact between the senses and the object. This stage does not occur in the case of visual or mental perception, where physical contact between the object and the senses is not necessary, while the remaining four senses must have it before apprehension.

Arthavagraha, is again the apprehension of an object in its most general form.

After sensing the object in its general form, we have a natural desire to know the object in detail. This desire is followed by a proposition or suggestion of a certain class, quality or the individual. This is called *Iha*.

The above proposition is followed by the judgment which transfers the probability into a decision. It is called *Avaya*.

This judgment is further confirmed in the stage of *Dharana*, where the impression takes a firm root in the mind and can revive later on as memory. It leaves a definite impression in the subconscious mind.

Sruta Jnana

The *Sruta* is just like *Sruti* in the Vedic tradition. It is the knowledge based on scriptures or the words of authority.

While describing it in detail the Jains enumerate their canonical literature of the period after Mahavira which is divided into *Angapavittha i.e.* occupying the position of a limb in the body of canon personified and *Anangapavittha* (not occupied as a limb). The pre-Mahavira canon was divided into fourteen *Purvas*.

It should be mentioned here that Jains do not regard their scriptures a eternal or the words of some eternal being. In every cycle of time, new pontiffs are born and give their sermons as they like. Those sermons are arranged into book by their chief disciples known as *Ganadharas*. In addition the contribution of *Srutakevalins* (the sages of possessing the knowledge of complete fourteen *Purvas*) and of those with a minimum knowledge of ten *Purvas* also are regarded as *Agamas*. The composition of *Ganadharas* is regarded as

Angapavitha, while that of other as *Anangapavitha*. In the post-Mahavirian tradition there are twelve Angas. The number of not-*angas* is uncertain.

Leaving aside the canonical literature when *Sruta* is considered in its widest sense it enters into the province of *Mati* and it is difficult to draw a clear line of demarcation between the two. Jinabhadra holds that all knowledge is associated with word and , therefore, terminates into *Sruta,* the sphere of *Mati* is confide to the presentation of data. The classification of that data come under the province of *Sruta. Mati* contributes the stuff and compares them with raw jute and rope made thereof. It is for this reason that *Mati* and *Sruta* are accepted as existing in every being.

Umaswati in his *Tattwartha* expresses a different view. He expands the sphere of *Mati* and contracts that of *Sruta*. He confines *Sruta* into canonical literature and all types of perceptual and conceptual knowledge are included into *Mati*. He says that the sense cognition, memory, recognition, induction and deduction, all are different types of Mati. This enumeration of the various types of Mati provides clue for the division of knowledge by the logicians.

Avadhi Jnana

The Avadhi is an extraordinary perception akin to clairvoyance. Generally, it is regarded as supernatural power obtained through penances or Yogic practice. But in the kingdom of heaven and hell it is acquired with the birth. Perhaps, Jains have regarded extraordinary knowledge as a necessary equipment for enjoying the extreme types of both, happiness as well as pain. Avadhi is confined to material objects only as its objects.

Manahparyaya Jnana

Manahparyaya jnana means the reading of thought waves. It is obtained when soul is extraordinarily purified through a high order of conduct. Only a monk can have it.

Kevala Jnana

Kevala jnana means the knowledge of the absolute. It dawns when obscurance is totally removed and all the power of soul get their full manifestation. It is same as realization in other systems.

The word *Kevala* means absolute. In the aphorism of Patnjali as well as in the system of Sankhya, *Kaivalya* means the knowledge of distinction between consciousness and matter. In Buddhism it is interpreted as the highest knowledge. But in Jainism, it is interpreted as omniscience. Etymologically, the word *Kevala* does not mean 'all'. It appears that the sense of omniscience is later innovation.

In Indian systems omniscience is regarded a supernatural power obtained through Yogic practices. Nowhere, except Jainism it is held as a necessary equipment for salvation. Jains also included it among *labdhis; i.e.* supernatural powers, which are not necessary steps in the path of salvation. In Buddhism the knowledge of four Great Truths is sufficient for obtaining *Nirvana,* Omniscience is an equipment of Bodhisattva only, who adopts the carrier of preaching others and converting them to his order. In Brahmanical school it is an epithet of God. It can also be possessed by the ascetics of high order. The Jain Tirthankara compares well with the Bodhisattava of Buddhism. He also adopts the carrier of preaching others. Thus, it appears that omniscience came to be accepted as an equipment of Tirthankara only. Its inclusion into the special embellishments of Tirthankaras indicates that in ordinary case *kevala* did not mean omniscience. Later on, logical conclusions led to its acceptance in other soul as well. One can visualize two reasons behind it. Firstly, according to Jainism, knowledge is the nature of soul. It does not depend upon external help for its full manifestation. Consequently, the souls which are entirely free from the *karmic* obscurance, cannot have any difference regarding knowledge. Thus, in party with the Tirthankaras other souls also came to be recognized as omniscient. Secondly, according to the theory of non-absolution all objects have a relative existence. Thus, a complete knowledge of one object is impossible without knowing all objects. The Ayaranga announces. "One who knows one object, knows all the objects, and who knows all the objects, knows only one object."

The *Upanisad* also propose the knowledge of all through the knowledge of one. But their approach is different. According to them the effect is only a manifestation of the cause : and therefore, one, who knows the effect automatically. *Brahman* is the cause of entire Universe. Thus, the knowledge of *Brahman* leads to the knowledge of entire universe. But, Jainism believes in plurality. It holds that the cause and the effect both are equally real. Thus the knowledge of one cannot lead to the knowledge of the other. But, at the same time, they are correlated; consequently the knowledge of one is incomplete without knowing the other. In this way the knowledge of entire plurality becomes a necessary condition for complete knowledge of one thing.

The soul is admitted for Infinite Bliss and Infinite Energy. One cannot interpret 'Infinite' as 'All'. Similarly, in the case of knowledge and intuition also 'Infinite' cannot give the idea of all. Any how, the concept of omniscience is firmly rooted in Jaina tradition and has come to be recognized as an integral part of their theology.

Influence of Logic

The above division of knowledge is an original contribution of Jainism. It is found in canonical literature and serves as the nucleous of Jain theory of Knowledge. In the later period, as a result of the contact with logicians, Jains also have remodelled their terminology in accordance with the prevalent logical terms.

The first stage of this development is noticed in the *Tattwartha* (200 A.D.) and the *Niryuktis* (400 A.D.). They divided the above mentioned five types into *Pratyaksa* (Immediate) *Paroksa* (mediate) cognitions. But, the definitions of *Pratyaksa* as well as *Paroksa* were their own. They held that the cognition arising direct from the soul, without the assistance of senses or mind was *Pratyaksa*. While, that mediated by the senses etc. is *Paroksa*. Thus the first two types of *Mati* and

Sruta were regarded as *Paroksa* and the remaining three as *Praktyasa*. We can notice here, that in spite of the introduction of two terms from logic, there is no change in the spirit.

In the *Nandi* (400 A.D.) perception is divided as sense-perception and No-sense-perception. Thus due to the influence of other systems the sense-cognition also came to be recognized as perception, but, there was no attempt for adjusting the same in the old scheme. In the later part of the same treatise, all stages of sense-cognition have been included into *Paroksa*. It only shows that a necessity was felt to recognize sense-cognition also as perception.

Akalanka (800 A.D.) has suggested the final solution. He accepted the sense cognition as *Samvyavaharik Pratyaksa, i.e.* perception according to the common usage.

Akalanka is regarded as the father of Jaina Logic. The shape given by him was accepted as final. No important change has been introduced later. He divided knowledge as given on next page.

Epistemology

According to Jainism the appearance "This is a jar" means "I know a jar." It means the appearance of the self as well as the jar. According to the Naiyayika the appearance—"This is a jar" apprehends the mere object. The cognition and the cognizer are apprehended by a subsequent appearances which he calls *Anuvyavasaya*. But, Jainism holds that all the three, the object, the cognition and the cognizer, are apprehended in one and the same appearance.

Both the self as well as the jar possess objective existence. According to Jainism there is no appearance without a corresponding object. All notions of relation, causation, generality or class exist externally. Thus Jainism is a strong devotee of *expriori*. There is nothing a *Priori*. Still, we cannot say that Jainism is empiricist in the western sense of the term. Modern empiricists regard senses only as the source of knowledge. Inference and other types of mental deliberations they hold, are mere deductions. The mind does not contribute

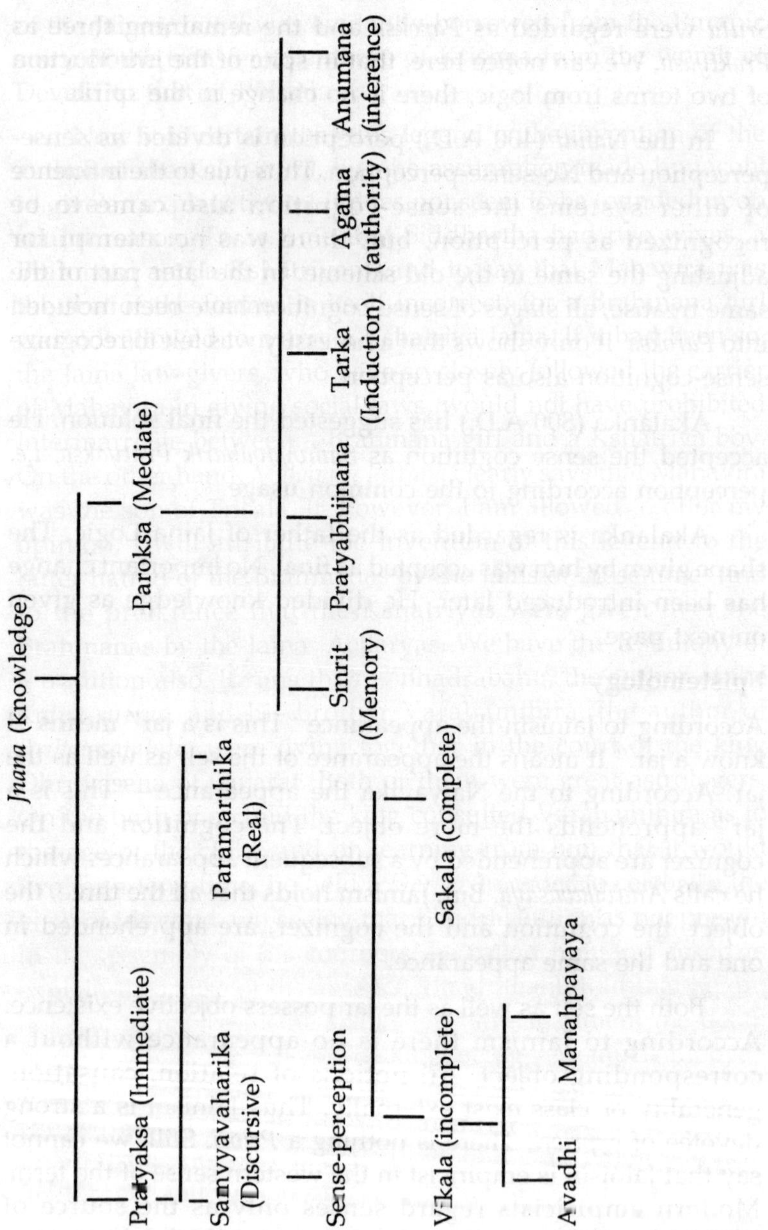
Jnana (knowledge)
Pratyaksa (Immediate)
Paroksa (Mediate)
Samvyavaharika (Discursive)
Paramarthika (Real)
Sense-perception
Smrit (Memory)
Pratyabhijnana
Tarka (Induction)
Agama (authority)
Anumana (inference)
Vikala (incomplete)
Sakala (complete)
Avadhi
Manahpayaya

any thing new. Its activities are confined to the act of feeling or deduction. But, according to Jainism mind and soul have their independent contribution towards knowledge. Of course, that contribution is not subjective. It is also objective. Thus, we can say Jainism is empiricist with three-fold organs of experience, *i.e.* the sense, the mind and the soul. Though, in reality soul is the only organ, others are mere accessories; yet the above differentiation takes the helping cause also into consideration. In the first two categories of knowledge the soul works with the assistance of the senses and mind. In the third category it works independently. But, in all cases, whether assisted or not assisted, it is only a discoverer and not creator. Jainism holds that knowledge is a discovery and not projection.

Compared with rationalism the Jainism is against the theory of mere subjective existence. All the same it holds that there are some objects which cannot be known through senses. The same is the case with intuitionist. It admits that there are objects which can be known trough intuition only. But, it differs that they do not exist in intuition only.

According to Dignaga and Dharmakirti the particular objects exist externally. But, all concepts of class, relation etc., are subjective. The Sankhya holds an opposite view. According to him universals are objective while particulars are subjective. The German Philosopher Kant also holds certain categories of interpretations as subjective while the thing-in-itself as objective. But according to Jainism both universals and particulars, the percepts and concepts, the categories of interpretation as well the thing-in-itself have an objective reality. No appearance without external existence, is the keyword of Jainism.

Illusion

According to Jainism illusion does not mean false appearance. No appearance is false. The appearance of rope as a snake is as true as its appearance as a rope. The rope is not absolutely different from snake. It also possesses certain qualities common with the snake. In darkness, only those qualities are discovered while the distinguishing ones are not realized. The common qualities assisted by the complex of fear, produce the appearance of a snake, which is not without objective basis. It is regarded false, because, in later stages the distinguishing qualities get prominence. The change occurs only in the attitude of the subject. Formerly, he was holding it as a snake and denying the existence of rope. Now, he holds the same object as rope and denies the existence of snake. In reality the object is both, snake as well as a rope, in relation to their respective qualities. Both appearances are true. The common distinction of true and false depends upon the pragmatic consideration of serving the useful purpose. The illusive snake cannot bite and, therefore, the appearance is regarded as false. But, we cannot say that it does not do any function common with the real snake. In that case the fear also would not have been there.

Vidyananda holds that there is no qualitative difference between the appearance held as valid and invalid. All of them are apprehensions of truth in part. The complete apprehension is possible in the stage of omniscience only. Absolute validity rests in that knowledge only. The validity of incomplete knowledge is judged on pragmatic valuation or on the attitude of the subject as it is in the ethical aspect. In their objective consideration there is no difference between the two.

Relative Existence

It is essential to know here that according to Jainism every existence is relative. The same object can exist in as many forms as there are relations. And this is an acceptance of subjectivism in another form. It makes no difference if one holds that the object is devoid of all concepts or that it possesses all concepts in different relations. After all the judgment formed on the basis of relations is the choice of subject only. It is his business to form a judgment on the basis of a particular relation. The only difference is that in Jainism it is a choice while in idealistic systems it is subjective creation. The point may be clarified through the following illustration : three ladies are sitting together and a gentleman comes from outside. One of the ladies says "There is my husband." The other say "There is my brother." The third says "There is my son." The Buddhist will say that all the three concepts of husband, brother and son are subjective. But the Jain would say "No, all the notions are objective." The gentleman under consideration possesses all the three qualities, in different relations. The ladies made their choice according to their respective relations. There is no concept without relation. It can be asked : the first child at its birth cannot possess the quality of being a brother. But he comes to possess that quality when the second child is born. How, the second child, without any physical relation with the first can produce a new quality in the latter? The Jain reply is that physical contact is not necessary for generating a quality. Thus, the sphere of objectivity in Jainism, is so wide that it loses the very sense of it.

A question can be raised again; whether all the attributes of an object, the original as well as the derivative, stand on the same level of reality. In the example quoted above the attributes of being a husband, brother or son are not original. They have been derived from the relations with different persons. But, the quality of being a human being is original. If there is any difference between these two types of attributes, that must continue in knowledge also. It means that we shall have to make some distinction between the knowledge of original qualities and the desired ones.

The Jaina reply is this : as far as the existence is concerned both stand on the same level. But, the pragmatic outlook creates an apparent gradation. To the child of a professor the factor of his being a father is more real than that of professorship. To his mother he is more son than a professor or father. To a student he is a professor more than anything else. To his servant he is a master. To a disinterested person all the factors stand on the same level. But he also takes into consideration mainly those factors as have a universal value; and here lies the difference between original and the derivative attributes. Those with universal valuation are regarded as original while those with a limited sphere of valuation are regarded as derivative.

Jainism takes four factors into account for existence. Dravya (person), *ksetra* (space), *Kala* (time) and *Bhava* (state) when an individual exists in relation to the above factors belonging to his own; personality, he is thought real. In respect of the relation other than his own, he is non-existent.

We can compare these categories with those of Kant with; certain reservation.

Theory or Presentation

According to Jainism the object is presented to the subject direct without any *via* media. According to Sankhya the object itself is never perceived. It is reflected into the mode of *Buddhi* and that reflection only becomes the object of perception. The existence of the object itself is inferred through that reflection. But, Jainism does not believe in the theory of reflection. Of course, Kunda has compared the soul with a mirror and shown a liking for this theory. He also proposes that in reality an omniscient sees himself only and as all the object are reflected into the self, he comes to know the objects also. His view can be compared with Vijnana Bhiksu, but it lacks support from Jaina tradition. The canonical literature defines knowledge as the illuminer. The school of logicians also supports the same view. Yasovijaya compares soul with the sun, having a natural faculty of illumining the objects. For this purpose it does not require any physical contact with the object. Kunda Kunda also says, "The omniscient neither enters into the objects nor is entered into by the object . Still, it perceives all the objects.

The Soutrantika School of Buddhism admits two factors as the regulator of knowledge. Firstly, it cognizes the object from which it is produced. Secondly, the cognition takes the form of the object. As knowledge is self-luminary it perceives the modified form and infers the object through that. Jainism does not enter into these complicacies. It does not admit object as the producer of knowledge nor believes in the theory of model change. It believes in attention or *Upayoga* only. The consciousness is like a lamp in one's hand. It is always burning with its glaring light. One is required to direct it towards the object for apprehension. This, direction is known as *Upayoga*.

II

AUTHORITY AS A SOURCE OF KNOWLEDGE

The major part of our knowledge is derived from the assertions of other persons. None can say that even a half of his beliefs, is based exclusively on his own experience. Nevertheless every intellectual tries to establish his claim as a rational being. To be called irrational, illogical or a person led by the assertions of other persons, hurts our sense of pride. Inspite of this it is a fact that we cannot dispense with authority as a source of knowledge. Our quantum of knowledge would reduce considerably and the life would come to a stop if belief in authority is given up altogether. We believe in the theories of scientists, in the railway time table, in different charts and hundreds of other statements merely on the basis of authority.

Thus, we see that resort to authority is indispensable for accumulation of knowledge. But, there are divergent views regarding its reliability. Some schools of thought totally reject authority as a reliable source of knowledge. They are not prepared, to accept any statement without putting it to the test of reason or experience. But, their claim is confined to theory only. In practice they do believe in the words of propounders of their respective systems. There are others who introduce some criterion for its validity. In doing so, either they cross the boundary knowledge is concerned all systems subordinate its validity to logic. This we can say it is secular authority tarianism. Those accepting the person with extraordinary knowledge also fall into two categories. The first category consists of those admitting extraordinary knowledge as manifestation of spiritual power attained through the removal of obscurance. They stress upon the spiritual purity, the removal of passions, leading to the purity of knowledge as well. This is mystic authoritarianism.

The second category consists of those believing in the inspiration by God. They are in a way intuitionist. Those believing the *Vedas* as composed by God and seen by the sages through their penance, come in this category.

The Sankhya Mimansa systems believed that the Vedas were composed neither by personal not impersonal being. They are traditionalist.

Those believing in intuition or tradition attach intrinsic validity to the Vedas, but, in order to avoid clash with experience, restrict their sphere to ethics or imperceptible objects.

The common people measure the prestige of an authority in proportion to :

1. the prestige is its original exponents,
2. the number of its adherents,
3. the time through which it has lasted.

I need not discuss here how logically feeble these grounds are.

The modern politics attaches too much importance to number without a regard for quality. The court of law observes both the number of witnesses as well as the quality. The quality is two-fold. Firstly the witness should have a first hand knowledge of the incident and secondly he should be above partiality. These criteria correspond to those of Jainism and Yoga systems.

In the present democratic set-up of the political institutes the number is supreme. The opinion of two persons is invalid against that of three persons. This view is supported in the light of pragmatism. Truth, as William James holds, is beyond our approach. No proposition or decision is final. The verdicts of scientists and other so called authorities may change any time. In this position of responsibility of a decision is borne by three in place of two. This view can be useful when there is a tussle between two courses of action with equal strength or when there is a question of choice or taste. But, in finding truth the view of one specialist is far more weightier than hundreds of common men. The democratic way is only a short cut to settle differences. It is not a correct approach to truth.

9 PHILOSOPHICAL AND RELIGIOUS PRINCIPLES OF JAINISM

It is considered that as distinct from the Vedic religion, Jainism is not an *'apaurusheys'* (man-made) religion *i.e.* it does not possess divine origin. This teaching was created by persons, each one of them is known as a *Jeena, i.e.* a conqueror (removing all the obstacles on way to salvation) or a Trithankar—boatman across the current (of existence).

The basic principles of Jainism are the following :

1. Initially every human soul is invested with an envelope of materialistic particles called *karmas,* attaching it to impure earthly tasks.
2. Every human being must strive for liberation from this dependence and for achieving perfection of the condition of soul, in which it acquires four new qualities, unlimited faith, unlimited knowledge, unlimited force and unlimited bliss.
3. A human being must hold the material envelop under control of his soul, since only after complete mastery over the envelopes binding force, the soul can reach perfection.
4. A human being can reach perfection by his own efforts. Nobody can help him on this path. Everyone carries full measure of responsibility for all that he does.[1] This last principle objectively rejects God.

The basis of Jain philosophy is faith in the objective existence of two categories (conceptions)—*Jiva* (living) and

Ajiva (without living), which are uninterrupted interaction, giving rise to the phenomenon of life.[2]

A human being can accomplish the feat of stopping this interaction and of liberating itself gradually from the attractions of all that relates to *Ajiva* and can accomplish the feat of securing the condition of *Moksha*—complete freedom, salvation.

For securing Moksha, every Jain must efficiently master the thought of the seven so called *Tattvas*: (1) living (spirit), (2) non-living (matter), (3) penetration of matter into the soul, (4) connection of the matter with the soul, (5) mastering of this penetration by the soul, (6) liberation from the influence of matter, and (7) *moksha*.

Jiva (we will translate it as soul) is wholly eternal and intransient, but it consists of innumerable multitudes of individual souls, invested in most varied material envelopes or bodies. These may be bodies of people, animals, insects and even plants. There are categories of beings manifesting only one sense, one aspect of soul-touch. These are immovable—*'Sthavara'* (these are plantations, air, water, fire, land). There are beings—*'Trasa' i.e.* moveable. Amongst then, there are those who have two senses : touch and taste (for example, worms), and who have three senses : touch, taste and smell (beetle), who have four sense : touch, taste and smell and sight (bee), who have five senses—the above four and hearing (people, animals and birds).

Inasmuch as the existence of soul in every living being is acknowledged, the doctrine of *ahimsa i.e.* non-violence, absence of injury to life is adhered to in the strictest possible manner.

This doctrine prescribed absence of injury even to plants and those beings, which possess only one sense. But in as much as such a prescription is not compatible, say, with agricultural practice, Jain preachers introduce the explanation that only conscious harm to living beings is strictly prohibited but harm which is caused by necessity is not.[3]

Five conceptions form a part of the category of *Ajiva i.e.*

non-living. *Pudgala*—matter, *Dharma*—means, environments, stimulation movement or action, *Adharma*—means or environment, stimulating absence of movement (for example, land), *Akasha*—expanse and *Kala* (time).

All these are primordial and in their essence are unchangeable. Only conditions can change, in which they manifest themselves.

Consciousness in originally natural to each soul but the material *karmas*, giving birth to various barriers disturb the finding of real knowledge.

Cognition can be secured by means of feelings, and mind and by means of soul, which has liberated itself from *karma* (this is the highest form of cognition).[4]

The soul, having secured the condition of perfection—*kevala* can cognize the real nature of all things; it can accept everything relatively and conditionally in the remaining steps of path to salvation.

Every affirmation is not absolute but relative and this was given rise by the objective condition of each real existing substance, since with the substance there are two basic groups of indications : unchanged and changing (accidental). All indications exist in reality.

Changing indications are connected with uninterrupted cycle of birth and destruction, while the unchanged indications are the cause of uninterrupted existence of real substance.

All substances with the exception of time (*kala*) possess extent in space. Soul is also related to the category of substance, having extent in space, but with the reservation that it exists in it but does not fill it and be combined simultaneously with other substance (let us say with other soul).[5]

Individual qualities, inherent in every human soul are conditioned by the influence of all *karmas* on the souls of preceding generations. Dependence on *karmas* engenders passions, which should be mastered. On this path the competence of the 24 preachers (*Jinas*)—who are called

Tirthankars—boat men across the current (existence or passions), can be helped.

They are called Tirthankars because of this only.

Correct faith, correct cognition and correct conduct are known, because of this, as three jewels (*triratna*) in the ethics of the Jains.[6]

All that exists was eternal and would remain eternal. There was no creator of the universe, similar to Hindu gods Brahma and Prajapati.

Time is divided in three eras—past, present and future. In every era lived 24 Tirthankars. In the Jain scripture '*Kalpasutra*' and in the glossary '*Abhidhana Chintamani*' composed in the twelfth century by the Jain acharya. Hemchandra and in a number of other works, the life and selflessness of these Tinthankars and the miracles, which they performed, are described. The continuity of their life is measured in units, called 'sea of years', which is equal to one trillion units if time, called '*palya*' and they are equal to the time, necessary for ravaging a big cave, filled with trimmed hair, taking out one hair at a time in a century.[7] And only about the last but one Tirthankar (Parshva), it is said that he became an ascetic at the age of 30 and reached perfection at age of 70. These realistic figures testify according to our opinion to the fact of his existence as a historical person whose memory preserved towards the time of the blossoming of Jainism and creation of its cannon.

Each era consists of six epoches, called '*ara*'. In the cause of these epoches, humanity passes the path of great happiness to great grief and again to great happiness. In the first five *aras*, people become huge and strong and live for long. But by the sixth *ara*, growth of people decreases to one eubit and the continuity of life reaches up to 16 years. In the following six *aras* everything passes in the reverse order.

In deep antiquity human beings received all that was necessary for life from the godly trees.[8] All people were equal. Happiness reigned everywhere. But the trees gradually started giving less and less fruits and humanity was threatened with ruin. At this time, the first Tirthankar Rishabha appeared. Having given laws, knowledge, sword, agriculture, trade, cattle-breeding and ink, he saved the people.[9] He created books on sciences and religions but the language of these books was forgotten. They are, however, retold in various languages. His son ruled in Bharatkshetra *i.e.* in India[10] it is not possible to explain from Jain legends, in which territory life of the society was going on up to this time.

It is not difficult to discover in this legend an attempt at original interpretation of the most ancient history of humanity from the stage of primitive community—existing mainly by collectivism, until the period of class relations.[11]

According to Jain notion there are several worlds, situated one above the other. Thus there are two lower worlds, where demons of various categories live. In the lowest world 15 categories of demons live, they subject the soul of sinners to torments. In the following world also, demons and spirits live. The spirits are called '*bhavanpati*' and demons are divided in two groups—black (*vyantara*) and white (*vana vyantara*). Those who are regarded as spirits and semi-gods in Hinduism (for example, *yaksha* and *gandharva*) are also called demons. Also those who are called demons in Hinduism (*Pishachcha* or *rakshasa*) are designated as demons.

The middle world is situated above the two lower worlds. In this world there is land with all its inhabitants. According to ancient geography of Jainism, the middle world consists of eight wheel-like continents, separated by oceans and in the centre the holy mountain of Meru is situated.

There is also an upper world, where gods and the holies live; this world is near the summit of the mountain Meru.

Above everything, on the very summit of the mountain Meru, the Zenith of the unverse—*Siddha* shila is situated. Here in sparkling eternity, the Siddhas who have liberated their souls lead their lives.

The souls of those people, who are nearer to perfection

and called *devatas* live down the summit of mountain Meru, in the heaven—*swarga*. They serve the *Siddhas*. Here the Hindu gods—Indra, Shiva, Brahma, Hanuman, Ganesh and others and also Buddha live, they being *devatas*. It is considered that God Vishnu, after his incarnation as Rama became a *Siddha*. Hindu gods are usually portrayed in the Jain temples in the form of small figures, standing in humble pose before the portrayals of Tirthankars and Siddhas.

Several Hindu deities have found a place as god-patrons or god-protectors of Tirthankars. Most probably the striving of the Jain community to popularize its own religion widely is reflected in their admission of Hindu gods.

The goddess-mother cult made its appearance in Jainism. It was very difficult to accommodate this cult with the teaching of strict ascetism. Buddhism could not overpower the force of this most ancient cult and it found a place in Buddhism in the form of Tantrik Buddhism. In Jainism, another solution was found—the place of goddess-mother was taken by goddess messengers (shasana devi). Every Tirthankar has his own goddess-messenger, connecting him with the world of mortals. Goddess Padmavati is thus associated with Adinath etc. These deities are referred to in a number of Jain books but their functions are described most fully in the texts of Digambaras, who have secret texts devoted to these deities, wherein their forms, names, symbols, weapons etc., are described.[12]

Jains revere these goddesses and some goddesses of Hindus - Saraswati (goddess of learning). Laxmi (goddess of prosperity) etc. Jains have their own 16 goddesses of knowledge. The Jains also worship caste deities and patron deities of the family.

One can see the images of all these holies and gods in the temples (mainly in those of Shvetambaras, who adopted more elements of Hinduism than Digambaras). Orthodox Jains try to fight against these deviations from the principles of religion but it is not possible to eradicate them, since they have made their appearance in Jainism very long ago.

Images of Tirthankars are worshiped in the temples of both the sect (excluding the sub-sect of Digambaras – taranapanthis and the sub-sect of Shvetambaras – sthanakavasi).

Digambaras have simple, unadorned images of nude males, standing upright or sitting on crossed exposed legs, while the Shvetambaras have often images wrapped up in cloth and adorned by jewellery and gold. Usually their eyes are made of precious stones.

Many elements go into the ritual of worship of the images, although it is not obligatory to perform all these every time. Those offering prayers through the medium of the priest of the temple sprinkle and saffron on the image, place in front of it burning aromatic sticks - *agarbatties* - say prayer, place near the image flowers, rice, fruits, sweetmeats. Most often the ritual of worship consist in the prayer-doer revolving clockwise round the image three times and saying brief prayer : Namo arhantanam, Namo siddhanam. The morning prayer of the ordinary members of the community is also very short : 'let the sinful thoughts which visited me last night be forgiven'.[13]

Philanthropy and donations for maintenance of temples are considered great religious services.

Every day the priest of the temple washes the images with milk and on the festival days, by special aromatic composition and adorns them with flowers.

The stanakavasi and taranpanthi sub-sects have prayer-houses, where their monks live and where their holy books are read.

Jains make pilgrimages to their holy places, where according to their superstition their Tirthankars were born and had secured enlightenment or had died.

The following are the fond places of pilgrimage :

Bihar

(1) City of Parasnath, near which the mountain of Samata

is situated. Here according to legend, Parshva and a number of other holies secured Nirvan. On this mountain and round about there are many Jain temples.

(2) City of Papapuri (or Pavapuri) where Mahavir died. This city is situated not far from the capital of the State *i.e.* Patna. Here on the lake one of the most Jain temples is situated.

(3) City of Rajgir. Here, according to legend, 20th Tirthan was born. There is a rocky mountain near the town on which the Jain ascetics performed penance in the course of many centuries in front of the people, coming to see them.

(4) Bhagalpur, where the 12th Tirthankar was born.

Rajasthan

(1) Mount Abu, on the summit of which the whole town of magnificent temples is situated.

(2) The village of Rakhab-Dev near the city of Udaipur. Here there is an ancient temple of the first Tirthankar– Rishabha. The most interesting feature of local culture is worship of the carved image of Rishabha, made of black marble not only by the Jains but also Vaishnava (regarding the carved image as incarnation of Vishnu) and Bhils (calling it their own god Kala-ji *i.e.* black god.). This is one of the most eloquent confirmations of the assumption about the ancient and initial connections of Jainism with the cult of Vishnu-Krishna and with the pre-Aryan cult.

(3) City of Ranapur on the west of the State, near the city of Jodhpur.

Gujarat

Temples on the mountain of Girnar, where according to legend, the 22nd Tirthankar-Arishtanemi (or Neminath) submerged in *Nirvan.* The image is carved from black marble.

South Sharavanbelgol in the State of Mysore is regarded as the holiest place of pilgrimage. On the mountain of Shravan belgol, temples of Tirthankars, Parshva and Neminath, built in the tenth-twelfth centuries are situated. The gigantic statue of Gomateshwar, son of Rishabha, carved out of rock is also standing here."[14]

Usually these pilgrimages are connected with festivals and fasts. Jains observe many festivals and fasts of their own religious community. They observe many festival andfasts of the Hindus too.

The following are purely Jain festivals :

1. Jalyatra—ablution in the river of the sacred wheel—siddhachakra—which is taken twice in a year—in spring and in autumn—solemnly to the river and back.
2. Festival of Mahavir Jayanti—The birth anniversary of Mahavir is celebrated on the 13th day of the first half of Chaitra (March-April). Both the Digambaras and Shvetambaras celebrate the birth anniversary.
3. Jina-panchami (by Shvetambaras and Digambaras in October-November) or Shruta-panchami (by Digambaras in May-June) is the festival of holy books, when worship of these books takes place. They are decorated with flowers.
4. Virashasana jayanti (only the Digambaras observe this) the day of the first preaching by Mahavir after securing enlightenment (in July-August).

The following fasts are observed :

1. Paryushana—strict ten days' fast in August-September (by the Digambaras) or eight days' fast (by the Svetambaras). It is accompanied by prayers, processions and worship of holy books.
2. Ashtanhika—(only by the Digambaras) three times in a year.
3. Fast of four full-moon nights in the year (when Svetambaras illuminate their temples).
4. Both the sects also observe fasts (which are not very strict) on the 4th, 8th, 12th days of every month.

From the Hindu festivals Jains observe the following :

1. Divali—the autumn festival of lights which the Jains

regard as the day of achievement of *Moksha i.e.* full liberation, by Mahavir.

2. Rakshabandhan—the day by the end of July, when the sister ties a special lace—amulet on the wrist of brothers. The Jains regard this day as a festival of mutual friendship and amity.
3. Ganesh Chaturthi—day of the god Ganesh (is observed only in Maharashtra and Mysore, where the Hindus celebrate it very solemnly).
4. Anant Chaturdasi—the day of reverence to the great serpent Naga, regarded as a symbol of infinity.

Several other local Hindu festivals are also observed.

Jainism, similar to Hinduism, accepts the idea of religious suicide, but as distinct from Hinduism, Jains always considered that quick methods of suicide are worthless and the people making use of them are reborn as demons. The Jain ascetics choose the method of slow death from hunger and thirst. Moreover, death itself is not their aim. The aim is to renounce all the requirements of the flesh and thus atone for all sins, connected with the flesh.[15]

Only the ascetics are permitted religious suicide. Any other suicide is strictly condemned by Jainism, as violent interruption of the process of liberation of soul from the power of *karma*.

Notes and References

1. J.L. Jaini, *Outlines of Jainism,* pp. 195-96.
2. Warren, *Jainism,* pp. 50-51.
3. "Jainism," Shri Vallabh Suri, Jain Literature Series, Pushpa. 2, pp. 9-10.
4. S. Chatterjee and D. Datta, *An Introduction to Indian Philosophy,* p. 74.
5. *Ibid.,* p. 90
6. *Ibid.*
7. This information is cited from the works of F. Bushanan,

Particulars of the Jains; N.T. Colebrooke, *Observations on the Sect of Jains.*

8. Analogical legends exist amongst the Dravidian hill tribes, in particular with Kadar tribe, living in north Kerala (W. Ruben, *Uberlegung tur Geschicte der Religion,* p. 213).
9. I. Minayevl, *Information About Jains and Buddhists.*
10. Retold from the article : "Notices of the Jains received from Charukirti Acharya, their chief Pontiff at Belligola, Mysore".
11. It is true, that it is hardly possible to connect Rishabha with the period of the beginning of class relations. Jain legends say that marriages between brothers and sisters were widespread during his life-time, that he himself was married to his sister and gave two of his sons – Bahubali (Goutameshwer) and Bharat – in marriage to his own two daughters (V.A. Sangave, *Jaina Community,* p. 162). This myth enables us to accommodate the notion about Rishabha in much more ancient stage of development of the society.
12. 'Praci Jyoti' Digest of Indological Studies, Institute of Indic Studies, Kurukshetra University, 1963, December, p. 35.
13. E. Thomas, *The Early Faith of Ashoka.*
14. The list of places of pilgrimage is given mainly from the book of N. von. Glasenapp, *Heilige Statten Indiens.*
15. U. Thakur, *The History of Suicide in India,* pp. 103-106.

10 THE STRUCTURE OF JAIN COMMUNITY

As is already indicated, the entire Jain community is divided into two sects – Digambaras and Svetambaras.[1]

Digambaras in their turn are divided into five sub-sects – bisapanthi, terapanthi taranapanthi (or samayapanthi), gumanapanthi and totapanthi.

The difference between them consists in observance or non-observance of one of the other fine points of ritual (thus, bisapanthi present flowers, fruits and sweetmeats to the images of Tirthankars and Terapanthi present only rice), but the first two sub-sects do not visit the temples of other sub-sects.

Svetambaras have three sub-sects : pujera (or murtipujaka or deravasi or mandirmargi), dhundhia (or bistola or sthanakavasi or sadhumargi), and terapanthi.

Pujeras dress up and richly adorn Tirthankars in their temples, their ascetics bind their mouths with white cloth but they can wear yellow dress. The dhundias have not got images of Tirthankars at all, and their ascetics wear only white. Terapanthi is rather a big sub-sect and strictly observe ascetism. They also do not worship the images of Tirthankars.

The spiritual like of all these sub-sects is led by the heads - Acharyas. Still petty groups, headed by their mentors – Acharyas – exist in the sub-sects. These groups are called sanghas and still smaller sub-groups – gana, gachcha and sakha - exist in those sanghas. Contradictions and disputes constantly arise amongst them about various questions of ritual. Many groups have their own temples and separate schools for religious education of the young. These schools are called *gurukulas* or *patha shalas.*

Every group has its own ascetics. The interesting feature of the internal structure of these groups is the system of mutual control between laymen and ascetics. For breach of rules of conduct or prohibitions, not only the laymen but also the ascetics can be expelled from the community and this practically takes place sometimes in out days too. Even Shripujya (head of ascetics of a given group) can be expelled by its members.

Some such sanghas also arose which strove to even out contradictions inside the community and they evaluated this to the level of their programme o religious teaching. Thus, the sangh, known as the yapya, existing in Andhra accepts, as the Svetambaras do, the truth of canonic books and the possibility of salvation of women also, but like the Digambaras, it upholds the customary ritualistic nudity of body and all the rules prescribed for the ascetics.[2]

As has been already mentioned division into castes penetrated in the Jain community and the custom of inheriting the profession in each caste (mainly by the north Indian Jains) got partially established. Here it is quite in place to remember the words of Jawaharlal Nehru, which briefly and aptly characterise this process. It is exceedingly interesting and significant that during the stretch of a protracted segment of Indian history, the great people more than once warned against priesthood and the rigid caste system, and strong movements took place against them. Nevertheless, as though it was predestined, castes slowly developed and almost imperceptibly spread and caught in their pernicious clutches all the spheres of Indian life. The rebels, rising against the old religion and which was in many respects highly distinctive from it, reconciled with the caste system, as a result of which, it continues to exist in India almost as a branch of Hinduism.[3]

As distinctive from Hinduism, there are no rigid caste prohibitions or prescriptions in Jainism. No caste enjoys privileged position, even though a stratum of Brahmins proper has formed amongst Jains. Judging from the traditions which have come down from word of mouth and the works of Jain literature, a numberless sub-sects and castes arose mainly in the medieval period, commencing from the 2nd half of the 1st millennium. It is apparent that the historical process of settlement of the Jains in India, conversion of individual groups of population and also the process of adoption of the caste system by the Jaina community was reflected in the rise of such petty sub-groups in that community.

This idea is confirmed by the fact that the Jain tradition preserves the names of tens of preachers, who supposedly formed those groups and moreover, interpreted canon in various ways and prescribed different religious practices to their groups.

But the makers of the religious canons of Jainism, in no way expressed their own attitudes to castes and did not introduce any prohibitions or prescriptions in this connection.

Some of the castes of Jains are extremely small in numbers. Thus amongst the Svetambaras, almost no caste (excluding the five strong castes) has more than 500 members. Amongst both the sects, there are some castes which consist of 10-12 persons each.[4]

Notwithstanding the fact that not all the caste institutions were adopted by the Jains, the ideas about higher and lower position of this or that caste exists all the same. Thus many castes of the Jains are divided into two groups—visa and dasa. Scholars are unable to explain the origin of these groups, but it is certain that these groups are endogamous and that the position of the latter group is lower than that of the former. The numbers of the latter group are not even allowed to enter the temples in some places, even though untouchability practically does not exist amongst Jains.

Marriages of widows are allowed amongst the castes of visa group, while amongst the castes of dasa group, such marriages are prohibited.[5] It is possible to assume that the dasa caste goes back genetically to those ancient groups of Jains which had their origin in the non-Aryan people, while visas have their origin in the groups of Jain-Aryans, which were formed much later.

It is characteristic that marriages of members of visa castes with those of the dasa castes are prohibited, while marriages between the members of visa castes of Digambaras and Svetambaras and equally between those of the dasa castes of both the sects are not censured.

In several castes of Western India, in which a part of members profess Jainism and another part, Hinduism, Jains as a rule belong to visa group and Vishnuites belong to the dasa group. It is obvious that here members of higher castes were converted into Jainism in those times, when the rulers patronised this religion (as it happened, for example, in Rajasthan and Gujarat).

Marriages between such Jains and Vishnuites are allowed.[6]

Jain castes, like the Hindu castes, are divided in exogamous groups—gotras. Gotras are traced to kin groups and exogamy is observed rigidly to the present day.

Osaval (or Osvala), shrimali, poravada (partially Digambaras) of the Svetambara castes and Agarvala, Khandelvala, Paravara, Khumbada (partially Svetambaras) of the Digambara castes are the most numerous ones in northern and western India. In south India, where practically all the local Jains belong to Digambara sect, such fractional division into castes does not exist amongst them Here there are four big castes—saitavala (this caste is not in Mysore), chaturtha, panchama and bogara or kasara and three small castes-Upadhyaya, Kamboja and Harada.

The Digambaras of the south do not marry and do not practically keep any connection with members of Jaina community living in all the other regions of India. Apparently ancient and deep differences divide this group from the other Jains.

An interesting feature of the life of south Indian Jaina community is that here the priests are the high caste Hindus, tracing themselves to ancient Aryans, support patrilineal system of inheritance and while giving daughters in marriage give dowry, but the rest of the Jains have no such institutions. As distinct from priest the rest of Jains (so-called laymen) support most ancient customs, which are preserved even to this day by the Dravidian peoples (as by the hill and jungle tribes). Sister's son and not his own children inherit by right the property of the deceased.[7]

Along with these survival of matriarchal relations, Jains preserve the custom of payment of *'dahej'* (bride-price) in monetary form and also in the form of presents and transfer of part of property to the father of the bride in conformity with the marriage contract.

Amongst the priests in the south, marriages of widows are prohibited and amongst the rest of the Jains, they are allowed (with the exception of regions towards the south of the city of Madras).[8]

Marriages between priests and laymen are prohibited.

Each of the four big castes in the south is led by its own spiritual leader (bhattaraka) who, occupying intermediary position between ascetics and laymen, can individually resolve disputes between the members of the caste and expel from it whomsoever he considers it necessary.

The institutions of bhattarakas arose in medieval ages amongst the Digambaras of north India and spread out from there wider and wider and flourished in southern regions.

In the course of several centuries, leadership is everyday life of the members of the community and control over their conduct and performance of religious obligations was concentrated in the hands of the bhattarakas. Specially trained students directly helped them.

But in course of time bhattarakas started to claim divine power, and came in conflict with one another, dragging in this enmity the groups, led by them and gradually exhausted their authority. Manifestations of dissatisfaction with the power of bhattaraka began. Thus the sub-sect of Digambaras *viz.* terapanthi appeared in the beginning of the eighteenth century in the form of a group, expressing its protest against this dominance.[9]

Side by side with the temple—priests there is a chief village priest—gramopadhyaya in each Jain village. He as well as all the other priests—non-ascetics—can marry. But the head priest of the district—dharmadhikari—is an ascetic and all the priests of this district are subordinate to him.

All the priests and heads of the castes must see whether the members of the community follow the correct mode of life and observe the correct conduct. Great attention is paid to correct conduct, since it must ensure perfection of the soul on its path to salvation. The conduct of ascetics must be perfect –'*sakala*' and such perfection is not demanded of a layman (the mode of their conduct is called *vikala*).

Every Jain believes that his life consists of various stages of existence of his bodily envelops and he must rationally satisfy the requirements of his body in conformity with each stage.

Entering into marriage is fully obligatory for all except ascetics. Marriages of Jains take place according to the selection by the parents, as is common with the members of other religious communities in India.

It was prescribed in ancient times, in conformity with the Jain philosophy, to give the daughter in marriage, soon after attaining puberty, since unproductivity is tantamount to murder and this stands in contrast with the doctrine of non-violence. That is why, child marriage was widespread in the community. such marriages were stopped comparatively recently, after the Sarda Act in India about instituting criminal proceedings against persons guilty of child marriage adopted in 1931 by the British administration was brought strictly in operation.

Special religious ceremonies are performed in connection with various incidents in life. Marriage is the most serious and important step in the life of a Jain and is accompanied by many *rites.* As distinct from Hindus, Jains do not consider marriage a god-pleasing act but a feature of service to society, since people who do not marry are subjected to all sorts of temptations. They remain childless, which undermines the principles of society's life.

As distinct from Hindus, Jains do not consider that it is preferable to have only sons who are supposed to perform funeral ceremonies, since they do not prescribe sacrificial offerings to the spirits of the ancestors and do not regard the cult of the ancestors as a path towards liberation of the soul.

The Jain canonical books do not support the prescriptions regarding marriage *rites.* That is why these *rites* widely depend on local customs.

If Hindus acknowledged eight forms of marriage, described in the 'Laws of Manu' (brahma, daiva, arsha, prajapatya, asura, gandharva, rakshasa and paishacha), the Jains regard only the first four forms as acceptable, because these marriages take place with the consent of parents of the bridegroom and the bride. The Jains consider remaining four forms of marriage sinful, since the gandharva form of marriage takes place only with mutual consent of the young and the remaining three forms are connected with '*dahej*' (bride-price) or with her forceful abduction (*rakshasa*). However, in ancient times, *rakshasa* form of marriage was widespread amongst Jains, from which once more one can venture to reflect upon the initial connection of this religion with non-Aryan peoples.

Most often marriages of brahma and prajapatya forms mean handing over of the bride to the bridegroom by her father in the presence of witnesses.

In the south of India, cross-cousin marriage is preferred and the very best form of it is the marriage with the daughter of mother's brother, while in the north cross-cousin marriages are not recommended and not practiced.

Until recently the form of marriage, in which there is exchange of sisters was widely prevalent, but with the spread of western education it is almost forgotten, as it is at variance with the interests of girls.[10]

Amongst almost all the families dowry is given for the daughter but among the lower castes of Jains, the asura form—a marriage with '*dahej*' (bride-price—this form is often met with also among lower castes of Hindus) is practiced.

All marriage negotiations must be confirmed by the panchayat of the caste.[11]

In general outlines the marriage *rites* of all the Jains are similar.

Usually a month before the marriage, betrothal takes place. On that day the father of the bride presents gifts to the father of the bridegroom in the presence of witnesses. Soon after this, the father of the bridegroom gives ornaments as gifts to the bride. On the marriage day both the fathers ask all those present whether they agree with the proposed marital union. Then the father of the bride joins the young people couple's hands asking them to observe all the precepts of the faith. As with Hindus, the marriage *rite* ends with the couple passing seven times round the holy fire[12] and during this time, the couple takes an oath to lead a highly moral life and to be friendly. After completing the last of the seven circle, the marriage is considered to have been performed. This ceremony also indicates that the marriage is indissoluble. Marriage ceremony takes place everywhere in the home of the bride.

Polygamy is not rejected in Jainism but is very rarely found at present. While judging from references to this custom in Jain texts, it can be said that earlier it was much widespread. Usually the reason for bringing a second wife in the house is childlessness of the first wife or lack of vitality of her children. But her consent for her husband's second marriage while she is living is necessary. There are practically no divorces, though the usual right allows divorce, provided either of the couple detects secret defect of the other. Only in the saitavala and bogara castes in the south, divorces can be effected more or less freely.

As a whole, the position of women in the Jain community is never humiliating and although the fuels regarding their entry into nuns' order are stricter than those for men, it is considered all the same that women can even become Tirthankars and preaches of the faith (Digambaras consider that the 19th Tirthankar Malli was a woman).

In the sphere of education, chances for both boys and girls are almost equal, although girls are brought up more as housewives and would be mother than as specialists in some sphere of social activity.

It is worth emphasising that widows have the right to inherit husband's property—a fact testifying to the preservation by the Jains of the survivals of the high social position of women. According to Jain law, a widow has a right to inheritance, even though sons are born in marriage (there is no such right in Hinduism) and even the division of children's portions depends on the desire of the widow.[13]

Jain religion prescribes performance of various ceremonies in the course of family life, directed to ensure satisfactory conception, normal development of focus and satisfactory birth. Not earlier than twelve days after its birth, the child is named and special ceremonies are performed on this occasion. Special *rites* are also performed on the day on which the child starts to sit, on the day when it is given solid food for the first time, on the first birthday and on the day of commencing learning (at the age of 5). At the age of 8, children pass through the ceremony of dedication in the temples (this *rite* does not exist in Gujarat) and holy threads are placed through the shoulders of the children. This is also done amongst higher Hindu castes. The completion of learning at the age of 14 to 16 is also observed by special *rite.* After this, they are ready for marriage.

After having married, every Jain is obliged to think of good earnings, so as to support his family, to support the community, to help monks and to engage in philanthropy. This is considered as one of the reasons for engaging themselves in trade and enterprises.

After fulfilling all the obligations of family life, the head of the family passes through the *rite* of dedication to asceticm and after leaving home, can lead the mode of life of an ascetic, performing various rites and ceremonies prescribed in the holy book *Adi Purana* (ninth century A.D.).

For the Digambaras fulfillment of 53 *rites,* or passing through 53 stages are prescribed. Death and access to heaven and descent on the earth are considered such stage, which will enable a Jain to be born as a would be Trithankar and to gradually turn into arhata and secure full liberation—*Moksha.* Svetambaras, in conformity with the holy book *Achharadinakara* (beginning of sixteenth century) must pass only 16 such stages, the last amongst which is death.

Digambaras and Svetambaras burn the bodies of the dead, bathing and then wrapping them in new clothes before burning. The ashes are prescribed to be thrown in water, as in the case with Hindus. The nearest relatives of the dead are considered 'impure' for ten days.

There are no funeral ceremonies amongst the Jains of the north and the south but in Karnataka those ceremonies are performed one month in a year. In general, the Jain law prescribes mourning the death of an ascetic for not more than a minute of Kshatriya not more than five days, of Brahmin not more than 10 days, of Vaishya not more than 12 days, and of Shudra not more than 15 days.

All these *rites* are performed in different regions of India with different degree of relativity, since for the most past, these *rites* were introduced in Jain practice in medieval period and were borrowed mainly from Hinduism.

Jains are liable to expulsion from the community for committing murder, adultery, falsehood, stealing and for amorous affairs with non-Jains.

Jains ascetics must lead the life of a wanderer, not living in one place for more than a month (only in rainy seasons they can live in one place up to four months). They must move about only on foot and only during daylight. In the dark period of the day and night they must not walk and must not eat also, because being unable to see, they may crush or swallow some insect.

Amongst Digambaras, ascetics are divided in three classes, anuvrata, mahavrata and nirvana. To be an anuvrata, it is necessary to leave the family, to clean-shave the head, to give up holy threads and live at the temple. An anuvrata must dress himself in clothes of saffron colour and must always carry with him earthen vessel for alms. While moving about, he must sweep the road before him with a bunch of peacock feathers (so as not to crush some insects).

The mahavrata ascetics may wear only loin-cloth. The hair on his head are pulled out from their roots by his pupils. He must eat rice only in a day on his palm.

The nirvana ascetic must be always nude, eat rice, placed in his palm by somebody and must not move after sunset.[14] His hair is also pulled out from the roots by his pupils (for this custom, even the Buddhists ridiculed Jains, saying that they thus violate their own concept of not subjecting living beings to evil and pain).

Svetambara ascetics differ in that they wear white dress, bind their mouths with stripes (according to one explanation, so as not to swallow some insect, according to the others, so as not to profane air with their breath) and carry in their hands whisks on sticks to sweep the road. Monks and nuns must have their hair pulled out.

They must feed themselves on alms. Moreover, they must not ask for alms and wait until given voluntarily (they called this means of collection of alms, 'madhukari'). By this term they mean, they treat themselves like bees, which take very little honey without depriving the flowers of it, and yet finally gather enough quantity for themselves.

Members of Shudra Caste cannot be ascetics.

Jainism does not prescribe ceremonial purification from sins, as is done in Hinduism. That is why Jains must avoid sin in the strictest manner. Inasmuch as causing harm to living beings is regarded as the greatest sin, Jains are prescribed strict observance of extreme caution in all their work, especially household work, such as chopping wood, sweeping floor, cleaning vegetables, cleaning hearths etc.

Not only ascetics but many laymen also filter water through cloth, so as not to swallow even the minutes living beings, which may turn out in it and they do not move about with the coming of darkness.

Notes and References

1. H. Jacobi considers that the division took place in the second century after Mahavir's death (H. Jacobi, *Jaina Sutras,* Part I p. XXXV).
2. V.A. Sangave, *op. cit.,* pp. 54-65,398.
3. J. Nehru, *Discovery of India.*
4. V.A. Sangave, *op. cit.,* pp. 75-76.
5. *Ibid.,* p. 91.
6. Ch. Krause, *The Social Atmosphere at Present Jainism.*
7. V.A. Sangave, *op. cit.,* p. 110.
8. *Ibid.,* p. 111.
9. *Ibid.,* p. 292.
10. *Ibid.,* p. 163.
11. *Ibid.,* p. 165.
12. In so far as Jainism does not prescribe worship of fire, several scholars consider that this *rite* was borrowed from Hinduism (M. Mackenzie, *Accounts of the Jains*).
13. V.A. Sangave, *op. cit.,* p. 192.
14. M. Mackenzie, *Accounts of the Jains.*

11 LITERATURE AND ART OF THE JAINS

The most ancient works of Jain literature, which are ascribed to Mahavira, were written in Ardhamagadhi language. This was '*prakrit*' (*e.g.*, popular, spoken language) of eastern Gangetic regions, a language of Indo-Aryan groups, a language of Aryans which had spread out in the environment of local Kshatriyas, and later of wider strata of population.

It is not known to us in which language Mahavira preached and to what extent Ardhanmagadhi had spread in ancient Bihar in the middle of the 1st millennium B.C. The written works of Jain literature appeared much later.

According to a legend, Mahavira expounded his sermons orally and his nearest followers (*ganadharas*) copied down his sermons, giving them the form of books (*ganipitaka*). On the basis of these books special teachers (*Upadhyaya*) taught the whole order of Shramanas.[1] According to another legend of the Jains, the sermons of Mahavira were understood by all the people, irrespective of the language which they spoke.

Jains highly value Ardhamagadhi as the language of their holy writings and study it. Many Jain works—literary, philosophical or scientific—were written in Sanskrit. Jain inscriptions dated second century A.D. in the so called hybrid Sanskrit, representing a mixture of local colloquial dialect and Sanskrit, have been found in Mathura. Literary Sanskrit partially stands as a language of Jain writings only from the middle of the 1st millennium A.D. As a result of its fusion with central Indian dialects, a special variety of Sanskrit—the Jain Sanskrit[2] has developed.

To the extent to which Jains settled in various regions of India, they used the language of these regions. The Apabhransha language, which are closer to new Indian analytical languages that the ancient Indian inflicted languages occupy a significant place in the much later Jain literature. In the second millennium A.D., Jain literature appeared mainly in new Indian languages, since Jains always strived to popularise their teachings amongst wide mass of people, who did not know Sanskrit. The Jain literature not only developed in Indo-Aryan languages, but in Dravidian (mainly in Kannada) also in as much as thousands of Jains lived there and biggest monasteries and temples are situated there.

The religious-philosophical terminology of Jain literature is traced back to Indo-Aryan terms. Uptill now no research is made regarding manifestation and reconstruction of the ancient strata of the languages of Jain canonic books. That is why it is not possible to say anything about the real connection, existing between the Indo-Aryan group and the other groups and about the manner in which the process of the forcing out of the ancient vocabulary by the Sanskrit and Ardhamagadhi vocabularies took place.

Accepting the then existing tradition, Mahavira left his pupils—*Ganadharas*, 14 books or sections as—puvva (*purva*)—containing the principles of religion. Six generation of *Ganadharas* remembered them by heart and later, when under the reign of Chandragupta Maurya, a big group of Jain monks headed by Bhadrabahu left for the south (it is considered that the reason for this was a long famine, sweeping the land of Magadha), only one monk named Sthulabhadra, who remembered all the *puvvas* remained back. Then an all Jain Synod was called in the city of Pataliputra and a canon was formed for the first time which is known as '*Siddhanta*' or '*Agama*'. The first 11 parts or *Angas* form its base. It is considered that the 14 *puvvas* which were committed to memory were brought in the 12th *Anga*, which got the name of *Ditthivaya* (*Drishtivada*). But later, the initial *Ditthivaya* was lost and what was preserved was a record of 14 *puvvas* of the

4th Anga.[3] There are in all 45 parts in the canon; 11 *angas*, 12 *upangas*, 10 *painnas* (which are considered to be mixed texts of various origins). 6 *chhedasutras*, 4 *mulsutras* 3 and 4 independent texts.

Bhadrabahu, who after his return from the south did not acknowledge the canon, allegedly wrote '*Kalpasutra*' (which is a part of the fourth *chhedasutra*).

Having returned from the south the monks saw that much had changed in their absence and that the rest had forgotten the prohibition of not wearing dress and not moving about in white clothes and that the canon had been composed without the participation of the Bhadrabahu and his associates. Then the community was split into Digambaras and Svetambaras,[4] and Digambaras refused to acknowledge the canon, declaring that all real holy texts were forgotten.

With the passing of time, the canon of *Siddhanta* was partly forgotten and partly modified in the process of the spread of Jainism in India. Then a new Synod was convened in the town of Vallabhi (Gujarat) in the middle of the fifth century A.D. and the canon was re-constituted.

The canonic text contains both prose and verses. The metrics in all the early Jain texts is not vedic but fold-metrics. The Aryan metrics is very rarely found in the texts in Ardhamagadhi.[5] The first *Anga,* in which the rules of life and conduct of Jains is described is considered to be the most ancient.[6]

Sharp polemics with the Brahmins and satirical attacks on their teaching form the characteristic feature of canonic texts, reflecting hostile relations with the representatives of Vedic cults. An extract from the 3rd *Anga* '*Suyagadangi*' (1.7) can serve as an example of such sort of texts: If it is true that it is possible to secure perfection by means of baths in cold water, then frogs, tortoises and serpents reach high perfection, and if water washes away wicked acts, then it must wash away the kind acts also. Brahmins believe that they reach perfection by daily enkindling fire, but if so, smiths and other similar handicraftsmen must reach the highest holiness.[7]

The themes of Indian epics are also found in Jain literature. For example, there is a legend about Draupahi, the wife of the five Pandavas and about her polyandric marriage, in the 6th *Anga*.

The 6th Anga contains a legend about Krishna, about the destruction of his kin and the attack on his city—Dwarka. All this has been described as in *Mahabharat* but Krishna himself is described as a Jain—a circumstance, again reminding us of the known interlacing of Krishnaism and Jainism.

Interesting narration about the unsuccessful and unhappy rebirths of a human being as result of the law if *Karma* appears in the 11th *Anga*.

Exposition of scientific views on the questions of astronomy, geography, cosmogony, science of conception of time, etc. is found in the *upangas*. Also the principles of architecture, planning of cities and decoration of buildings are laid down there. Music, dance, art, erotics, methods of teaching actors etc. are also described. All this creates before us a picture of ancient Indian society.

'*Kalpasutra*' is one of the latest parts of the canon but it is revered by the Jains as the highest of all the parts. It consists of three sections : the life of 24 Tirthankars is described in the first, different groups in the community and their leaders in the second (inscription of first century A.D. remind of these leaders as historical personalities) and the third contains the rules of the conduct of ascetics.

Mulsutras contain, interesting material—fables, parables, and dialogues of ascetics, in which disputes with Brahmins are carried and their ideals are subverted.

Very little is known about the canon it Digambaras. I. Minayev observed that they took an hostile attitude towards Europeans and did not show their books to anybody,[8] but it is known that their canon is also divided in 12 *Angas*, though it is noticed from its contents that it differs from the canon of Svetambaras.

Collection of stories (often composed according to the principle of 'story of set frame ') is interesting in non-canonical literature. One comes across themes of different episodes in those stories. A peculiar form if given to these and all other themes to show therefrom how conversion to Jainism facilitates moral correction of man. The most known collections are : '*Kathakosha*' (eleventh- twelfth century, the author unknown), '*Kathakosha*' containing 500 stories written by Shubhashilagami (fifteenth century) '*Kathamahodadhi*' by the famous Jain writer Somachandra (fifteenth century) and '*Katharatnakara*' by Hemavijaya (seventeenth century).

The following story would serve as a model of the stories appearing in such collections (eleventh to twelfth cetury).

A girl had a wicked stepmother, who compelled her to do all sorts of heavy work. Once while she was grazing her cow, she fell fast asleep. A black serpent, who was followed by a hunter of serpents awakened her and requested her to save him. The girl hid the serpent and he promised her by way of gift that he would fulfill any desire of hers, for her asking. Then the girl requested him to create shade above her, so that she could hide her cow, from the sun. The serpent created a shady garden all around by his power of magic and from that time it went wherever the girl went. Once she saw in the garden a young king, who fell in love with her and decided to marry her. Knowing this, her stepmother started machinations to substitute her own daughter, but the serpent smashed all these machinations and helped the kind girl to secure her happiness.[9] This story with a moral calls upon people to observe the doctrine of ahimsa.

There are many stories about the life of Tirthankars and other holies, whom the Jains worship. Such stories are called '*Charitra*' or '*Charita*' which is a universal literacy term in Indian literature for this genre. The widely known *charita* is a work of Jain monk. Hemachandra, who was a distinguished religious worker, scholar and politician of the twelfth century. The work is called *Trishashti _ShalakaPurushacharita* (life of 63 best persons).

Hemchandra wrote the treatise *Yogashastra* for the ruler Kumarapala, which praises Jainism and fiercely attacks Hinduism as an amoral, unjust religion, which does not know the real doctrine of *ahimsa*.[10]

There is also another type of such stories, which is called '*Prabandha*'. They describe the lives of distinguished monks and laymen. This literature contains many interesting testimonies to the life of the representatives of various strata of the society. Such stories were composed by both Svetambaras and Digambaras.

Jain prose usually alternates with insertions in verses (this is an ancient principle of compositions in prose in the whole of India).

Yashustiluka written by Somadeva, a Digambara, in the tenth century is a famous story in prose and poetry. Its theme is also intended to propagate the omnipotence of Jainism. It tells about the king of Maridatta, who once decided to sacrifice a girl a boy from the Jain community but suddenly thought that they may be the children of his own sister, who had become a Jain nun leaving her family. After inquiries, it was revealed that, that was exactly so. The children narrated the story of their previous births from which it became clear that all the great poets, such as Vyasa, the author of *Mahabharata*, Kalidasa, Bana and others treated Jainism with deep reverence. Startled by what he learnt, the king became a Jain.

Poetry occupies an important place in Jainism. Many religious-lyrical verses, known as *stotras* were composed in Sanskrit. However, many others were also composed in *Prakrit* and in new Indian languages. Various miracles which ensured conversion of people into Jainism, are described in those *stotras*. Such polemics with Brahmins (for example, in the poem *Subhashita Ratna Samdha*–collection of marvellous treasures of speech) are contained in the poetic expositions of Jain ethics, especially in the works of Digambaras-poets. The author of *Subhashita Ratna Samdha*, Amitagati, also composed other works, which contain dogmatic disputes with Brahmins and sharp criticism of their morals, rules of conduct, god-worship etc.

Anthologies of Jain poems and collections of aphorisms were also composed. Out of the latter, the most widely known are the *Gothakosha* by Munichandra Suri (twelfth century) and Gathasahasri by Samayasunder (seventeenth century). They are valuable because they are great stories of ancient aphorisms and apophthegms in verses. The following lines can well serve as specimen of the aphorisms in these collections :

One can never walk along two roads simultaneously,

One cannot sew with a needle whose both ends are sharpened,

One cannot simultaneously accommodate within oneself sinful joy and the path of salvation.

Many literary works of Jains deal with the question of religious dogmas, philosophy, ethics, grammar, astronomy, cosmogony etc. This form of literature is supplemented at present by new treatises and discourses by Jain monks-scholars.

Saddarshana Samuchhaya (ninth century) by Haribhadra, is one of the most remarkable old treatises on religion. In this book the author makes an attempt to put an end to the enmity which had flared between the sects and to convince people that one must not blindly reject everything that disagrees with their views and that it is necessary to search for rational essence in every religion, including Hinduism. Only thus can they aspire to comprehend reality.

The book *Jivaviyara* (tenth century) by Shantisuri is also interesting. All the beings, living on the earth and their paths of rebirths are described in this book. The level of development of various sciences of that time—botany, zoology and geography is reflected in this book. The book contains interesting myths also.

The Jain teachers paid much attention to the spread of religious education among the members of their community. This was attempted not only through oral sermons and readings of canonical texts (to popularise the texts, simplified stories were composed for laymen) but also through special illustrations to these texts, carved on slabs of stones.

In is said in *Anuyogadwara Sutra* that cognitions given to the members of the community were divided in earthly ("*laukika*) cognitions and religious philosophical ('lokottara') cognitions. All the sciences belong to the first and teachings about discipline and obligations of members of the community and especially of the monk belong to the second category. Also all questions connected with religious teachings and philosophical conceptions belong to the latter.

Every Jain desiring to go through learning had to be initiated in learning by the mentor, *Upadhyaya,* and then had to learn from the teacher, *Acharya.* This system exists even at present. Many educational and explanatory texts were prepared and essence of Jainism was expounded in a simple way so as to be easily understood.

All the Jain literature was created to propagate Jainism and was above all subjected to this aim. Hence wide use of motifs of folklores and folktales was made in the literature. Folk languages and dialects were used precisely for this reason. Usually merchants, handicraftsmen and also *shudras* appear as characters in Jain literary works. The literature received great popularity due to these reasons.

Jains contributed a great deal to the development of literature in dialects and stood out to some extent as forerunner of those educators, who fought in later Middle Ages against the dominance of Brahmanic language—Sanskrit—and defended the dialects. Creations of Jain writers played a great role especially in the development of literature in Dravidian languages. South Indian writers narrated and developed the themes of the literary works of the Jains in many of their own works.

In modern times, popular propagandistic literary works are produced. They expound philosophy and ethics of Jainism.

Presently the famous written sermons and verses of

Acharya Shri Tulsi, the leader of terapanthi sub-sect of the Svetambaras are much in use.

Art

The Jain community also contributed to Indian art. Having started from the second half of the last millennium B.C. Jains created beautiful and exceedingly plastic statues of their Tirthankars.

Two such images carved out of stone were found during excavations in Lohanipura (not far from Patna). They belong to the epoch of Mauryas (fourth to third century B.C.) One of them is a male torso, done in strict realistic manner and is magnificently polished. It is considered to the most ancient iconsgraphical sculptural image.[11]

Note should be taken of the remarkable similarity of this torso with the small torso from polished sandstone, found in Harappa. Both the sculptures portray nude males. Notwithstanding the fact that the hands, heads and feet of the sculptures are broken off, it is seen that the portrayed personages stand fully erect. The holies are portrayed by the Jains in that posture which is called *kayotsarga,* and it shows the personage at the moment when the soul leaves the body, *i.e.* at the moment of conversion into a *Siddha*. Does not this clear-cut similarity once again confirm the belief that some ideas of the people of Mohenjo-daro and Harappa subsequently appeared in Jainism.

There are no known portrayals of nude male figures standing erect, in Indian plastics, except those of the Tirthankars. That is why we can consider the above referred images, statues as a link connecting the most ancient stage of development of sculpture in 3rd-2nd millennium B.C. with the sculpture of the next 20-25 centuries.

The search for a direct link between the above referred statues enables us to presume that other forms of plastics of Indus Valley civilisation found their continuation in the sculptures and reliefs, done in India from the fourth-third century B.C. and in the articles of handicraftsmen (small metallic plastics, earthen figurines, children's playthings etc.) Fixed, unchanging form is a characteristic of the Jain sculpture throughout the history of Jain art.

The Jain as well as Buddhist architecture at the early stage of its development is represented by cave-temples. The most ancient temples are those in Bihar, dated fourth-second centuries B.C. and in Orrisa and Gujarat, dated second century A.D. The upper arches of these big and deep caves support the columns (usually smooth). At some places the outside wall is decorated with simple reliefs portraying the figure of nude Tirthankars and the branch of the holy tree 'Bo'.

There are many cave-monasteries especially in Orissa, in the Udaygiri and Khandagiri mountains. Images of other ancient religious symbols, such as mutli-headed serpents, tridents, swastika, women pouring water from the pitcher (apparently this symbol is connected with the cult of water) are also seen in those monasteries. One also comes across multi-figure compositions on friezes, portraying scenes from Jain legends.[13]

The presence of great number of cave-temples and cave-monasteries in Jainism and Buddhism testifies to the great antiquity of traditions, adopted or probably preserved by these religions. The Aryan cults could not have been connected from time immemorial with cave-prayer-halls, owing to the climatic conditions of those places, where those cults had formed and developed. In India, cave happen to be beautiful shelters from heat and rain, and even the extremely laborious process of carving artistic caves in the rocks could not prevent them from creating those shelters.

Can this not be the reason for not coming across temple structures in the ruins of the cities of the Indus Valley? It is not possible that the prayer services were directed by monks, living in the mountains and sheltering themselves from the sun and the rains in the caves? Coming to the city, they possibly gave sermons directly in the houses of their followers, as the Jain sermons directly in the houses of their followers, as the Jain *Acharyas* often do in present day India.

The Jains also erected stupas, cylindrical structures with arched tops, standing on quadratic platform. The Jain stupas are preserved on plates (beginning of our era) on which images of Jeenas were carved. Judging from these plates, one can see that the foundation of the stupas were ornamented with reliefs, columns were erected along the sides of the stupas and sculptural figures were planted.[14]

Jain stupas of our era were discovered in Bihar, Central India, and in the north-west (in Taxila). Cave-temples (significantly less than Buddhist because Jainism did not call upon people to have mass prayers) were erected in various regions of India, depending on the spread of Jainism. The temples in Badami and in Aikhol (District Bijapur) in the region of Khandesh, near Nasik and in other places are also well known. These temples are dated sixth-seventh centuries A.D. They were created in a great number and later on they were dressed with rich reliefs and sculptures.

Jains created monolithic ground temples, carving them in rock tracts. These temples have all the characteristics of so-called Dravidian style—stepped raising of roofs, crowned with circular screws, abundant columns with figures and sculptures, ornamental walls, etc. Majority of Jain temples are concentrated in the south, in the region of Khasan in the State of Mysore. Shravanbelgol is the centre of Jainism in the south. Besides temple buildings which are called *'basti'*, here are many *'bettas' i.e.* enclosed grounds, in the middle of which, carved images of Jain holies are raised. Several of these carved images reach tremendous size, as, for example, the statue of Gomateshwara (who is considered to be the son of Rishabha, the first Tirthankar), carved from a rock in 980-990 and reaching almost 20 metres are erected in the south Kanara district.

The temples of the tenth century in Central India—in Khajuraho—are also famous. Here the style of decorative carving was already taking shape.

Towards the eleventh-thirteenth centuries, the style of Jain temples fully blossomed in west India. By this, a complex of temples on Mount Abu in the south of Rajasthan was built. These temples are famous throughout the world. They are dressed in rich and refined carving on marble, that no other temple elsewhere can be a match for them.

There is a famous monument in colossal relief, carved out in the fifteenth century on the surface of a rock in Gwalior. Many places in Gujarat are also famed for temples which are beautifully and lavishly ornamented. There are whole towns of temples in Kathiawar and Palitana, which, along with the temples on Mount Abu are the centres of mass pilgrimages (and also tourist centres). Erection of temple-cities is a distinctive feature of Jain art. This feature had developed in Jain art much more forcefully than in the art of Hinduism.

There are also famous temples richly ornamented by carved images and sculptures (for example the temple built in 1840 by the head of the trade of the town, Nagar Seth in Ahmedabad, where many prosperous Jain merchants and usurers lived.)

An overwhelming majority of temples are built in the name of Tirthankars but there are also temples of messengers goddesses of Tirthankars, where usually a big statue of the head goddesses of the temple, small statues of the remaining 23 goddesses (or their portraits in relief) ad the statue of the Tirthankar, who commands the goddess are found.

The so-called Jain tower or the tower of Victory in Chitore is very popular. It was created in the twelfth century. The whole tower is covered with carved ornaments and several hundred figures of nude Tirthankars are portrayed on it.

The symbolical portrayals of the river Ganges and the river Jamuna in the form of beautiful women is widespread in the Indian sculpture. This has found place in the sculptural ornamentation of Jain temples as well.

One constantly comes across the portrayals of Jeenashwars in the sculpture, in reliefs, in frescoes and in miniatures. They are portrayed only in two postures, either in the posture of a nude person standing erect, or a person sitting with legs tucked in, in the posture of a *yogi*. The latter posture is also well known to us from the seal of the Indus Valley. There the person sits in this posture with horned headgear and surrounded by animals. This figure is usually interpreted as ancient portrayal of God Shiva.

If we juxtapose this posture which is called *yoga* posture or *yogas* in India, with the fact that the most ancient philosophical work of the Jains, the'*Book of Wisdom of Arhatas*' ascribed to Rishabha himself was called '*Yoga*' and also that this posture is the classical echelon of the posture of Tirthankars for 25 centuries (and possibly much longer) then all this brings back to our minds the thought that there is possibly ancient connection between Jainism and the Indus civilisation. It is apparent that the teaching of *yoga* and this posture connected with it penetrated in the faiths of later period and Buddha and many Hindu gods were portrayed in this posture. This posture is most popular with all the ascetics and hermits in India.

All the Tirthankars are portrayed in an almost uniform manner in the Jain temples and it is possible to distinguish them practically from only special signs, usually placed on the pedestals of these sculptures and sometimes from the special colour of the portrayals. Thus,

(1) Rishabha has yellow colour, and the sign is an elephant.

(2) Ajita—yellow colour, sign, an elephant.

(3) Sambhava—yellow colour, sign a horse.

(4) Abhinandan—sign a monkey.

(5) Sumati—yellow colour, sign a bird.

(6) Padmaprabha—red colour, sign, a lotus.

(7) Suparshva—golden colour, sign a swastika.

(8) Chhandraprabhe—while colour, sign, a half-moon.

(9) Pushpadanta—white colour, sign, a makara.[16]

(10) Sitala —golden colour, sign a sitala (four-petalled rosette).

(11) Sreyan—golden colour, sign, a rhinoceros (according to another tradition, an eagle).

(12) Vasupujya—red colour, sign, a buffalo.

(13) Vimala—golden colour, sign, a wild boar.

(14) Ananta—yellow colour, sign, a falcon (with Svetambaras) or a bear (with Digambaras).

(15) Dharma—yellow colour, sign, a vajra.

(16) Shanti—yellow colour, sign, an antelope.

(17) Kunthu—yellow colour, sign, a goat.

(18) Ara—yellow colour, sign, Nandavarta (cryptogram in the centre of which swastika is portrayed, but according to another tradition his sign is fish).

(19) Malli—blue colour, sign, a jar (Digambaras consider that Malli was a woman)

(20) Munisuvrata—black colour, sign, a tortoise.

(21) Adinath or Naminath —yellow colour, sign, a blue lotus.

(22) Neminath or Arishtenemi—dark colour with red shade sign, a shell.

(23) Parshva—blue colour, sign, a serpent.

(24) Mahavira or Vardhamana—golden colour, sign, a lion.[17]

It is difficult to explain the symbolism of these colours and signs at the present level of study of Jainism. The suggestion that there is a connection between these signs and totemic representations of pre-Aryan peoples of India (these representations are preserved by many peoples even to this day) appears most probable. *Devatas*–various Hindu gods are usually portrayed round the statues of Tirthankars, and also on their pedestals. Such statues are placed in the cave-temples and ground temples in niches. Very big statues of *Siddhas* to whom people come to worship are placed on open grounds, as has already been mentioned. There is a *siddachakra*—the holy wheel—in every temple of Svetambaras. This is a seven—edged plate, on which holy words are inscribed and five figures of Parameshthians *i.e.* people in the five stages of salvation are portrayed. Often the engraving on these plates reaches artistic perfection.

Jain holies were also portrayed in bronze, in the form of small statuettes, or big figures. But this branch of the art was not as strongly developed as, for example, the bronze sculpture of the Hindu or Buddhists. The portraits of Tirthankars are made from various material—gold, silver, and precious stones.

Jain paintings had remarkably developed. As is common with all Indian painting, it starts with frescos. The frescoes in Jain temples in Sittanavasala near Tanjore (Madras) dated seventh century A.D. are much more famous than other Jain frescoes of the early medieval period.

Here, the rocky surface was at first covered with a 0.51 cm. layer of pounded stones, clay, cowdung and rice husks, as is the case with all the wall-paintings in India. Later, a thin layer of white gypsum was superimposed and the painting was done on the moist surface of this white gypsum.

A big picture on the ceiling of the temple in Sittanavasala is well preserved. A magic lake with blooming lotuses and with girls taking bath (apparently nymphs—*apsaras*) is portrayed on the ceiling. Also cows and elephants are standing and swans are swimming in the picture. This picture shows perfect skill in workmanship.

Paintings on the walls and ceilings of temples in Shravanbelgol, Kanchipuram and Tirumalai (Madras) and in a number of other places are distinguished for high workmanship and skill.

Jain miniature developed mainly in the west, in Gujarat. Here are very slender multi-coloured illustrations to the Jain texts, and mainly to Kalpasutra, describing the life of Mahavir and other Tirthankars and also illustrations to Kalikacharya Katha, in which disputes of Jain monk Kalika with unjust ruler Gardabhilla are described.

There is a common feature of the manner of portrayal from which it is possible to distinguish Jain miniature of Gujarat. The artists drew human face in such a manner that three-fourths of it was visible. The eye on the distant half of the face was always drawn fully, as on the full-face portrait, but the cheek under it was not drawn at all, with the result that this eye looks as if hanging in the air.

The Gujarat school of miniature blossomed in the fifteenth-seventeenth centuries. During this period, drawings were done on paper but before this, they were done on palm leaves (such a drawing dated thirteenth century is preserved in a temple in Patan).[18]

A distinctive branch of Jain art is the making of wooden utensils for ritual purpose. The author of this book had the opportunity of seeing these articles from near. They are hollowed out and turned by hand from unbroken pieces of wood. Their sides are as the sides of porcelain cups. These tureens are of various capacities and cups and bowls are of various forms. Majority of them are painted red and the outside edge is decorated with narrow strips of black-golden ornament.

The heads of Jain monastery community usually use such utensils for meals. The cooked food is served in big bowls and is distributed from small bowls. Milk and water are also poured out from small bowls.

The paints are durable and such utensils serve their masters for a long time.

As regards artistic handicrafts, Jains have mainly developed jeweller's art. Many Jains are engaged in the trade of gold ornaments and jewellary ornaments and that is why the production of these ornaments is often concentrated in their hands.

II

It has been stated in the last chapter that the greater part of the life of Mahavira as described in the Jaina Granthas is imbued with myths which mar the real value of these works. Some of these myths are rather curious, and a few of them are given below as typical of the rest.

The first of them relates to his previous births. The *Mahavira Purana* gives a long and a cumbrous list of his innumerable previous births with a detailed description of some of them. The value of this description is incomprehensible unless it be only to illustrate the Karma philosophy of the Jains, or it only shows the bitter hatred of Jaina writers towards Brahmans. He is said to have existed even before Swami Adinath. He had the fortune of being the son of Bharata Chakravarti and grandson of Swami Adinath. This made him proud. Through pride he began to preach falsehood, and consequently had to undergo several existences. This myth shows how one is rewarded for the good or the bad acts of his previous births. It may be only to this end that this myth has been connected with the life of so great a personage as Mahavira. The *Kalpa-sutra* on the other hand, says nothing about this. It only asserts that Mahavira, leaving his long and happy divine life, only for the good of the world and the attainment of *Nirvana*, came to this world as a *Tirthankara*, descending from the great Vimana, the all-victorious and all-prosperous Pushpottara, to take the form of an embryo in the womb of his mother. Both the above quoted Granthas state the date of his entering the womb of his mother as the sixth day of the latter half of Ashadha.

The second myth of the transfer of embryo is also connected with this. It runs thus both in the *Acharanga-sutra* and the *Kalpa-sutra*. "Here, forsooth, in the continent of Jambudvipa, in Bharatvarsha, in the southern part of it, in the southern Brahmanical part of the place Kundapura he took the form of an embryo in the womb of Devananda, of the Jalandharayana Gotra, wife of the Brahmana Rishabhadatta, of the Gotra of Kodala....

"Then in the third month of the rainy season, the fifth fortnight the dark (fortnight) of Aswina, on its thirteenth day, while the moon was in conjunction with Uttaraphalguni, after the lapse of eighty-two days, on the eighty-third day current, the compassionate god (Indra) reflecting on what was the established custom (with regard to the birth of the *Tirthankaras*), removed the embryo from the southern Brahmanical part of the place Kundapura to the northern Kshatriya part of the same place, rejecting the unclean matter, lodged the foetus in the womb of Trisala or the Vasishtha Gotra, wife of the Kshatriya Sidhartha, of the Kashyapa gotra, of the clean of Gnatris, and lodged the foetus of the Kshatriyani Trisala in the womb of Devananda of the Jalandharayana gotra.....

In connection with this story Professor Jacobi remarks :

"This legend is rejected as absurd by the Digambaras, but the Shvetambaras staunchly uphold its truth. As it is found in the *Akaranga*, the *Kalpa-sutra*, and many other books, it cannot be doubted that it is very old. However, it is not at all clear for what reason so absurd a legend could have been invented and have gained currency. Yet I may be allowed to offer my opinion on this dark point. I assume that Siddhartha had two wives, the Brahmani Devananda, the real mother of Mahavira, and the Kshatriyani Trisala; for the name of the alleged husband of the former, *viz.* Rishabhadatta, cannot be very old, because its Prakrit form would in that case probably be Usabhadinna instead of Usabhadatta. Besides, the name is such as could be given to a Jaina only, not to a Brahmana. I, therefore, make no doubt that Rishabhadatta has been invented by the Jainas in order to provide Devananda with another husband. Now Siddartha was connected with persons of high rank and great influence through his marriage with Trisala. It was, therefore, probably thought more profitable to give out that Mahavira was the son, and not merely the stepson of Trisala, for this reason, that he should be entitled to the patronage of her relations. This story could all the more easily have gained credence as Mahavira's parents were dead many years when he came forward as a prophet. But as the real state of things could not totally have been erased from the memory of the people, the story of the transfer of embryos was invented. The latter idea was not an original conception of the Jainas, but it was evidently borrowed from the Puranic story of the transfer of embryo of Krishna from the womb of Devaki to that of Rohini..."

Now it is certain that this legend is the invention of the author of the *Kalpa-sutra,* but the assumption made by Jacobi to give an explanation of it does not seem to be founded upon sound reason. To assume that Siddhartha had two wives, a Brahmani and a Kshatriyani, and to say that Mahavira was the son of the former is itself incorrect; for a Brahmana girl was not allowed to marry a Kshatriya Jaina. If it had been so, the Jaina law-givers, who have so closely followed the carrier of Mahavira in giving social laws, would not have prohibited intermarriage between a Brahmana girl and a Kshatriya boy. On the other hand, *Mahavira Purana* clearly says that Mahavira was the son of Trisala. If, however, I am allowed to offer my opinion, I will attribute the invention of this legend to the bitter hatred of the Brahmanas by the Jains of those times and to the preference that the Kshatriyas were given over the Brahmanas by the Jaina Acharyas. We have the testimony of a tradition also. It runs thus : "Bhadrabahu, the author of the *Kalpa-sutras,* and his brother Varahamihira, the author of *Brihat-samhita,* were living together in the court of the king Dhruvasena of Gujarat. Both of them were great astrologers. On the birth of a child the king consulted Varahamihira as to the age of the child, and on learning from him that it would live for a long time, he held a *Darbar* in order to celebrate the birth of his child. On seeing that Bhadrabahu was not present in the assembly of his courtiers, he called him and asked to explain the cause of his absence. Bhadrabahu told that he did not like to rejoice for he shall soon have to lament the death of the child after ten days. The king, being very much annoyed with this unexpected reply, sent him to jail, but after ten days the king lost his child, and admiring the foresight of Bhadrabahu, not only liberated him, but gave him a seat near his throne, and turned out Varahamihira."

How far this tradition is true cannot be said, but it shows that Bhardrabahu and Varahamihira were not on good terms and one hated the religion of the other. Now can it not be that Bhadrabahu, out of his hatred for the Brahmanas, might have invented this story of the transfer of embryos? Whatever it may be, it can be safely asserted on the authority of *Mahavira Purana* that Mahavira was the son of Trisala and not of Devananda as Professor Jacobi has assumed. As to his assumption that the story was borrowed from the Puranic story of the transfer of the embryos of Krishna from the womb of Devaki to that of Rohini, it cannot be said whether it were the Jainas or the Brahmanas who borrowed it from the other.

Another myth is that of the sixteen dreams. It is stated that the mother of Mahavira like those of every *Tirthankara* saw sixteen dreams on the night on which Mahavira is believed to have entered the womb of his mother. These dreams were :

1. A fine, enormous elephant, possessing all lucky marks, with strong thighs and four mighty tusks. This was supposed to foretell the birth of a Tirthankara.
2. A tame, lucky bull, of a whiter hue than that of the mass of petals of the white lotus illumining all around by the diffusion of a glory of light. This was supposed to foretell the birth of a great religious preacher.
3. A handsome, handsomely shaped, playful lion, jumping from the sky towards her face. This was supposed to foretell the birth of a child who will be a destroyer of his *karmas* (the enemies) and a possessor of limitless *Veerya*.
4. Shree, or Lakshmi, the goddess of wealth, of famous beauty, with the face of the full moon, on the top of Mount Himavat, reposing on a lotus in the lotus-lake, anointed with the water from the strong and large-trunks of the guardian elephants. This was believed to indicate that the child will be an anointed king.
5. A garland charmingly interwoven with fresh Mandara flowers coming down from the firmament. This meant that the body of the child will be a fragrant one.

6. The bright sun radiating his golden rays in all directions and shedding his lustre in all round Mount Meru. This indicated that the child will be a dispeller of the mass of darkness which is the symbol of ignorance.
7. The cow-milk-white full moon, the lover of Rohini, rising in the heavens and raising the waters of the ocean below. This portended the birth of a great religious preacher.
8. Two fishes, which meant that the child will be a happy one.
9. Two golden and costly vases, filled with pure water and indicating the birth of a child who will be constantly immersed in spiritual meditation.
10. A great lotus lake adorned with water lilies round which the black bees and the mad drones were hovering. This was supposed to foretell that the body of the child will possess all the marks of a perfect being.
11. The milk-ocean, white like the breast of Lakshmi, indicating that the child will be a Kevalin.
12. A costly throne of diamonds and rubies which meant that the child will be a master of the three *lokas*.
13. An excellent celestial abode shining like the disk of the morning sun.
14. The great king of the gods residing below this earth.
15. An enormous heap of jewels resembling Mount Meru and illuminating even the sphere of the sky. This was supposed to foretell the birth of a child who will be a possessor of right knowledge, right intuition and right conduct.
16. A great fire fed with much shining and honey-coloured *ghee* and in vehement motion.

The *Kalpa-sutra* says that a large meeting was convened by the king on this occasion, and learned men were asked to interpret the dreams. But from *Mahavira Purana* we learn that in the morning the queen herself came to the council of the king with all her maids. The king affectionately asked her to take her seat near him on the throne; and then he himself interpreted the dreams.

From these mythical descriptions we proceed to real facts in the life of our Lord Mahavira whose ideal and sublime life is to be written, as far as possible, in the life of each individual.

Notes and References

1. Muni Shri Nagraji, *A Pen-sketch of Acharya Shri Tulsi,* p. 5.
2. V. Ivanov and V. Toporov, *Sanskrit*, p. 27.
3. H. Jacobi, Jaina Sutras, Part I, Introduction, p. XLIV, supposedly assumes that the texts of the *puvvas* were contradictory and became unacceptable in the process of formation of Jain community, and it became necessary to compose a clear and systematized canon.
4. Inscription of first century A.D. show that at that time two communities of Jains were already known and various schools–ganas, existed within these communities (M. Winternitz, Geschishte der Indischen Literatur, p. 294).
5. B. Ch. Law, *India as Described in Early Texts of Buddhism and Jainism,* p. 265.
6. H. Jacobi, *Jaina Sutras,* Part I, Introduction. B. Ch. Law, considered this *Anga* as the earliest testimony to the tenor of life of the nirgrantha sect (B. Ch. Law, *India as Described in Early Texts of Buddhism and Jainism,* p. 268).
7. M. Winternitz, *Geschishte der Indischen Literatur,* p. 299.
8. I. Minayev, *Information About Jains and Buddhists.*
9. Retold from the book *Geschichteder Indischen Literatur,* by M. Winternitz, p. 325.
10. The Svetambara monk must daily read the first four chapters of this book.
11. *Bihar Through the Ages,* p. 251.
12. Walter Ruben also took note of the similarity of the portrayals

of nude : Tirthankars and the above-referred figures from the Indus Valley (W. Ruben, *Uberlegung zur Geschichte der Religion*, p. 226).

13. A.K. Coomaraswamy, *History of Indian and Indonesian Art*, p. 36.
14. *Ibid.*, p. 72.
15. B. Rowland, *The Art and Architecture of India*, plate 81a.
16. Mythological monster portrayed in the form of a crocodile with an upturned nose. Svetambaras consider that crocodile is the sign of Pushpadanta and Digambaras portray a crab as his sign. (P. Thomas, *Epics, Myths, and Legends of India*, p. 194).
17. The list is taken from the books—F. Buchanana, *Particulars of the Jains*, P. Thomas, *Epics, Myths, and Legends of India.*
18. A.K. Coomaraswamy, *op. cit.*, p. 120.

12 PENANCE AND NIRVANA

I

We have now reached the period in the life of Mahavira from which he begins to lead that houseless and hard life of a Jaina Muni in which he had to travel from place to place, except in the rainy season, all the eight months of summer and winter, preaching teaching the people as he travelled, and performing severe bodily mortifications for the destruction of the *karmas* and the attainment of *kevalgyan*. A very interesting and precise description of this part of his life is given in the Jaina Shastras mentioning the places which he visited and where he preached to the people the doctrine of Jainism during the course of his travels through the greater part of India. Though both the sources of our information, the Digambaras and the Svetambaras, declare that he travelled and performed penance for twelve years before the attainment of *Kevalgyan*, yet there is much discrepancy between the accounts given by the two. Thus the *Acharanga-sutra* says that Mahavira, soon after his Diksha of "the Renunciation" and after having formed the resolution of leading a devoted life of a Jaina Muni, neglecting his body, arrived in the village of Kummara, and then began his travels from that place. It does not say anything about the places which he visited. The *Kalpa-sutra* does not mention his first visit to Kummar; but it says that he stayed the first *Chaturmasa* or the rainy season of four months in Asthika-grama, three rainy seasons in Champa and Phristi-champa, and the rest of the eight in Vaisali and Vanijagrama. But this does not contradict the fact of his going to Kummar. It is possible that Mahavira might have first visited Kummar and then commenced his travels beginning with his first rainy season stay at Asthikagrama. Travelling for the Jaina Munis is prohibited for four months of the rainy season for fear of killing the insects and such other small creatures as are seen specially in that season and thereby committing *Hinsa* which is strictly avoided by the Jainas. In compliance with this *Agya* (order) Mahavira had to stay at one place during the rainy season and thus the fact of his staying in different places in different rainy seasons as given by the *Kalpa-sutra* is possible. Let us now see what the Digambara Granthas say about this. In the *Mahavira Purana* we read that he did not attain the fourth *Gyan* just at the time of renunciation. Just after his renunciation he performed constant meditation of six months in which he had to be quite motionless. Still he did not attained the fourth kind of knowledge. He had to undergo bodily mortification several times before he got it. At the end of six months he is said to have gone to a place called Kulpura. Kuladhipa, the ruler of that place paid his respect to his venerable guest; and it is at this place that Mahavira had his first *Purana* or meal at the end of a fast of six months. From this place he went to the city of Dashapura. Kula, the king of that place, came to see him and having gone round him three times and having washed his feet with his own hands offered him milk and rice for his breakfast. Having partaken of his hospitalities, Mahavira returned to the forest. He then visited several places and then began to perform twelve kinds of penances. Through this he obtained eight kinds of *Riddhis* and many kinds of *Siddhis*. There he had to bear the twenty-two Parishahas. He then observed the five *Mahavritas*, the five *Samitis*, the three *Guptees* and the eighty-four *Uttara Gunas*. He again visited several places. Once he went to Ujjain and there began his penance at a cemetery. Here a test of his perseverance was made by a certain Rudra, who, being struck with Mahavira's wonderful power of bearing bodily pain and of forbearance, at last came to him and asked his pardon for the mischief he was intending to him. We shall give this anecdote later on. From Ujjain, Mahavira went to Kaushambi, and then again returned to the forest and entered his self-meditations. It was now that he attained the fourth, the *Manhparyaya Gyan*. Then he is said to have observed the vow of silence for twelve years and to have performed severe penance. This shows that Mahavira performed his penance for twelve years at one place and the above mentioned travels were made before this time. This fact brings us to and unexpected difficulty. We have already learnt that Mahavira renounced the world on the tenth day of the first half of *Magsir* in his thirty-first year *i.e.*, when he was thirty years, seven months and twenty-seven days old. He is then said to have performed penance for six months. So that, before commencing his meditations he was about thirty years and two months old, *i.e.*, he was in his thirty-second year when he began his *Dhyana* for twelve years. This shows that at the time of attaining *Kevalgyan* he was about forty-three years and two months old *i.e.*, he attained *Kevalgyan* in his forty-fourth year. But it is further stated that it was on the tenth day of the latter half of Vaishakha when he was forty-two years old, i.e., he obtained *Kevalgyan* in his forty-third year. Thus there is a difference of about one year between the two computations. Moreover, this does not take into account the time for which he travelled before entering his *Dhyana*. However, this difficulty can be overcome by supposing that Mahavira's renunciation took place in his thirtieth year and not when he was thirty years old. It was what perhaps the Digambara Acharyas meant to in indicate.

Further, we learn from Bhagawati that Mahavira met Gosala two years after his Renunciation at a place called Nalanda, near Rajgriha, and the two ascetics lived together for six years in Paniyabhumi. Now this is not consistent with the facts given above. According to *Kalpa-sutra*, Mahavira went to Paniyabhumi after his obtaining *Kevalgyan* and stayed there only for one rainy season.

There is a further discrepancy between the two authorities about the mode of his life during these years. In the *Kalpa-sutra* it is said that, after his Renunciation, Mahavira, wore clothes for a year and a month, and after that time he walked about naked. On the other hand, *Mahavira Purana* says that he had abandoned the twenty-four Parigra has, and as clothes were one of them, he had to abandon them too.

After the end of his twelve years' penance he obtained *Kevalgyan*. Both the Digambaras and the Svetambaras assert that this took place in his forty-third year on the tenth day of the latter half of Vaishakha near a place called Grimbhakgrama on the northern bank of the river Rijkul not very far from Parashnatha hills. They also say that this took place in the field of a certain farmer Samaga or Samaka. Mahavira at that time was sitting upon a Ratna Shila below a Sal tree in a squatting position with joined heels, exposing himself to the heat of the sun. He had to perform severe meditation there at the end of which, having destroyed the four *Ghatiya karmans*, he reached the highest knowledge and intuition called *Kevala*, which in infinite, supreme, unobstructed, complete and full.

His Travels and Preachings for Thirty Years

We have now reached the end of the second great period in the worldly career of Lord Mahavira. In the beginning of this period of twelve years we found him a *Sanyasi*, disgusted with the world, determined to renounce it and attain the ever-lasting life of bliss and happiness, *Nirvana*, by a constant study of his self and by performing severe bodily mortifications or *Yoga*. At the end of this period we find him in the full realisation of his hope, a Jina or a conqueror of the *Karmas*, the eight great enemies of the soul, and a *kevalin*, that is, an omniscient lord comprehending all objects; he could know all conditions of the world and the thoughts of men. His knowledge pervaded all things; and by reflecting on his self and the world he had reached the highest intuition and knowledge. Such was our Lord Mahavira as we find him in the beginning of the third great period in his life. From this begins the third great act in his life. This period comprises thirty long years of travels and preachings. He having known the great Law, proceeds to teach the same to all the human beings in this world. The whole of this period was spent in travelling and preaching except in the rainy seasons when for fear of killing small creatures and thereby committing *hinsa*, he had to suspend his mission and to pass four months in one place under the patronage of some mighty chief. In fact, it was a life of hard work and severe austerities. He passed it 'in teaching his religious system and organising his order of ascetics,' which as we shall see later on, was patronised by the mighty kings of northern India. Mahavira was convinced of the necessity of his penances in the last twelve years of his life and did not think his years wasted, for he knew that it was through his penances that he had obtained the nine *Labdhis* and the *Ananata Chatushtaya*. It may be remarked here that there is not much difference between the accounts of this period as given by the Digambaras and the Svetambara Acharyas. The difference, if any, is of details rather than that of main outlines. Before commencing his travels there is one fact worthy of note. Soon after his obtaining *Kevalgyan*, Mahavira was visited by Gautama Indrabhuti who became his first pupil and was raised to the position of the head Ganadhara of a Chief Pontiff. His story is one of great interest, and we will give it later on. He followed his master for the last thirty years of his life and obtained *Kevalgyan* at the very time when Mahavira attained *Nirvana*. Mahavira began by first preaching to Gautama, then to the people around him, and then he began his travels.

He travelled through many parts of India, and preached the high doctrines of Jainism and *Nirvana* to people professing different creeds and religions. It was his earnest desire that people should give up their wrong beliefs and follow the true path to happiness. He preached on both the sides of the Ganges. First he preached in Magadha and the country round Kundalpura, where he was received with due greeting. From Magadha he proceeded to Bihar where he visited Shravasti, Vaishasti and many other places. He is said to have extended his travels as far as the foot of the Himalayas. In the *Kalpa-sutra* a list is given containing the names of the places where he passed his rainy seasons. According to that authority "he stayed four rainy seasons in Vaishali and Vanijagrama, fourteen in Rajgriha and the suburb of Nalanda, six in Mithila, two in Bhadrika, one in Alabhika, one in Paniyabhumi, one in Shravasti, and the one and the last in Papa in king Hasthipal's office of the writers." Now we see that some of these names do not occur in the *Mahavira Purana*; but there is not much difference. There it is also mentioned that he travelled and preached throughout the countries of northern India. In Videha he was patronised by Chetaka, the ruling chief of that country. Kunika, the king of Anga, also welcomed the great preacher. He is said to have gone even to Kaushambi. Shataneeka, the ruler of the place, had heard much about his preachings and severe penances. He paid high reverence to the great preacher and entered his holy order. During these thirty years, Mahavira is said to have converted to Jainism Magadha, Bihar, Prayag, Kaushambi, Champapuri, and many other powerful States in the north of India. But the place where he spent a large part of his life and where he was much loved by the people was Rajriha, the then metropolis of Magadha. Shrenika, the powerful king of that place was one of the greatest champions of Jainism and a staunch follower of Mahavira. They are said to have met each other under very auspicious circumstances. When Mahavira went to Rajgriha he put up at Mount Vipulachala in the vicinity of the country. King Shrenika, hearing the happy news of the arrival of the great preacher in his capital, went to see him with all his ministers and whole of his army. He was charmed with the divine splendour of the Lord and of Samosaran or the great religious assemblage. Having paid his due greetings, he took his seat in the gallery reserved for men. He is said to have put sixty thousand questions to Mahavira and all of them were answered by Gautama Indrabhuti at the command of his master. To our great misfortune no account, not even a very small one, has been left of this interesting discussion. Shrenika was satisfied with the answers and entered the holy order of our Lord. It is said that Gautama also related the previous births of Shrenika and his relations.

Some few remarks may be made here upon Mahavira's method of preaching. He did not travel from place to place like an ordinary *Sadhu* unaccompanied by any one. On the other hand he was followed by many men who had entered his order. His order was known as the Samosaran. This consisted of about fourteen thousand *Munis* according to both the Digambaras and the Svetambaras. Wherever they went a magnificent hall of audience was erected for them, containing many galleries for different orders of men. They had among them many Arjikas or nuns too. The pillars of the hall were set with jewels and Mahavira used to sit upon a costly throne of diamonds and rubies and pearls. Such was the Samesaran, they say in which Mahavira used to preach wherever he went.

It is said that Mahavira preached to the people in his *Anakshari* language which was unintelligible to the people. Gautama, who was specially sought for this purpose, explained it to them in Magadhi.

Another thing worthy of note is his doctrine of conversion. He paid no regard to caste or section. His order was open to all kinds of men who would hear him and profess the doctrines of Jainism. Gautama Indrabhuti, the head of the order, was a Brahama at first. We thus see that Mahavira converted men of all castes to Jainism.

Thus travelling from place to place, with the whole of his order of ascetics, preaching the *Karma* philosophy to the people, and converting countries after countries to Jainism under the mighty patronage of the kings of those countries, Mahavira passed the last thirty years of his life.

II

This laborious and hardy period of the later life of Mahavira described in the previous chapter brings us to the end of it. The three acts of great drama have been performed and there remains very little to be said as an epilogue. Birth and death, like the opposite poles in a magnet, are always seen together. One is never found without the other. They are constantly following the soul like two policemen attending a prisoner between them. He who is born must die some day or other, and he who is dead must be born in some form or other. Night and day, like a black and a white mouse, are always trying to gnaw with their sharp teeth, the slender rope of our life. They must succeed some day or other, and their success is nothing but the end of that life. Such end must come to each of us, but the end of that noble life of our Lord was not an ordinary one. He passed "never to come again." It was a death which liberated his soul for ever from his two great enemies, birth and death. This is what the Jainas mean by saying that he attained *Nirvana*.

Nirvana, as already explained, is the goal in the long race of every man's life. It is what the gods and men are always struggling to reach at in their repeated births. It was for the attainment of this *Nirvana*, the condition of unlimited happiness, unimpedable valour, and liberation from all the cares and miseries of this world, that Mahavira had to pass through so many repeated births and deaths, and, as we learn from the Jaina Shastras, it was for this purpose that he came to this world. Whatever it may be, he obtained it at the end of his life, and a description of the manner in which he obtained it will be found interesting.

As to the place where he died all the sources of our information assert the same thing. In the *Kalpa-sutra* and in the Buddhist works he is said to have died at Papa. In the Digambara Shastras and in the modern times, too, it is known by the name of Pavapuri. The place has been thus described by Mr. J. L. Jaini :

"A small hamlet of moderate dimensions, and of mudhouses mostly, Pavapuriji is a place lovely in its simple surroundings and lovelier still in its sacred traditions. There are several *dharmashalas* (resting-place) for Jaina pilgrims. There are about half a dozen temples, erected by the Svetambaras and Digambaras. Many pilgrims of both sexes proceed to the place chiefly on the Divali occasion, the day on which Lord Mahavira attained *Nirvana* and then up to the month of March, when the attendance begins to fall. The main temple, which contains the *charanas*, sacred foot-impressions, of Lord Mahavira, stand in the middle of a tank, covered with lotus leaves and other aquatic plants of various kinds. Many fish float in the water and make a very funny sight by their incessant fitting. Sometimes a bigger fish would attack a shoal of smaller fish and make them dart down into the water in great confusion. At present no lotuses are blooming in the tank but it is easy to imagine how charming the tank must look when white and red lotuses dot its surface and the fish dance in its pellucid depths through the mazes of the lotus-stems. The sun also may then be imagined as converting every stray drop of water that the ever-busy tails of the fish have cast on to a lotus, into a pearl of the most beautiful pink colour. The insulated temple of our Lord is reached by a bridge of stone. In the temple itself is a low chamber, facing the east are 3 niches; the central one, the largest of the three, contains the foot-impression of Lord Mahavira; the niches on the right of it, of his disciple Gautama Swami; and that on the left those of Sudharmacharya."

Hastipal, the ruler of this place, was, as we have already learnt, a patron of Mahavira, and he had made great arrangements for the reception of the great preacher. Almost all the ruling chiefs of the country had assembled there. People from all parts of the country flocked there to hear him. He preached to them for six days constantly. Then came the seventh day. It was the fifteenth day of the first half of Kartika when the moon was in conjunction with the asterism Svati. Mahavira was sitting upon a high diamond throne in the centre of a magnificent hall specially erected for his preaching in the forest in the vicinity of a large tank. All men from the beggar to the mighty king, were round him. They had formed themselves into twelve societies consisting of the different grades of society. It was a dark night and hence the whole of the hall had to be illuminated with the brightest light. His pupils were all around him excepting Gautama Indrabhuti, who is said in the Svetambara Shastras, to have been on a mission. For the whole night he was preaching to them. in the fourth *prahar* of the night all men fell asleep. Mahavira, through his *Sukla-gyan* saw that his end was come. He assumed a particular position known as the *Samparyanka,* and attained *Nirvana* just when it was twilight. In the morning when the people got up they saw to their great sorrow that their Lord was gone. There was no help. They began to grieve but Gautama comforted them. Then they celebrated his cremation with great pomp. The news of his death reached far and wide and the people had illuminations and *sabhas* in several places. They thought it more worthy to rejoice than to weep on the occasion of the liberation of their Lord from the bonds of this world. It is said that the modern festival of Divali took its rise from this great incident. The word Divali is a corruption of the Sanskrit work *dipavali* which means a "row of lamps." It refers to the illumination that is held every year on the Divali festival. This illumination is but the imitation of the great illumination held on the occasion of the death of Mahavira. The people have forgotten the great incident which gave rise to this national festival, but they have tenaciously stuck to it through so many centuries. It is also said that the modern Hoi a or Hatri, worshiped after some days of Divali, is also an imitation of the great hall at Pavapuri in which Mahavira breathed his last.

13 MASS POPULARITY

I

The admiration for Mahavira which we have in modern times is not due only to Jaina literature and the Jaina Acharyas, but it is due to a great extent to the faith which his followers and pupils had in him; and to say something about his followers will not be out of place. It may be safely remarked that the Digambaras and the Svetambaras who differ so much from each other about many facts in the life of Mahavira, are almost of one opinion as regards the statement about his followers and the difference, if any, is very slight.

The excellent community of Mahavira in his life-time was a large one and used to travel with him from place to place. It consisted of four orders, each having its own head and different rules of life. The first order consisted of fourteen thousand members who were known as the *Munis* or the Shramanas. They held the highest position in the whole community and had very strict rules of living for them. These rules are given in the Jaina Shastras. Further, this order was divided into nine Ganas of schools each of them being under one head who was known by the name of Ganadhara or a teacher of one school. There were eleven such Ganadharas who were the first and the chief disciples of Mahavira like the twelve apostles of Christ. Seven of these had the charge of one school each, and the remaining four taught the remaining two schools, two of them together having the charge of one school. The names of these Ganadharas or the Sthaviras are as follows :

I. Indrabhuti of the Gautama-gotra, whose Gana (school) consisted of five hundred Shramanas (*Munis*);

II. Agnibhuti of the Gautama-gotra who had the charge of five hundred *Munis;*

III. Vayubhuti of the Gautama-gotra who instructed five hundred *Munis;*

IV. Arya-Vyakta of the Bharadvaj-gotra whose school consisted of five hundred *Munis;*

V. Sudharma of the Agni-Veshyayana gotra. He had the charge of five hundred *Munis;*

VI. Mandikaputra of Manditputra of the Vashista-gotra who instructed two hundred and fifty Shramanas;

VII. Mauryaputra of the Kashyapa-gotra whose order had two hundred and fifty *Munis;*

VIII. Akampita of Gautama-gotra;

IX. Achal-vrata of the Haritayana-gotra. Both of them instructed together three hundred Shramanas each;

X. Maitreya;

XI. Prabhas. Both were of the Kandinya-gotra and had the charge of three hundred *Munis* each.

The following Table will make this still clearer :

Table 13.1

No.	*Name of the Ganadhara*	*Gotra*	*Number of Munis in the order*
I	Indrabhuti	Gautama	500
II	Agnibhuti	Gautama	500
III	Vayubhuti	Gautama	500
IV	Arya-Vyakta	Bharadvaja	500
V	Sudharma	Agni Veshayana	500
VI	Manditpura	Vashistha	250
VII	Mauryaputra	Kashyapa	250

(Contd.)

(contd.)

VIII	Akampita	Gautama	300
	Achal-vrata	Haritayana300	
IX	Maitreya	Kandinya	300
	Prabhas	Kandinya	300

This shows that there were nine Ganas at the head of which there were eleven Ganadharas. It is also said that Indrabhuti was the chief disciple of Mahavira and exercised an authority over other pupils. Of these eleven, only Indrabhuti and Sudharma survived Mahavira, obtaining their salvations after his Nirvana. We will know much about them shortly. The rest died in his lifetime as Kevalins.

From the above list we learn that there were only four thousand and two hundred *Munis*, but it has been stated that there were in all fourteen thousand *Munis*. Perhaps the rest lived as apprentices, and were not taken in the order.

The above division of the *Munis* is according to their Ganas. There is further classification according to their merits and spiritual attainments. According to *Kalpa-sutra* among these there were three hundred sages who knew the fourteen *Purvas* and the twelve *Angas* of the *Jina-Vani*; thirteen hundreds sages who were possessed of the Avadhi-knowledge and superior qualities; seven hundred *Kevalins*; seven hundred *Munis* who could transform themselves, and, though no gods, had obtained *Riddhis* or the power of gods; five hundred sages who could know the thoughts of all beings; four hundred professors who used to discuss with men of other religions, and who will never be defeated; seven hundred male and fourteen hundred female disciples who were perfect; and eight hundred other sages. These make together only six thousand and eight hundred. The rest of them perhaps were of inferior merits. According to the Digambaras there were three hundred *Munis* who knew by heart the twelve *Angas* and the fourteen *Purvas*; thirteen hundred *Munis* possessing Avadhi-knowledge; seven hundred *Kevalins* or those who had

Kevalgyan; nine hundred sages who could transform themselves; five hundred *Munis* who had the four kinds of knowledge; twelve hundred professors; and nine thousand and nine hundred ordinary *Munis.* This, too, gives in all fourteen thousand and eight hundred *Munis* which is greater than the other number by eight hundred.

The eleven pupils of Mahavira were all converts to Jainism and, as such, they strictly adhered to the cause. They were greatly attached to their Lord. The story of Gautama Indrabhuti, the chief disciple, is a very interesting one. He was the son of a Brahama named Vasumati. He is said to have been a learned pandit and a writer of Hindu Granthas. He was very proud of his learning. Once upon a time a certain old man went to him and said, "O, Revered Sir, my Guru, Mahavira, gave me a poem, but before explaining it to me he entered his deep meditations. No one can explain me its meaning. I have heard much about your learning that you are well versed in the Vedas and the Puranas. I think I cannot live without having explained to me the meaning of this poem. I hope, therefore, that you will be kind enough to save my life by explaining to me the meaning of this sloka." Indrabhuti promised to comply with the Brahamana's request provided the Brahama promised him to become his pupil on his having explained him the meaning of the sloka.

Gautama fell into confusion. He could not know what is meant by the three *Kalas* and the six *Dravyas.* He could not understand the *Panchastikaya,* the seven *Tattvas* and the six *Leshyas.* And he could not give a wrong explanation, for he was afraid of Mahavira. He, therefore, thought it propel to come to Mahavira and there explain the meaning of the sloka as he understood it, so that he may not be charged with the guilt of having explained the sloka wrongly. Having thus concluded he went to Mahavira with his five-hundred pupils and his two brothers Vayubhuti and Agnibhuti. In the way he began to think that if he could not explain it in the absence of Mahavira how would he be able to explain it in his presence, but his brother induced him to go there. On his first seeing

Mahavira, he was struck with the spiritual valour of the great Yogi. His pride went off and he saluted Mahavira by falling before him and then requested him to preach to him. Mahavira explained to him the doctrines of Jainism. Being struck with the truth of the doctrines and the learning and wisdom of the Lord, he left his home, became a *Muni* and entered the order of Mahavira. His 500 pupils and 3 brothers did the same. He remained faithful to his master throughout his life. Mahavira was greatly pleased with him and hence raised him by and by to the position of a Ganadhara with his two brothers, and then to that of the chief Ganadhara. When Mahavira died he is said to have been on a mission to convert somebody. He became a *Kevalin* just when Mahavira died. After Mahavira he was the leader of the order. He died twelve years after, having lived fifty years as a monk, and altogether ninety-two years.

Another disciple who survived Mahavira and Sudharma. The Pattavali of the Kharataragachha states that he was the son of a Brahmana of Kollaga. He succeeded Indrabhuti to the position of the chief Ganadhara. He was a great preacher. The well known Jambu-Swami was one of his pupils. He was succeeded by Jambu-Swami, who was the last *Kevalin* and obtained his salvation at a place near Muttra.

From the order of the *Munis* we come to that of the Arjikas or the nuns. This is said to have consisted of thirty-six thousand nuns. These were the women who had entered the order of Mahavira. They are distinguished from ordinary women by the fact that they are not allowed to mix in worldly matters. They are female *Munis*. They have strict rules of conduct like the *Munis*. At the head of these nuns was Chandana. In the Digambara Shastras she is said to have been the daughter of Chetaka, the mighty ruler of Vaishali or Vishalpura. Further we learn from *Kalpa sutra* that Chetaka was the maternal uncle of Mahavira. Thus Chandana must have been the cousin of Mahavira. The Digambaras say that Chetaka was the father of Trisala. This shows that Chandana was Mahavira's mother's sister. Whatever it may be, one thing is clear that she was closely related to Mahavira. The anecdote, showing how she became an Arjika, runs thus :

"One day, Chandana had been to the pleasure gardens for taking a walk. A certain Vidyadhara, being fascinated by her beauty, took her off, but in the way, thinking of his wife, he left her in the forest. She was weeping there, when a certain hill-man came there and took her with him to kaushambi and sold to a rich man named Virshabhasena. The man kept her for sometime in his house, but as she grew young, his wife, Subhadras, became jealous of her beauty. Chandana was illtreated by this Subhadra in all kinds of ways. She was given the worst kind of food to eat and wretched clothes to put on. Sometimes she was beaten too. After sometimes it happened that Mahavira came to that place and began to preach there. She was disgusted with the world, became an Arjika and entered the holy order. By and by she was raised to the position of the head Arjika."

The third order consisted of one hundred and fifty-nine thousand lay votaries with Sankhasataka at their head. These lay votaries are called the Shravakas and correspond to the Grihasthas of the Hindus. The rules of conduct for this order were not so strict as those for the *Munis*. They were allowed to live with wives and children with some limitations. The Digambara Acharyas give the number only as one hundred thousand.

The fourth order consisted of three hundred thousand female lay votaries or Shravikas with Sulasa and Revati at their head. In the *Kalpa-sutra* their number is given as three hundred and eighteen thousand Shravikas.

Such were the four orders of which the community of Mahavira consisted in his life-time. After Mahavira they were led by Gautama Indrabhuti for twelve years and after him by Sudharma for twelve years. After Sudharma Acharya his head pupil Jambu-Swami led the order for twenty-four years. A long list of such leaders is given in the *Kalpa-sutra* known as the list of the Sthaviras, and also in the Pattavalis.

II

"Character is one of the greatest motive powers in the world", wrote one of the best writers of the last century, and strange it would seem, as it really does, how Mahavira did such a great work in life, if nothing is said about his character. Great men are not great only because they were looked upon to be so by the surrounding people, but also because they have done great things. Character is one of the chief factors in the accomplishment of such deeds, and no man has ever become great, not what we ordinarily mean by great but really great, without being one of good character. It is rather a fruitless task to try to find out the elements which composed the real greatness of Mahavira, for he was a *Tirthankara*, and, as such, must have possessed almost all the forty-six qualities of an Arhat; but it would not be out of place to give a glimpse of some of them. The three great elements of the character of a great man are bodily valour, intellectual excellence and mortality. Of the first Mahavira is said to have been possessed to a high degree or Ananta. He had a very strong and a well-formed body which was beautiful and fragrant and is said to have been seven cubits high and to have the yellow colour of gold. As a proof of this statement we have already learnt the anecdote of his having tamed a wild and a ferocious elephant while playing with his friends in a garden when he was a young prince of eight years. The auspicious mark of lion that is seen on his images in modern times might have perhaps been given to him to show his great bodily valour. It has already been noted that in the Svetambara Shastras he is said to have married and led the life of a house-holder for thirty years, while in the Digambara Shastras he is said to have been one of five *Bal-brahmacharis*.

As to his intellectual excellence there is nothing to show that he was regularly educated in the ordinary way. In the Jaina Shastras knowledge is said to have been of five kinds. They are *Mati, Shruti, Avadhi, Manahparyaya* and *Kevalgyan*. Of these Mahavira is said to have been born with the first three. The fourth, as we have seen, he attained at the time of his Renunciation and fifth one he obtained in his forty-third year. This is all we know about his education. He acquired learning through *Yoga*. He was also a great speaker. He always spoke the truth. As to his morality there is no doubt that he was a type of virtue. He was a great preacher, and knowing that example is better than precept, he did what he preached to others. He strictly followed the principles of the gospel that he preached, and observed them in his practice also. Forbearance is one of the ten high virtues with the Jainas, and Mahavira patiently bore the abuses and even the ill-treatment of the wild tribes of Vajra-Bhumi, and Shuddha-Bhumi, when he preached to them the doctrines of Jainism. He was never angry, and led a life which is a Jaina model of purity and piety. We have already learnt of his attachment to his parents. He did not only love them but was very obedient to them. Thus he is said to have intended to renounce the world several times, but would not do so against the wish of his parents. It is also said that he was greatly obedient to his elder brother. Nothing is so necessary as perseverance for one who wishes to become a great Yogi, and Mahavira is said to have been a man of great perseverance. Soon after his Renunciation, "it happened that a certain cowherd with his cows came to the place where he was sitting all absorbed in his meditation and calling upon, Mahavira to look after his cows that he left to graze there, himself went away to the village. Mahavira being engaged in his meditations, could not hear him and the cows went astray. The cowherd, when he came back from the village, did not find the cows there, and began to reproach Mahavira and actually dealt two or three blows to him. Happily, some acquaintances of Lord Mahavira came there. They rebuked the cowherd very much and informed him the real character of the saint." The story though illustrating the great mental powers of Mahavira, has somewhat the colour of absurdity. Mahavira, being the son of a great king and a noble saint, must have been known to all men, and specially to the subjects of his brother. The cowherd's not recognising Mahavira, who was the brother of the king of that country in which the cowherd lived, is a fact beyond our perception. However, as it stands, it shows that Mahavira was free from anger.

Somewhat similar anecdote is given in the *Mahavira Purana*. "Once he was deeply meditating upon himself at a cemetery called Devoktamukta near Ujjain. A certain Rudra in conspiracy with his wife, Pavati, intending to test Mahavira's preservance began to interrupt him, but Mahavira did not leave his meditation. Having completely satisfied themselves, Rudra and Parvati began to praise Mahavira."

There were the great qualities of Mahavira which led him to do great things and in turn made him great.

Mahavira was a great teacher. It is a misfortune that we have got no direct information regarding his gospel. All our information is secondary and comes from the Acharyas. The Acharyas say that whatever they say is the word of Sarvagya, but how are we to convince others of his truth in the absence of any direct proof? The history of the Jaina literature, as given by our Acharyas, is likely to make them hesitate from taking it for granted that they say the word of Sarvagya. However, the history of the evolution of the Jaina literature as it stands, is as follows :

The whole Jaina literature known as the Syadvad Agama is divided into two main divisions the twelve Angas and the fourteen Angabahyashutras or the scriptures other than the twelve *Angas*. The last or the twelfth of the Angas consists of the five Parikramas, the Sutra, the Prathamanuyoga, the five Chulikas and the fourteen Purvas. All these form the twelfth *Anga*. This vast literature chiefly known as the Dwadashanga word of the Sarvagya has never been seen by any body, for it was never written down. It was preached by the *Tirthankaras* from time to time and was remembered by the people. Lord Mahavira taught the same thing to the people who were present in his sermons and who could understand the divine speech of their Lord. After Mahavira his Ganadharas, whose memory was the chief repository and means of continuance of the Siddhantas, used to promulgate the faith by word of mouth and tradition. Gautama Indrabhuti, Sudharma and Jambu Swami, the three consecutive *Kevalins* after Mahavira, held the pontifical chair for sixty-two years, and taking advantage of their highly trained memories, which could retain all the Agamas, propagated the traditions by word of mouth. These were followed by the five *Shruta Kevalins* who held the chair for hundred years. The memory of these was weaker than that of the *Kevalins* and hence they forgot the Angabahyas. Thus the knowledge of these Angabahyas shut from the world. Then came the eleven Ten-Purvins who remained pontiffs for about hundred and eighty-one years. They forgot four of the *Purvas*, and thus the four of the *Purvas* were no more known. These were followed by the five Eleven Angins who remained for hundred and twenty-three years. The memory of these was still weaker. They forgot all the fourteen *Purvas* and other parts of the twelfth *Anga*. Thus the twelfth Anga was no more known. Then came the four Four-*Angins* holding the chair for ninety-nine years. They could remember only for *Angas*. But after them came the five One-Angins. They remained pontiffs for hundred and eighteen years. Their memory was so week that they forgot every thing but one *Anga*. Thus only one *Anga* was known to the world. But after them no one had the knowledge of even of one complete *Anga*. The Acharyas, seeing that memory was growing weaker and weaker, thought it expedient to take advantage of the art of writing, and with the little knowledge of the *Agamas* left to them by the One-*Angins*, they composed the Shastras. This took place about 57 A.D. The above history is from the Digambara point of view. This tradition, notwithstandingour full faith in its reality is not likely to appeal to the reason of a modern critical reader, who is likely to assume that this is an invention of the Jaina Acharyas with the object of giving a scared authority and a colour of antiquity to all their writings, which are, as a matter of fact, of a later day composition. In the absence of any direct proof he cannot believe that the Jaina Shastras are a true representation of what Mahavira taught, and even if he assumes that the original compositions of the Acharyas are based upon the information given by the One-*Angins* he can hardly believe that the whole Jaina literature, vast as it is, is the out-come of the original compositions which are said to have been drowned by Shankaracharya.

14 APPROXIMATE DATE OF HIS NIRVANA

The last but not the least point about Mahavira that remains to be specially mentioned is the date of his salvation or the year of his death which in all probability is a most important point in the life of a great man. It may be remarked, before proceeding to enter into a serious discussion upon the more than one sources of our information concerning this matter, that it is difficult or rather impossible to give a final judgment upon this subject in a book like this which comes from the pen of an ordinary student who does not claim any share in the research work of the modern scholars. The demonstrations that are brought forward in the following few lines are not, as some one is likely to suppose, the result of any research work on his part. On the other hand all information on this point is a secondary one, being due to and only to the unceasing labours of scholars like Prof. Jacobi and Dr. Hoernle whose learning and tact should be admired and respected by every student of antiquity.

It has been observed above that there are many facts to shows precisely the year in which Mahavira died. In the first place we learn from the sacred books of the Buddhists that Mahavira was a contemporary of Buddha. Thus in Mahavagga and Mahaparinibhana Sutta, the two great Buddhist works, Mahavira is said to have been a contemporary of Buddha. He is mentioned by his prakrit name Nataputta. He is spoken of as one of the six opponent teachers of Buddha. Prof. Jacobi cites in his translation of the Jaina Sutras, besides the above quoted books, the Anuguttara Nikaya, Samanaphala Sutta of the Digh Nikaya, Sumangala Vilasini, a commentary by Buddhaghosha on Brahmagala Sutta of the Digh Nikaya, and the Magghima Nikaya, all of which that Mahavira was a great opponent of Buddha. "In the Magghima Nikaya it is related that the Nigantha Nataputta made Abhayakumara engage in a disputation with Buddha. The question was so adroitly formed that whether the answer was Yes or No, it involved Buddha in self-contradiction. But the plan did not succeed, and Abhaya was converted by Buddha." Further "in the Mahavagga VI, 31 (S.B.E., Vol. XVIII, p. 108ff) a story is told of Siha, the general of the Likhavis, who was a lay-disciple of Nataputta. He wanted to pay Buddha a visit, but Nataputta tried to dissuade him from it, because the Niganthas held the *Kriyavada*, while Buddha taught the *Akriyavada*. Siha, however, setting his master's prohibition at naught, went to Buddha on his own account, and was, of course, converted by him." Again in the Maghima Nikaya 35, a disputation between Buddha and Sakkaka, the son of a Nigantha, is narrated. From the same authority we learn that this Sakkaka was not himself a Nigantha. He boasts himself of having vanquished Nataputta in disputation. Now whatever the truth of these traditions, they put beyond doubt the fact that Mahavira and Buddha lived and preached at the same time. This means that Buddha was born before the death of Mahavira. Now Buddha, according to the western scholars, was born about 557 B.C. Therefore, Mahavira's *Nirvana* must have taken place many years after this date. This is all we know from the Buddhist works. We learn nothing as to the priority of one over the other. The Jaina Shastras, however make this point a little clearer.

This means that in the Tirtha of Parshva-Natha (that is during the period between the Arhatship of Parshva-Natha and Mahavira) Buddhakirti, a monk learned in Shastras, a disciple of Pihitashrava was performing was performing penance on the banks of the river Sarayu near a city called Palashnagara. He saw some dead fish floating by him. He thought that there was no *hinsa* in eating a dead fish : for there was no soul in it. Having come to this conclusion, he left his penance, put on red clothes and began to preach the Buddhist religion. This proves that Buddha began to preach his doctrines before Mahavira became and Arhat. Now we know that Buddha began to preach when he was 39 years old, that is, in B.C. 518. Therefore, Mahavira's Arhatship must have taken place about or after this time. And since he lived thirty years as an Arhat, the probable date of his *Nirvana* must be somewhat near B.C. 488.

But this is far from the actual date of Mahavira's *Nirvana*. The now commonly accepted historical date of Mahavira's *Nirvana* is B.C. 527. And let us see how far does this agree with facts.

15 MODERN PERIOD OF DEVELOPMENT OF JAINISM

Towards the twentieth century, the south Indian part of the Jain community was numerically very small. According to the 1901 census, there were 7 Jains (6 according to the data in 1941) per ten thousand of population in Madras. In Hyderabad, it was 18 (15 in 1941) and in Mysore 25 (45 in 1941). Approximately the same picture was seen in northern India : in 1901 in UP and Punjab there were 18 to 20 Jains per ten thousand of population (19 to 13 in 1941). But in western India, the ratio was different. In 1901 in Ajmer Marwar, there were 418 Jains per ten thousand of population, in Rajputana 349, in Baroda 247, in Bombay, 123. Towards the middle of the twentieth century, the number of Jains in the west also decreased. According to the 1941 census, in Ajmer-Marwar there were 323 Jains per ten thousand of population, in Rajputana 247, in Baroda 164. Only in Bombay the number of Jains increased to some extent. It was 127.

In 1950-1960, an increase in the Jain community was observed. In comparison with 1951, it increased by 25.17% (according to 1961 census, Jains formed 0.46% of the population of India)

Highest increase was seen in the local groups in the eastern regions of India in the regions intensively developed by the Indian Governmet recently. Though the numerical strength of these groups in absolute figures is small, in terms of percentages, their increase is quite remarkable : In Assam, it is more than; 127% (in all nearly 9.5 thousand Jains), in Andhra, nearly 85% (in all 9,000 Jains). In Orissa, nearly 84% (in all 2.3

thousand Jains). In Bihar the number of Jains increased almost by 116% (in all 17.6 thousand).

In western India the increase in the community is extremely insignificant. In Rajasthan it is in all 13.8% (total Jain population 409.5 thousand), in Gujarat 9.3% (total Jain Population 409.8 thousand). In the remaining States Jains are most numerous in Maharashtra (485.7 thousand), Madhya Pradesh (248 thousand) and Mysore (174.4 thousand). In other States their number does not exceed 40-50 thousand.

Evidently, a sharp increase in the community in the above - mentioned regions can be explained by the fact that the Jain bourgeois seeks and finds a sphere for investing its capital precisely in those regions, where intensive capitalist development has started.

In their own times, the leader of the community started taking measures to eliminate the reasons for the fall in the number of members of their community. There were two tendencies, differently interpreting these reasons and taking different measures to overcome them.

One of the tendencies can be called conservative. The representatives of this tendency argue this out by saying that the community as a whole has forgotten the ancient rules of conduct, that the standard of being exacting and strict has fallen down and that the community; is having more faith in western type of education. First and foremost, they appeal to the laymen to give more of their time and energy to the teachings of canonic books. They also appeal with equal force to the monks to give more attention to expounding and propagating the canonic texts. The advocates of this tendency demand new rules of conduct, which will prohibit marriages of Jains with Hindus and will also restrict all except business connections with them. They also demand that journeys to foreign countries should not be allowed and especially Jain students should not be sent abroad for education.

Other tendency is represented by those who demand softening of caste restrictions, fusion of numerous small sects into a stronger unit, spread of education and assigning more extensive rights to women in social life.

The leading personalities of the community with affiliation to this tendency often raised the question as to how to fight against the failings of the community. They saw biggest evil in the caste system with its restricted rules regarding marriages and called upon the community to return to the ancient form of the community, in which castes had not yet penetrated.

Instead of caste division they offered the suggestion to divide the community in big endogamic groups according to the linguistic regions of India. They assume that this will also ensure the strengthening of the position of the Jain community in every State since the efforts of its members to better the position of the community as a whole within the limits of a given region would be directed in more organised manner.

As far back as in the 1920s an attempt was made in Punjab. There was created an endogenous unit out of several Jain castes. It was called Bhavada.[1] The castes comprising this group have more or less equal position. That is why this new community was comparatively more stale and there are more chances of intercaste marriages in this group even now. But this could not become a rule.

Analogical groups of castes were formed in other regions of India also—in Bengal, Rajasthan and Gujarat. It is reckoned that persons converted to Hinduism and also persons who had earlier joined Arya Samaj, which did not recognise castes are returning back to the Jain community and that in general the proselytising activity can be extended under new arrangement of the community.

Positive suggestions to abolish prohibition of widow marriages are put forward in order to fight against the decrease in the numerical strength of the community. These suggestions received adequate and wide support in the south but they are not very popular amongst the northern and western Jains.

Both the chief sects formed a number of organisations on an all-India scale for strengthening their positions.

Organisations of Digambaras are the All-India Digambara Jain Parishad, with its centre in Delhi, the All-India Digambara Jain Mahasabha with its centre in Delhi, and the All-India Digambara Jain Sabha with its centre in Mathura. The Svetambara organisations are All-India Svetambara Jain Sthanakavasi Conference with its centre in Bombay, and Shri Jain Svetambara Terapanthi Mahasabha with its centre in Calcutta. Almost all the sub-sects of Svetambaras have their all India organisations.

A number of organisations of local importance also exist. Their influence, sphere of activity and popularity is less than that of the organisations mentioned above. Thus, there are Jain youth organisations, children's aid societies and a huge number of philanthropic societies, as philanthropy is raised by Jainism to the level of one of the main religious services.

All the big organisations have branches in various states and also press-organs in English and local India languages.

The community as a whole manifests a tendency to review the prohibitions and restrictions and to reconstruct the pattern of life, conforming to the demands of the times. That is why the advocates of the conservative tendency press those who stand for reformatory changes.

In the conditions of capitalistic development of the country, the Jains constitute one such group of population before whom wide possibilities for investing capital unfold themselves. They, therefore, are in acute need of overcoming the barrier, which interferes with their coming closer and having intercourse with other social groups. It was the Marwari Jains, who started to play an especially great role in the economic life of India towards the end of the nineteenth and in the twentieth century.

Many big financiers and entrepreneurs of modern India, for example Mr. Birla, come from the Jain community, mainly from Osavala or Osval caste and from Shrimali caste (which are thus called from their place of formation—town and the surrounding district Osa or Osya and the town of Shrimali in Marwar).[2]

Important groups of Marwari-Jains live not only in all the big cities of India, but also in a number of other countries–Pakistan, Burma, various States in Africa, England and America.

The castes of Jain baniya-traders and also baniy; as from otheı western regions constitute a medium, which has given rise to many representatives of big Indian bourgeoisie.

Mr. S.P. Jain one of the Jain industrialist, warns his community against excessive aspirations for monopolistic domination in industry. "The interests of the business world as a whole demand that the strong industrial groups allow new people in the industrial sphere."[3]

People, similar to the author of the above lines are the spokesmen of the growing reformatory tendency in Jainism.

In the modern epoch of religious movement, sectarian traditions, aspirations to reorganise religious communities–all this is above all noticeable amongst the so called middle classes *i.e.* petty and middle bourgeoisie with which the handicraftsmen often side in these movements. A part of intelligentsia, representing these same social strata also participate in these movements. It is characteristic that the ideologies of modern Jainism, as also of any other modern religion depart from the purely theological positions and strive to attach social content to the new religious movements, including in their programme quite a number of purely social demands or claims. The leading personalities of the Jain community resolved for example to award a prize of a lakh of rupees to the best writer (in 1966, this prize was awarded to Shankar Kurup from Kerala). They conduct all-India seminars on the questions of culture, sciences, etc.

The movement, known as *anuvrat i.e.* movement for the moral revival of the society is an interesting attempt to conduct the new line in modern Jainism, which tries to unite and coordinate new social-economic conditions with the ancient religious dogmatics.

Terapanthi–the big sub-sect of the Svetambaras, which

consists of more than 700 *shramanas* (ascetics) and lakhs of laymen server as a basis of the movement. Acharya Shri Tulsi, one of the ascetics from the family of prosperous Rajasthani Jains of Oswal caste is the initiator of this movement. He became the head of the entire sub-sect (9th in succession from its formation) in 1936, at the age of 21.

In the course of number of years, he travelled on foot (as this has been prescribed for Jain monks) with a group of monks in the western and northern regions of India, giving sermons on the teaching of Terapanthi. He paid and continues to pay great attention to the spread of education among members of his sub-sect and especially among monks and nuns.

In March 1949, Acharya Shri Tulsi announced the beginning of the *anuvrat* movement and himself headed it. His thesis about antidogmatism serves the basis of his teaching. He thinks that the synthetical approach to contemporary problems is the best approach and that one must not be carried away either by ancient or by ultra-modern ideas, especially by blind imitation of the West. In his opinion the main problem confronting Man is liberations from vices.

He sees the essence of the conflict between communism and capitalism in that the accumulation of wealth in one pole gives rise to the attempts towards aggression.and destruction from the other pole. He therefore appeals to resolve this conflict by reducing to the minimum grabbling operations and by restricting grabbing instincts. He calls upon the society to negotiate and peacefully resolve all internal conflicts.

However, Acharya Shri Tulsi's appeal to review the traditional approach to philanthropic activity and also to reconsider whether it is necessary to give alms to beggars was something new for Jainism, as for all the Indian religious faiths. He preaches that it was only because religion promises posthumous bliss for this help that the society could compel the rich to part with certain part of their wealth in the name of help to the poor. But the more that is given to the poor, the more will be the number of the poor in this world.

Like the leaders of the movement of Sarvodaya,[4] Acharya Shri Tulsi asserts that it is possible to satisfy human needs only by organising cooperatives and by drawing in all the members of society for joint effort. He considers that only that nation has the right to be proud, which does not have beggars and not that which bases itself on charity to seven million.[5]

Acharya Shri Tulsi, like Shir Vinoba Bhave, the head of the Sarvodaya and Bhudan (gift of land) movement, considers that gift of land is not on an act of charity but an act of redistribution of land on the basis of justice. According to these theoretists, the slogan 'Don't accumulate riches' under mines the very basis of poverty and leads to real freedom, equality and fraternity.

In the opinion of Acharya Shri Tulsi, in a socialist State like India it its the government which must direct social life, realize just distribution of riches and adjust a just mutual relationship between various groups in the society. This programme is a reflection characteristics of many bourgeois scholars and a part of Indian bourgeoisie, looking upon State as a public organ above classes.

All the anuvratis are supposedly sub-divided in three categories : *praveshak anuvrati* (beginner), *anuvrati* and *vishishta anuvrati* (distinguished, perfect)

It is required of the first category that they must overcome sinful temptations surrounding their life and avoid moral degradation. It is required of the second category that they must be highly moral citizens of their country, serving as an example to all around them by their own life. It is required of this category that they must delve deep into the social problems and search for ways to their solution *i.e.* to be in search of a possible way for creating a society without violence and exploitation.

It is worth noting that a certain number of persons, professing other faiths—Aryasamajists, Sikhs, Vishnuties and Muslims - joined the *anuvrata* movement.

The *anuvratis* worked out the following suggestions for the moral uplift of the society, in their annual conferences and local weekly meetings :

(*1*) The entrepreneurs and traders must not resort to false weights and measures, must not sell in black market and must not participate in various machinations

(*2*) Students must not resort to unclean methods during examinations and must not participate in disorders.

(*3*) Government employees must not take bribes and must not use their position as employees to harm others.

Great attention is paid to work of students. Student organisations, such as Anuvrata Vidyarthi Parishads, or Anuvrata Samiti have been formed in a number of big cities. Students, connected with the anuvrata movement are forbidden to participate in political struggle.

The anuvrata movement is evaluated by its participants and leaders as a movement, revolutionary in its final analysis, as it pursues as its aim a cardinal reconstruction of the society by means of a change in the cognition of its members. Anuvratis say that they accept the ideal of equality from the communist teaching but do not accept the appeal to violence. So far as capitalism is concerned, they approve of the ideas of capital as an instrument of organised commerce and business but they object to its excessive accumulation and exploitation.[6] Thus they wish to hold back the proletariat from violence by re-educating the capitalists.

According to the teachings of anuvratis, humanity degrades itself because people try to acquire food and clothes by any means (non-violent as also violent). According to them, it is so because of the materialists who teach that food is the main thing. Anuvratis consider that it is necessary to suppress one's desires and aspirations to save humanity from hatred, mutual struggle (and in the final analysis from atom bomb).

They want the capitalists to 'realise' their shortcomings and cease to aspire for profit. The anuvratis persistently urge that the rich should cease defying wealth and then wealth will surely lose all its power before the people.

They consider class war as an 'unwise business' and building of a classless society, a 'fantasy' and even an 'absurdity'.[7]

In the sphere of relations with other religious communities, anuvratis appeal for tolerance and manifestation of friendly feelings.

They include in their programme also other burning problems of social life of modern India, right up to such of them as family planning, but the measures suggested by them for this reduce themselves to restrict conjugal relations or even totally abstain from them. They suggest for the struggle against prostitution 'to create such an atmosphere in the society, which would make the evil impossible' and also suggest banning of films which show 'tempting dancing women'. Anuvratis associate themselves with the struggle against child marriage, insisting on 18 years for the male and 15 years for the female as the marriageable age. They forbid in their community late marriages (after 40-45 years).

They protest against the dowry system, describing this custom as 'the dominance of materialism in out times', although as is known, the roots of this custom are embedded in the past and they have no relation whatsoever with materialism as a philosophical system.

Censuring smoking, consumption of alcoholic drinks and meat, anuvratis profess restraint in eating and simplicity in life. They even protest against wearing silk dresses and ornaments, as this leads people away from simplicity and naturalness.

Anuvratis also urge not to be carried away by festivals (especially the 'amoral' festival of Holi) and various earthly joys. Instead, they propose that 'Day of Non-Resistance' should be observed every year, keeping away on this day from all excesses and temptations. They urge that one should fast and do some good on that day.

In regard to caste relations—one of the most burning

social problems, anuvratis, following Gandhism, rise against discrimination of the untouchables.

On the whole, this movement does not have massive repercussions and is limited mainly to the members of the Terapanthi sub-sect.

* * *

Thus, from all the above, it follows that Jainism is one of the most ancient religions of India, enduring on its path of historical development quite a number of conflicts with other religious-philosophical systems and undergoing many changes as result.

Adopting caste institutions in the medieval period, is ensured greater stability for itself in comparison to Buddhism, in the environment of Hindu caste society. This helped it to preserve itself up to four times.

Jains engaged and continue to engage themselves mainly in industrial and trade-usury activities. It represents from its class nature the middle and big, trading, industrial and financial bourgeoisie.

Owing to the break-up of the community in a large number of endogamic castes, a decrease in numbers is observed, but a number of reforms are carried out under the leaders of the community and wide proselytising activity goes on in those regions, where in Independent India emphasis is laid on speedy development of economics (mainly in the eastern regions of the country). This is accompanied by finance cooperative support to the new members of the community. All this led to an increase of 25% in its members in the last 10-15 years.

In spite of the fact that Jains constitute only 0.46% of the population of modern India, they play a noticeable role in the life of the country, occupying several key positions in its economy.

Notes and References

1. Ch. Krause, *The Social Atmosphere, at present Jainism.*

2. Hasmukh D. Sankalia, *Studies in the Historical and Cultural Geography and Ethnography of Gujarat,* p. 144.
3. Quotations from the book Modern Indian Bourgeoisie, by L.I. Reisner and G.K. Shirokov, p. 67.
4. Sarvodaya (literally-universal prosperity, universal well-being) is a term introduced by M. Gandhi for the first time which express the ideal of classless society based on the principle of non-violence - *Ahimsa.*
5. Muni Shri Nagaraji, *Pity and Charity in the New Pattern of Society,* p. 14.
6. Muni Shri Nagaraji, *The Anuvrat Ideology,* p. 14.
7. *Ibid.,* p. 129.

16 CONCLUSION

The picture of the Brahmanas in *Jataka* literature is quite different from the one given in Brahmanical literature. It is gloomy, especially in *Jataka* literature. The Brahmanas are pictured as greedy, shameless, and immoral. While the shamelessness of the Brahmanas is clear from *Junha Jataka*, the *Sigala Jataka* shows that they were quite greedy. That their moral standards were not quite high is clear from the *Sambhava Jataka*.

Brahmanical literature on the other hand makes it abundantly clear that the Brahmanas enjoyed certain special privileges. For certain offences, for instance, they received milder punishment than those belonging to other classes. They were exempt from taxes. In the matter of treasure-troves, they were more favourably treated than the members of other classes. As a matter of fact, these privileges were granted only to learned Brahmanas, not to all of them. Moreover the Brahmanas did not occupy a privileged position in the eye of law. A criminal, whosoever he was, was executed, as is evident from a number of passages in the *Jatakas*, one of which also speaks of the execution of a Brahmana.

Vaisyas

The *Vaisyas* were not homogeneous in their occupation but followed different professions. They were known as *Gahapati* or *Gahavai, Kutumbika* and *Sethis*. *Gahapati* or *Gahavai* means, literally, a householder, but it seems to have constituted the high and rich middle-class families owning land and cattle. Jaina texts mention a number of *Gahavais* who were adherents of the Jaina faith. One such *Gahavai* was Ananda, a rich landowner of Vaniyagama, who possessed a large number of cattle, ploughs, and carts. Parasara was another *Gahavai*, prosperous in agriculture (kisi) and hence known as *Kisiparasara;* he had six hundred ploughs. Kuiyanna is described as another *Gahavai* who is said to have owned a pretty large number of cows.

The expression *Kutumbika* is used to denote the head of a family, but during this period, he belonged exclusively to the Vaisya community. We find him both in cities and in villages; in the former mostly as businessman, dealing in corn, practicing trade and money - lending and in the latter as a well-to-do cultivator. Some of the *Kutumbikas* figure as very rich citizens.

The *Sethis* were the richest aristocratic section of the Vaisya caste. They are represented as respectable tradesmen, enjoying a high position of honour among the members of their caste. They rendered various services to the king and tradesmen. It appears from the *Jataka*s that some of them occupied an official position in the royal court. Nanda is mentioned as an influential Sethi of Rajagriha. Anathapindika had spent considerable wealth for providing residence for Buddhist *Bhikshus*. They were usually charitable, and spent a good portion of their wealth in charities. Their sons received education along with the Kshatriyas and the Brahmana youths, and offered the teacher a handsome honorarium.

The Sudras

The word *'Sudra'* denotes a number of castes. In the contemporary Jaina and Buddhist literature we do not find a specific mention of a caste called *'Sudra'*. But the occupation and status of a class of people living in those days make it clear that they were none other than the Sudras. Both Mahavira and the Buddha tried their best to improve the general condition of these down-trodden people.

Specific names to the *Jabalopanished.* From the time of the early *Dharmasutras*, these four *Asramas* with their successive stages became well known. The *Apastamba Dharmasutra* says,

"There are four *Asramas, viz.*, the stage of a householder, that of one staying in the teacher's house, the stage of being a *Muni*, and the stage of being a forest-dweller. Apastamba places the householder first among the *Asramas* probably on account of the importance of that stage to all other *Asramas*. To Gautama the four Asramas were *Brahmachari, Grihastha, Bhikshu* and *Vaikhanasa*. *Vasishtha Dharmasutra* names the four *Asramas* as *Brahmachari, Grihastha, Vanaprastha* and *Parivrajaka*. The Buddhist literature knew all the four stages into which the life of the three upper classes was divided.

The first part of man's life is *Brahmacharya* in which he studies in his teacher's house ; in the second part he marries and becomes a householder, pays off his debts to his ancestors by begetting sons and to the gods by performing *Yajnas*. When he sees that his hair is growing gray and that there are wrinkles on his body, he resorts to the forest, *i.e.*, becomes a *Vanaprastha*. After spending the third part of his life in the forest for some time, he spends the rest part of his life as a *Sannyasin*.

It is believed that the scheme of the *Asrama* was so devised that the individual may attain the four goals of existence, namely, *Dharma, Artha, Kama*, and *Moksha*. In the *Brahmacharya* stage, through the discipline of his will and emotion, he attains *dharma*. In the *Grihastha Asrama*, he marries, becomes a householder, tastes the pleasures of the world, enjoys life, has sons, discharges his duties to his children, to his friends, relatives and neighbours and becomes a worthy citizen, the founder of a family. He is supposed to attain *Artha* and *Kama* during this period. In *Vanaprastha*, he is called upon to resort to a forest life for pondering over the great problems of the life hereafter and to accustom himself to self-abnegation, austerities, and a harmless life. In *Sannyasa*, he may succeed in realizing the supreme goal of *Moksha* in this very life or he may have to continue to rise in spiritual height until after several births and deaths the goal is in view.

This *Asrama* system was related to the theory of the three debts—*Rishirina, Pitririna*, and *Devarina*—and through this tripartite system, an attempt was made to pay them off. The debt to the *rishis* was paid off by studying their works at the stage of *Brahmacharya,* the debt to parents by procreating the stage of Brahmacharya, the debt to parents by procreating sons and educating them at the stage of *Grihasta,* and the debt to gods by performing sacrifices at the stage of *Vanaprastha.*

It is difficult to accept the theory propounded by RHYS DAVIDS to the effect that the four orders of life were of Post-Buddhistic origin and that the Brahmanical class unable to cope with the progress of new ideas formulated the theory of *Asramas* according to which no one could become either a hermit or a wanderer without having first many years as student in the Brahmanical school. The theory of *Asrama* was formulated long before the advent of Buddhism. It is possible that the separation of the last two orders, and particularly the development of the last one, may be due to the development of ascetic ideas stemming from the rise of Jainism and Buddhism.

No attempt was ever made to make the four stages obligatory except the first stage. It was not compulsory for an individual to enter into other stages. This system was never imposed arbitrarily with state legislation, ex-communication, perpetual banishment, or execution. The hold of the *Asrama dharma* on the life of the people was rather loose. Had it been strictly imposed on the whole population, the consequences would have been disastrous. It seems that it was confined only to the superior communities like the *Brahmanas* without any binding obligation.

Family Life

Throughout this period the system most in vogue was the joint-family system, and it included father, wife, children, mother, minor brothers, and sisters. The relationship between the different members of the family was mostly cordial and affectionate. The father was the head of the family, and he was respected by all the members. His wife was the mistress who performed her household duties, looked after the members of the family, and was obedient to the master. The mother was highly respected by one and all. We hear of king Pusanandi who was greatly devoted to his mother. The mother on her part had great love for her children. When prince Meghakumara decided to embrace the life of an ascetic, his mother became unconscious and fell to the ground like a log of wood. She was sprinkled over with water, fanned with a palm-leaf, and was consoled by her friends. Her eyes were filled with tears, and using some of the most pathetic words, she persuaded her son not to give up worldly pleasures.

There are also instances which reveal that amity did not exist between one member of the family and the other. Daughters-in-law and mothers-in-law often sought refuge in nunneries to escape from the tyranny of one another. One daughter-in-law even conspired to kill her mother-in-law. In one case, four daughters-in-law drove their father-in-law out of the house. We have the case of a son who refused to marry on the ground that wives generally showed scant respect to their parents-in-law and even domineered over them.

The conception of proprietary rights came into existence in the family circle. The reason was that trade and commerce prospered highly, and the number of professions increased. The members of the family began to earn their living independently. Some of the *Dharmasutra* writers began to give due recognition to the self-acquired property of the son. Gautama says, "Among the brothers one who is *Vaidya*, need not give his own earning to those who are not *Vaidyas*." Vishnu clarifies the point a little further, saying that if the *Vaidya* had acquired his knowledge with the help of family property, he must share the property with others.

Formerly, the father had extraordinary powers. There was a time when the gift or a sale of a son was not regarded as beyond the power of the father. These practices came to be disallowed during this period, no matter whether this was due to a Sastric prohibition in the proper sense of the term or to an alteration in the conception about the extent of the father's right over the son. With the beginning of the *Vanaprastha* system, the joint-family system began to crumble. Before becoming a *Vanaprasthi*, the father had to divide his property among his sons. Sometimes he had divide his property among his sons against his will. The son started demanding his legitimate share in the property even against the wishes of the father. Some of the *Dhrmasutras* declared that a son, who would force a partition upon his father should not be invited to perform the latter's *Sraddha*. This shows that such a procedure was disapproved by the society, but the son had legal rights and could get them enforced through the court of law. Gautama says that sons have rights by birth. Apastamba opines that the connection of the son with inheritance cannot be broken.

Marriage

In the sixth century B.C., marriage was generally regarded as necessary and desirable for all. There are also exceptional cases where both males and females thought of leading an unmarried life by renouncing the world under the influence of religion. Sometimes such persons were unable to live up to their high ideals, and their lapses were furiously commented upon by the public. Hence it was the married who enjoyed real respect in society and felt elevated and dignified.

Forms of Marriages

From the Jaina and Buddhist sources, it appears that *Brahma, Prajapatya, Asura, Gandharva,* and *Rakshasa* marriages were common during this period. Marriages referred to in the *Dharmasutras* are of eight forms, *viz., Brahma, Daiva, Arsha, Prajaptya, Asura, Gandharva; Rakahasa* and *Paisachda*. *Brahma* and *Prajaptya* marriages were the most popular. In these two forms, marriage was settled by parents. Auspicious days were fixed for the marriage ceremony and the bridegroom's party reached the house of the bride on a fixed day. The bride was carried in a car to the bridegroom's place escorted by a number of people.

The *Asura* form of marriage , in which a wife was procured by paying a substantial amount to her father, was also prevalent. The minister Teyaliputta wanted to marry the daughter of a goldsmith. A merchant, after leaving his negligent wife, married another girl by paying a large sum. A robber, who had plenty of money, paid the desired amount, and married a girl. From Buddhist literature we know that the father of Isidasi had received a bride as price for her in her marriage.

The *Gandharva* or love marriage was also popular among the nobles of the time. In this form of marriage, both the bride and bridegroom made their own choice by falling in love with each other without the knowledge of their guardians, and were married without rites or ceremonies. The marriage of Udayana with Vasavadatta is well known. We hear of king Siharaha of Pundavaddhana who married a girl in the *Gandharva* way. Some *jataka* stories also refer to this type of marriage. The *Baudhayana Dharmasutra* refers with approval to the view of some thinkers that love unions ought to be commended as they presuppose reciprocal attachment.

People sometimes resorted to the *Rakshasa* form of marriage. The forcible carrying of the girl to be married was the essential feature of this kind of marrieage. There are many instances of elopement and abduction. Suvarnangulika, a maid servant of Udayana, was abducted by king Pajjoya, Ruppini by Kanha, Kamalamela by Sagarachanda, and Chellana by king Seniya. The Jaina texts also refer to the abduction of Dovait by king Paumanava of Amarakanka. This type of marriage figures frequently in the Jatakas, and it remained quited popular among the warrior class from very early times.

The Jaina and Buddhists texts of this period do not refer to the Paisacha, Arsha, and Daiva marriages which are known from certain Brahmanical sources. In the *Paisacha* marriage, the bride is either duped very often by making her overdrunk or physically overpowered by the bridegroom in order to make her yield to passion. Jainas and Buddhist do not regard it as marriage at all. When a daughter was offered in marriage to an officiating priest by the sacrificer, the marriage was designated as a *Daiva* one. This marriage was not practiced among the Jainas and the Buddhists, who might have included it in the category of *Brahma* and *Prajapatya* forms of marriage. In *Arsha* marriage, the bride's father received a bull and a cow at the time of his daughter's marriage. Since it was thought to be a variety of *Asura* marriage, it was probably not mentioned.

The most interesting type of marriage known as Svayamvara (self-choice) was confined originally to the Kshatriya class, where in a princess selected her husband of her own free will, from among the assembled suitors, or as a result of tournament or contest in the use of warlike weapons. There are several instances of this type of marriage. The *Nayadhammakaha* refers to the *Svayamvara* of Dovai which was attended by various prominent kings and princes. The *Uttaradhyayana* commentary refers to another *Svayamvara* marriage of the princess Nivvui.

Caste and Gotra Consideration

During this period, caste and family (*jati* and *kula*) became important factors in determining marriages in order to preserve the purity of blood. Brahmanas, Sethis, clansmen, treasures, and others are mentioned as solemnising marriages with the members of their respective castes of equal family status. The Jaina and Buddhist accounts are supported by the *Dharmasastras* which prescribe that the bride should be of the same caste. Generally, endogamy was in practice, and restrictions were imposed on the intermixture of castes.

During the Vedic period, *Gotra* denoted a cow-pen, but it came to be used in the sense of lineage or ancestry at this time. When king Prasenajit asked the *Gotra* of Angulimala's parents, the latter replied that his father was of the *Gargya Gotra*, and his mother of the *Maitrayani*. Opinions are divided about the consideration of *Gotra* in settling marriages. Some of the law-givers (*e.g.*, Gautama and Baudhayana) are silent on this point, but some of them prohibit *Sagotra* marriages. A verse in the *Kachchhapa Jataka* suggests that generally, parties united in wedlock belonged to different *Gotras*.

There are during this period a few examples of brothers marrying their own sisters. Buddhist literature speaks of the

Sakyas marrying their sisters for the sake of continuing their family line. Incestuous marriages were also prevalent among the Lichchhavis. Marriage with one's won cousin was also in vogue. Bambhadatta married his maternal uncle's daughter. The Jataka stories refer to the marriages of Kasi and Sivi princes with their maternal uncle's daughters. The sister of the Kosala king Prasenajit was married to Bimbisara, and his daughter Vajira was wedded to Ajatasatru, the son of Bimbisara. The marriage of Jyeshtha to Nandivardhana, the elder brother of Mahavira, also belongs to this category. Such marriages were not confined to the royal families, but were prevalent also among the common folk as is evident from several popular stories. Some *Dharmasutras* refer to the custom of marrying one's maternal uncle's daughter, but this practice was confined to the South.

Marriage was guided by two special laws among the Lichchhavis of Vaisali. One of them prohibited the marriage of a Lichchhavi lady with any outsider. This law was so strictly followed that the secret marriage of Simha's daughter with the romantic king Bimbisara of Magadha brought on the dreadful fight between the Lichchhavis and the Magadha people, resulting in the discomfiture of the former and their resolve to make "a requital of enmity (*Vairaniryatana*) even to the sons of the king." They were so particular about it that this resolution was got recorded and kept in a box duly sealed.

The second law was in connection with *Striratna* 'the jewel of women' (the most excellent women). According to this law, the *Striratna* was not allowed to be married for herself, but was t adorn and entertain the society in which she was brought up, for which she was called *Nagarasobhini*. She was thought to be one of the greatest treasures of the nation, a treasure which was not to be under the possession of an individual, however great he might be in position or in wealth. She was to belong to the whole *Gana*. At this time Ambapah, for example, was the most excellent girl, and was therefore made *Nagarasobhini*.

Inter-Caste Marriage

The system of inter-caste marriages was not a common practice. Only the people of higher classes practiced it, but not quite often. The marriage of a bridegroom belonging to a higher caste with a bride of lower caste was known as *Anuloma* marriage, and the marriage of a high-caste girl with a low-caste boy was named *Pratiloma* marriage. We find in a *Jataka* that a king saw a beautiful girl named Sujata, daughter of a greengrocer selling jujubes, fell in love with her and made her his queen consort. A *Jataka* describer *Senapati* Ahiparaka as marrying Ummadanti, a merchant's daughter.

INDEX

K

L

M